TWELVE

LARGE
PRINT

ALSO BY **SEBASTIAN JUNGER**

A DEATH IN BELMONT

FIRE

THE PERFECT STORM

WAR

SEBASTIAN JUNGER

TWELVE

LARGE PRINT

Twelve
Hachette Book Group
237 Park Avenue
New York, NY 10017

www.HachetteBookGroup.com

Twelve is an imprint of Grand Central Publishing.
The Twelve name and logo are trademarks of Hachette Book
Group, Inc.

Printed in the United States of America

First Large Print Edition: May 2010
10 9 8 7 6 5 4 3 2 1

Library of Congress Cataloging-in-Publication Data

Junger, Sebastian.
    War / Sebastian Junger. — 1st ed.
        p. cm.
    ISBN 978-0-446-55624-8 (regular edition) —
ISBN 978-0-446-56697-1 (large print edition)   1. Afghan
War, 2001 — Campaigns — Afghanistan — Korengal Valley.
2. United States. Army. Airborne Brigade, 173rd.   I. Title.
    DS371.4123.K67J86 2010
    958.104'7 — dc22

                                                    2009049493

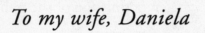

To my wife, Daniela

CONTENTS

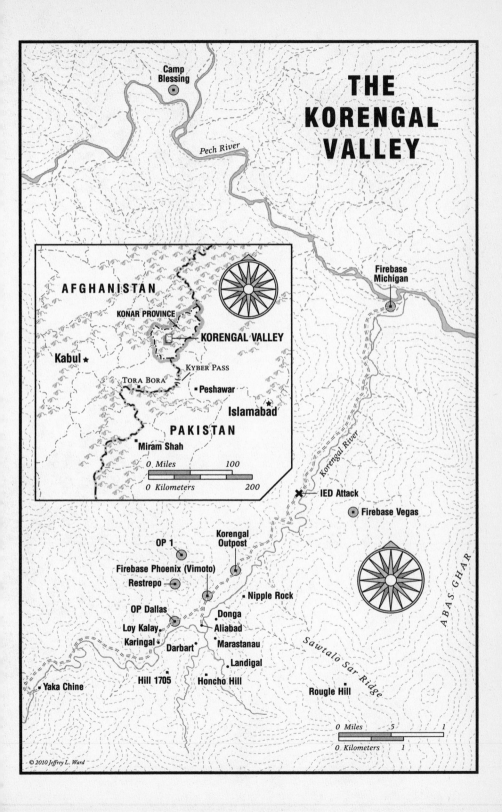

AUTHOR'S NOTE

THIS BOOK WAS THE RESULT OF FIVE TRIPS TO
the Korengal Valley in eastern Afghanistan that I
took between June 2007 and June 2008 for *Vanity
Fair* magazine. I was an "embedded" reporter and
entirely dependent on the U.S. military for food,
shelter, security, and transportation. That said, I
was never asked—directly or indirectly—to alter
my reporting in any way or to show the contents of
my notebooks or my cameras. I worked with a pho-
tojournalist named Tim Hetherington, who also
made five trips to the Korengal, sometimes with
me and sometimes on his own. Our longest trips
lasted a month. Tim and I shot roughly 150 hours
of videotape, and that material was aired in brief

AUTHOR'S NOTE

form on ABC News and then became the basis of a feature-length documentary, produced and directed by Tim and me, called *Restrepo*.

Many scenes in this book were captured on videotape, and wherever possible I have used that tape to check the accuracy of my reporting. Dialogue or statements that appear in double quotations marks ("…") were recorded directly on camera or in my notebook while the person was speaking, or soon thereafter. Dialogue recalled by someone later is indicated by single quotation marks ('…'). Some scenes that I was not present for were entirely reconstructed from interviews and videotape. Many scenes in this book are personal in nature, and I have shared those sections with the men involved to make sure they are comfortable with what I wrote. I hired an independent fact-checker to help me combat the inevitable errors of journalism, and a bibliography of sources that were consulted appears at the back of the book. In many cases I have shortened quotes from interviews and texts in order to ease the burden on the reader.

BOOK ONE

FEAR

By cowardice I do not mean fear. Coward-ice...is a label we reserve for something a man does. What passes through his mind is his own affair.

—Lord Moran, The Anatomy of Courage

NEW YORK CITY

Six Months Later

O'Byrne is standing at the corner of Ninth Avenue and 36th Street with a to-go cup in each hand and the hood of his sweatshirt pulled up. It's six in the morning and very cold. He's put on twenty pounds since I last saw him and could be a laborer waiting for the gate to open at the construction site across the street. Now that he's out of the Army I'm supposed to call him Brendan, but I'm finding that almost impossible to do. We shake hands and he gives me one of the coffees and we go to get my car. The gash across his forehead is mostly healed, though I can still see where the stitches were. One of his front teeth is chipped and looks like a fang. He had a rough time when he got back to Italy; in some ways he was in more danger there than in combat.

WAR

O'Byrne had been with Battle Company in the Korengal Valley, a small but extraordinarily violent slit in the foothills of the Hindu Kush mountains of eastern Afghanistan. He was just one soldier out of thirty but seemed to have a knack for putting words to the things that no one else really wanted to talk about. I came to think of O'Byrne as a stand-in for the entire platoon, a way to understand a group of men who I don't think entirely understood themselves. One valley to the north, two platoons from Chosen Company accumulated a casualty rate of around 80 percent during their deployment. Battle Company wasn't hit that hard, but they were hit hard enough. This morning I'm going to interview Justin Kalenits, one of the wounded from Chosen, and O'Byrne has asked if he could join me. It's a cold, sunny day with little traffic and a north wind that rocks the car along the open stretches and on the bridges. We barrel southward through the industrial dross of New Jersey and Pennsylvania talking about the deployment and the platoon and how strange it is — in some ways for both of us — to find ourselves in the United States for good. I spent the year visiting O'Byrne's platoon in the Korengal, but now that's over and neither of us will ever see it again. We're both dreaming about it at night, though, weird, illogical combat sequences that don't always end badly but are soaked in dread.

FEAR

Kalenits was shot in the pelvis during what has come to be known as the Bella Ambush. Bella was one of the firebases operated by Chosen Company in the Waygal Valley. In early November, fourteen Chosen soldiers, twelve Afghan soldiers, a Marine, and an Afghan interpreter walked to the nearby village of Aranas, met with elders, and then started to walk back. It was a setup. The enemy had built sandbagged positions in a 360-degree circle around a portion of the trail where there was no cover and the only escape was to jump off a cliff. By some miracle, Chosen held them off. Six Americans and eight Afghans were killed and everyone else was wounded. An American patrol hasn't taken 100 percent casualties in a firefight since Vietnam.

We turn into Walter Reed Army Medical Center and park in front of Abrams Hall, where Kalenits lives. We find him in his room smoking and watching television in the dark. His blinds are down and cigarette smoke swirls in the slats of light that come through. I ask Kalenits when was the first moment he realized he was in an ambush, and he says it was when the helmet was shot off his head. Almost immediately he was hit three times in the chest, twice in the back, and then watched his best friend take a round through the forehead that emptied out the back of his head. Kalenits says that when he saw that he just "went into awe."

WAR

There were so many muzzle flashes around them that the hills looked like they were strung with Christmas lights. The rounds that hit Kalenits were stopped by ballistic plates in his vest, but one finally hit him in the left buttock. It shattered his pelvis and tore up his intestines and exited through his thigh. Kalenits was sure it had severed an artery, and he gave himself three minutes to live. He spotted an enemy machine-gun team moving into position on a nearby hill and shot at them. He saw the men fall. He went through all of his ammunition except for one magazine that he saved for when the enemy came through on foot to finish everyone off.

Kalenits started to fade out from lack of blood and he handed his weapon to another man and sat down. He watched a friend named Albert get shot in the knee, and start sliding down the cliff. Kalenits's team leader grabbed him and tried to pull him back, but they were taking so much fire that it was going to get them both killed. Albert yelled to his team leader to let go and he did, and Albert slid partway down the cliff, losing his weapon and helmet on the way. He finally came to a stop and then got shot three more times where he lay.

Rocket-propelled grenades were exploding all around them and throwing up so much dust that the weapons were jamming. Men were spitting into the breeches of their guns, trying to clear them. For the next

8

hour Kalenits faded in and out of consciousness and the firefight continued as one endless, deafening blur. It finally got dark and the MEDEVAC bird arrived and started hoisting up the wounded and the dead. There was a dead man in a tree below the trail and dead men at the bottom of the cliff. One body fell out of the Skedco harness as it was being hoisted into the helicopter, and a quick-reaction force that had flown in from Battle Company had to search for him most of the night.

The last thing Kalenits remembered was getting stuck with needles by doctors at the base in Asadabad; the next thing he knew, he was in Germany. His mother had come home to a message telling her to get in contact with the military immediately, and when she did she was told that she'd better fly to Germany as fast as possible if she wanted to see her son alive. He was still alive when she arrived, and he eventually recovered enough to return to the United States.

O'Byrne has been quiet most of the interview. "Did anyone bring up the issue of walking at night?" he finally says. "On the way out, did anyone bring that up?"

I know why he's asking: Second Platoon left a hilltop position during the daytime once and got badly ambushed outside a town called Aliabad. A rifleman named Steiner took a round in the helmet, though he survived.

WAR

"*No—the lieutenant said, 'We're leaving now,*'" Kalenits answers. "*What are you going to say to him?*"

"*Fuck off?*" O'Byrne offers.

Kalenits smiles, but it's not a thought anyone wants to pursue.

1

KORENGAL VALLEY, AFGHANISTAN
Spring 2007

O'Byrne and the men of Battle Company arrived in the last week in May when the rivers were running full and the upper peaks still held their snow. Chinooks escorted by Apache helicopters rounded a massive dark mountain called the Abas Ghar and pounded into the valley and put down amid clouds of dust at the tiny landing zone. The men grabbed their gear, filed off the birds, and got mortared almost immediately. The enemy knew a new unit was coming into the valley and it was their way of saying hello; fourteen months later they'd say goodbye that way as well. The men took cover in the mechanics' bay and then shouldered their gear and climbed the hill up to their tents at the top of the base. The climb was only a hundred yards but it smoked almost everyone. Around them, the mountains flew up in every direction. The men knew that before the year was out they would probably have to walk on everything they could see.

The base was called the Korengal Outpost — the KOP — and was considered one of the most dangerous postings in Afghanistan. It was a cheerless collection of bunkers and C-wire and bee huts that stretched several hundred yards up a steep hillside toward a band of holly trees that had been shredded by gunfire. There was a plywood headquarters building and a few brick-and-mortars for the men to sleep in and small sandbag bunkers for mortar attacks. The men ate one hot meal a day under a green Army tent and showered once a week in water that had been pumped out of a local creek. Here and there PVC pipe was stuck into the ground at an angle for the men to urinate into. Since there were no women there was no need for privacy. Past the medical tent and the water tank were four open brick stalls that faced the spectacular mountains to the north. Those were known as the burn-shitters, and beneath each one was a metal drum that Afghan workers pulled out once a day so they could burn the contents with diesel fuel. Upslope from there was an Afghan National Army bunker and then a trail that climbed up to Outpost 1, a thousand feet above the KOP. The climb was so steep that the previous unit had installed fixed ropes on the bad parts. The Americans could make the climb in forty-five minutes, combat-light, and the Afghans could make it in half that.

Several days after they arrived, O'Byrne's platoon went on patrol with men from the 10th Mountain Division, whom they were replacing in the valley. Tenth Mountain had begun their rotation back to the United States several months earlier, but Army commanders had changed their minds and decided to extend their tour. Men who had arrived home after a year of combat were put on planes and flown back into the war. Morale plunged, and Battle Company arrived to stories of their predecessors jumping off rocks to break their legs or simply refusing to leave the wire. The stories weren't entirely true, but the Korengal Valley was starting to acquire a reputation as a place that could alter your mind in terrible and irreversible ways.

However messed up 10th Mountain might have been, they'd been climbing around the valley for over a year and were definitely in shape. On the first joint patrol they led Second Platoon down toward the Korengal River and then back up to a granite formation called Table Rock. Tenth Mountain was intentionally trying to break them off—make the new men collapse from exhaustion—and halfway up Table Rock it started to work. A 240 gunner named Vandenberge started falling out and O'Byrne, who was on the same gun team, traded weapons with him and hung the 240 across his shoulders. The 240 is a belt-fed machine gun that weighs almost thirty pounds; you might as well be carrying a jackhammer up a mountain. O'Byrne and the rest of the men had another fifty pounds of gear and ammunition on their backs and twenty pounds of body armor. Almost no one in the platoon was carrying less than eighty pounds.

The men struggled upward in full view of the Taliban positions across the valley and finally began taking fire halfway up the spur. O'Byrne had never been under fire before, and the first thing he did was stand up to look around. Someone yelled to take cover. There was only one rock to hide behind, and Vandenberge was using it, so O'Byrne got behind him. 'Fuck, I can't believe they just *shot* at me!' he yelled.

Vandenberge was a huge blond man who spoke slowly and was very, very smart. 'Well,' he said, 'I don't know if they were shooting at *you*...'

'Okay,' O'Byrne said, 'shooting at *us*...'

Inexperienced soldiers are known as "cherries,"

and standing up in a firefight is about as cherry as it gets. So is this: the first night at the KOP, O'Byrne heard a strange yammering in the forest and assumed the base was about to get attacked. He grabbed his gun and waited. Nothing happened. Later he found out it was just monkeys that came down to the wire to shriek at the Americans. It was as if every living thing in the valley, even the wildlife, wanted them gone.

O'Byrne grew up in rural Pennsylvania on a property that had a stream running through it and hundreds of acres of woods out back where he and his friends could play war. Once they dug a bunker, another time they rigged a zip line up between trees. Most of those friends wound up joining the Army. When O'Byrne turned fourteen he and his father started fighting a lot, and O'Byrne immediately got into trouble at school. His grades plummeted and he began drinking and smoking pot and getting arrested. His father was a plumber who always kept the family well provided for, but there was tremendous turmoil at home — a lot of drinking, a lot of physical combat — and one night things got out of hand and O'Byrne's father shot him twice with a .22 rifle. From his hospital bed, O'Byrne told the police that his father had shot him in self-defense; that way he went to reform school for assault rather than his father going to prison for attempted murder. O'Byrne was sixteen.

A shop teacher named George started counseling him, and O'Byrne spent hours at George's wood shop carving things out of wood and talking. George got him turned around. O'Byrne started playing soccer. He got interested in Buddhism. He started getting good grades. After eight months he moved in with his grandparents and went back to high school. "I changed my whole entire life," O'Byrne told me. "I apologized to all the teachers I ever dissed. I apologized to kids I used to beat up. I apologized to everyone and I made a fucking vow that I was never going to be like that again. People didn't even recognize me when I got home."

One afternoon, O'Byrne saw a National Guard recruiter at his high school and signed up. The unit was about to deploy to Iraq and O'Byrne realized he would be spending a year with a bunch of middle-aged men, so he managed to transfer into the regular Army. The Army wanted to make him a 67 Hotel—a tank mechanic—but he protested and wound up being classified as 11 Charlie. That's mortars. He didn't want to be a mortarman, though—he wanted to be 11 Bravo. He wanted to be an infantryman. His drill sergeant finally relented after O'Byrne got into a barracks fight with someone the sergeant didn't like and broke the man's jaw. The sergeant was Latino and spoke English with such a strong accent that often his men had no idea what he was saying. One afternoon when they were filling out information packets, the sergeant started giving instructions that no one could understand.

"He'd be like, 'Take your motherfucker packet and put it in your motherfucker packet,'" O'Byrne said. "And we're all like, 'What the fuck is he talking about? What's a "motherfucker packet"? And then he starts pointing to things he's talking about: 'Take your *motherfucker packet*'—which is a packet—'and put it in your *motherfucker packet*!'—and he points to his pocket. Oh, okay! You put your packet in your pocket!"

O'Byrne wanted to go to Special Forces, and that meant passing a series of lower-level schools and selection courses. Airborne School was a joke; he passed SOPC 1 (Special Operations Preparation Course) with flying colors; got himself selected for Special Forces; tore through SOPC 2; and then was told he couldn't advance any further without combat experience. 'You can't replace combat with training,' a black E7 at Fort Bragg told him. 'You can't do it. You can't replace that fucking experience. Get deployed, and if you want to come back, come back after that.'

O'Byrne thought that made sense and joined the 173rd Airborne, based in Vicenza, Italy. He'd never been out of the country before. He wound up in Second Platoon, Battle Company, which was already thought of as one of the top units in the brigade. Battle Company had fought well in Iraq and had seen a lot of combat in Afghanistan on its previous deployment. There were four platoons in the company, and of them all, Second Platoon was considered the best-trained and in some ways the worst-disciplined. The platoon had a reputation for producing terrible garrison soldiers — men who drink and fight and get arrested for disorderly conduct and mayhem — but who are extraordinarily good at war. Soldiers make a distinction between the petty tyrannies of garrison life and the very real ordeals of combat, and poor garrison soldiers like to think it's impossible to be good at both.

"I used to score three hundreds on my PT tests shit-canned...just drunk as fuck," O'Byrne told me. "That's how you got sober for the rest of the day. I never got in trouble, but Bobby beat up a few MPs, threatened them with a fire extinguisher, pissed on their boots. But what do you expect from the infantry, you know? I know that all the guys that were bad in garrison were perfect fucking soldiers in combat. They're troublemakers and they like to fight. That's a bad garrison trait but a good combat trait—right? I know I'm a shitty garrison soldier, but what the fuck does it matter? Okay, I got to shine my fucking boots. Why do I care about shining my goddamn boots?"

The weekend before they deployed to Afghanistan, O'Byrne and three other soldiers took the train to Rome for a last blowout. They drank so much that they completely cleaned out the café car. Traveling with O'Byrne were two other privates, Steve Kim and Misha Pemble-Belkin, and a combat medic named Juan Restrepo. Restrepo was born in Colombia but lived in Florida and had two daughters with a woman back home. He spoke with a slight lisp and brushed his teeth compulsively and played classical and flamenco guitar at the barbecues the men threw on base. Once in garrison he showed up at morning PT drunk from the night before, but he was still able to run the two-mile course in twelve and a half minutes and do a hundred sit-ups. If there was a guaranteed way to impress Second Platoon, that was it.

On the train Restrepo pulled out a little one-chip camera and started shooting video of the trip.

The men were so drunk they could barely speak. Kim was propped against the window. Pemble tried to say something about putting a saddle on a miniature zebra and riding it around. O'Byrne said his job in Rome was to just keep Restrepo out of trouble. "Not possible, bro," Restrepo said. "You can't tame the beast."

On the far side of the window the gorgeous Italian countryside slid past. "We're lovin' life and getting ready to go to war," Restrepo said, his arm around O'Byrne's neck. His face was so close to the camera there was almost a fish-eye effect. "We're goin' to war. We're ready. We're goin' to war...we're goin' to war."

The Korengal Valley is sort of the Afghanistan of Afghanistan: too remote to conquer, too poor to intimidate, too autonomous to buy off. The Soviets never made it past the mouth of the valley and the Taliban didn't dare go in there at all. When 10th Mountain rolled into the valley in 2006, they may well have been the first military force ever to reach its southern end. They were only down there a day, but that push gave 10th Mountain some breathing room to finish building the KOP at the site of an old lumberyard three miles in. The lumberyard was not operational because the Afghan government had imposed a ban on timber exports, in large part because the timber sales were helping fund the insurgency. Out-of-work timber cutters traded their chainsaws for weapons and shot at the Americans from inside bunkers made out of the huge cedar logs they could no longer sell.

They were helped by Arab and Pakistani fighters from across the border in Bajaur Province and local militias run by a veteran of the Soviet jihad named Gulbuddin Hekmatyar. Video made by insurgents during one attack shows tiny figures—American soldiers—sprinting for cover and trying to shoot back from behind ragged sandbag walls. The KOP is surrounded by high ground, and to mount an attack local fighters only had to scramble up the back sides of the ridges and pour machine-gun fire down into the compound. This is called "plunging fire," and it is hard to suppress or take cover from. The only way to fix the problem was to take over the high ground with small outposts, but those positions then also became vulnerable to attack. The battle plan for the valley became a game of tactical leapfrog that put the Americans into the village of Babiyal by the spring of 2007.

Babiyal was about half a mile south of the KOP and had ties to the insurgents, though it was not overtly hostile. American soldiers with 10th Mountain rented a residential compound from a local schoolteacher and fortified it with enormous cedar logs that locals had cut on the upper slopes of the valley. The position was named Phoenix, after the city in Arizona, and had its counterpart in Firebase Vegas across the valley. Unfortunately, all you had to do to figure out the tactical problems at Phoenix was to tilt your head upward at Table Rock. Insurgents could pound Phoenix from there and then just run down the back side of the ridge when the Americans started hitting back. One American was killed by an 88 mm recoilless round that shrieked through the narrow opening of his bunker and detonated; another was killed while running to one of the machine-gun positions during an attack. A soldier at the KOP was shot while standing at one of the piss tubes. An American contract worker was shot and wounded while taking a nap on his cot. Another soldier stumbled and drowned while wading across the Korengal River in his body armor.

At a brief ceremony at the KOP on June 5, Captain Jim McKnight of 10th Mountain took down his unit's guidon, climbed into the back of a Chinook, and flew out of the valley forever. Battle Company's guidon was immediately raised in its place. In attendance was a dark, handsome man of

Samoan ancestry named Isaia Vimoto; he was the command sergeant major of the 173rd and the highest enlisted man in the brigade. Vimoto's nineteen-year-old son, Timothy, was a private first class in Second Platoon, and after the ceremony Vimoto asked Battle Company's First Sergeant LaMonta Caldwell where his son was. Caldwell walked Vimoto over to the wire and pointed down-valley.

'He's down there at Phoenix,' he told him.

Vimoto had requested that his son serve in Battle Company because he and Caldwell were best friends. 'You tell him I said hello,' he told Caldwell before he left the KOP. 'Tell him I came out here.'

There had been some contact earlier in the day, and Second Platoon spotted what they thought was an enemy position on top of Hill 1705. A twenty-five-man element, including two Afghan soldiers and an interpreter, left the wire at Phoenix in early evening and started walking south. They walked in plain view on the road and left during daylight hours, which were two things they'd never do again — at least not at the same time. They passed the villages of Aliabad and Loy Kalay and then crossed a bridge over a western tributary of the Korengal. They started up through the steep holly forests of 1705, crested the top, and then started down the other side.

The enemy was waiting for them. They opened
fire from three hundred yards away with machine
guns and rocket-propelled grenades. A private
named Tad Donoho dropped prone and was
low-crawling to cover when he saw a line of bullets stitching toward him in the dirt. He rolled to
one side and wound up near PFC Vimoto. Both
men began returning fire, bullets kicking up dirt
all around them, and at one point Donoho saw
Vimoto open his mouth as if he were about to yell
something. No sound came out, though; instead,
his head jerked back and then tipped forward. He
didn't move again.

Donoho started shouting for the platoon medic,
but there was so much gunfire that no one could
hear him. It didn't matter anyway; the bullet had
gone through Vimoto's head and killed him instantly. One moment he was in the first firefight
of his life, the next moment he was dead. Donoho
shot through all twelve magazines he carried and
then pulled more out of his dead friend's ammo
rack. There was so much gunfire that the only way
the men could move without getting hit was to low-
crawl. They were on a steep ridge at night getting
raked by machine-gun fire, and everyone knew the
MEDEVAC helicopters would never dare attempt
a landing in those conditions; they were going

to have to get Vimoto and another man named Pecsek down to the road to get picked up. Pecsek had been shot through the shoulder but seemed able to walk. A staff sergeant named Kevin Rice hoisted Vimoto onto his back, and the men started down the steep, rocky slopes of 1705 in the darkness and the rain.

Captain Dan Kearney, the commander of Battle Company, drove down to Aliabad in a Humvee to help evacuate the casualties and remembers turning a corner in the road and hitting a wall of Taliban firepower. "I was blown away by the insurgents' ability to continue fighting despite everything America had to throw at them," Kearney told me later. "From that point on I knew it was — number one — a different enemy than I fought in Iraq and that — number two — the terrain offered some kind of advantage that I'd never seen or read or heard about in my entire life."

When Battle Company first arrived in the Korengal, O'Byrne was a gunner in Second Platoon's Weapons Squad. A squad is generally eight men plus a squad leader, and those eight men are divided into two fire teams designated "alpha" and "bravo." In a Weapons Squad, each team would be responsible for an M240 heavy machine gun. O'Byrne spent two months in Weapons Squad and then switched to First Squad under Staff Sergeant Josh McDonough. The men called him "Sar'n Mac," and under his tutelage First Squad became one of the hardest-hitting in the company, possibly the entire battalion. When his men didn't perform well, Mac would tilt his head forward and bore through them with an unblinking stare that could go on for minutes; while he was doing that he was also yelling. "Mac was just a fucking mule," O'Byrne said. "He was just so goddamn strong. His legs were the size of my head. His guys were his only concern. If one of us team leaders wasn't doing our job he got furious — because he cared. He just had a very rough way of showing it."

First Squad was line infantry, which meant they fought on foot and carried everything they needed on their backs. Theoretically, they could walk for days without resupply. O'Byrne was in charge of First Squad's alpha team, which included a former high school wrestler from Wisconsin named Steiner, an eighteen-year-old from Georgia named Vaughn, and a wiry, furtive oddball named Monroe. Each man carried three or four hand grenades. Two out of the four carried standard M4 assault rifles and a chest rack of thirty-round magazines. Another man carried an M4 that also fired big fat rounds called 203s. The 203 rounds explode on impact and are used to lob onto enemy fighters who are behind cover and otherwise couldn't be hit. The fourth man carried something called a Squad Automatic Weapon—usually referred to as a SAW. The SAW has an extremely high rate of fire and basically vomits rounds if you so much as touch the trigger. If you "go cyclic"—fire without stopping—you will go through 900 rounds in a minute. (You'll also melt the barrel.) O'Byrne's fire team probably had enough training and ammo to hold off an enemy force three or four times their size.

Every platoon also has a headquarters element composed of a medic, a forward observer, a radio operator, a platoon sergeant, and a lieutenant who had graduated from officer candidate school. Second Platoon went through two lieutenants during the first half of their deployment and then wound up with Steve Gillespie, a tall, lean marathon runner who reminded his men of a movie character named Napoleon Dynamite. They called him Napoleon behind his back and occasionally to his face but did it with affection and respect: Gillespie was such a dedicated commander that his radioman had to keep pulling him down behind cover during firefights.

Lieutenants have a lot of theoretical knowledge but not much experience, so they are paired with a platoon sergeant who has probably been in the Army for years. Second Platoon's sergeant was a career soldier named Mark Patterson who, at age thirty, had twelve years on the youngest man in the unit. The men called him Pops. Patterson was both the platoon enforcer and the platoon representative, and his role allowed him to keep an eye not only on the grunts but on the lieutenants as well. His face got bright red when he was angry or when he was working very hard, and he could outwalk just about everyone in the platoon. I never saw him look even nervous during a fight, much less scared. He commanded his men like he was directing traffic.

The men of Second Platoon were from mainland America and from wherever the American experiment has touched the rest of the world: the Philippines and Guam and Mexico and Puerto Rico and South Korea. A gunner in Weapons Squad named Jones claims he made thousands of dollars selling drugs before joining the Army to avoid getting killed on the streets of Reno. O'Byrne's soldier Vaughn was eleven years old when 9/11 happened and decided right then and there to join the U.S. Army. As soon as he could, he did. Danforth was forty-two years old and had joined the year before because he was bored; the others called him Old Man and asked a lot of joking questions about Vietnam. A private named Lizama claimed his mother was a member of the Guamese Congress. There was a private named Moreno from Beeville, Texas, who worked in the state penitentiary and had been a promising boxer before joining up. There was a sergeant whose father was currently serving in Iraq and had nearly been killed by a roadside bomb.

The Army has a lot of regulations about how soldiers are required to dress, but the farther you get from the generals the less those rules are followed, and Second Platoon was about as far from the generals as you could get. As the deployment wore on and they got pushed farther into enemy territory it was sometimes hard to tell you were even looking at American soldiers. They wore their trousers unbloused from their boots and tied amulets around their necks and shuffled around the outpost in flip-flops jury-rigged from the packing foam used in missile crates. Toward the end of their tour they'd go through entire firefights in nothing but gym shorts and unlaced boots, cigarettes hanging out of their lips. When the weather got too hot they chopped their shirts off below the armpit and then put on body armor so they'd sweat less but still look like they were in uniform. They carried long knives and for a while one guy went on operations with a small samurai sword in his belt. The rocks ripped their pants to shreds and they occasionally found themselves more or less exposed on patrol. A few had "INFIDEL" tattooed in huge letters across their chests. ("That's what the enemy calls us on their radios," one man explained, "so why not?") Others had tattoos of angel wings sprouting from bullets or bombs. The men were mostly in their early twenties, and many of them have known nothing but life at home with their parents and war.

The men who were killed or wounded were replaced with cherries, and if the older men got bored enough they sometimes made the cherries fight each other. They'd been trained in hand-to-hand combat, so they all knew how to choke someone out; if you do it right, with the forearm against the carotid artery, the person loses consciousness in seconds. (They die in a couple of minutes if you don't release the pressure.) Choking guys out was considered fine sport, so soldiers tended to keep their backs to something so no one could sneak up from behind. Jumping someone was risky because everyone was bound by affiliations that broke down by platoon, by squad, and finally by team. If a man in your squad got jumped by more than one guy you were honor-bound to help out, which meant that within seconds you could have ten or fifteen guys in a pile on the ground.

O'Byrne's 203 gunner, Steiner, once got stabbed trying to help deliver a group beating to Sergeant Mac, his squad leader, who had backed into a corner with a combat knife. In Second Platoon you got beat on your birthday, you got beat before you left the platoon — on leave, say — and you got beat when you came back. The only way to leave Second Platoon without a beating was to get shot. No other platoons did this; the men called it "blood in, blood out," after a movie one of them had seen, and officers were not exempted. I watched Gillespie get held down and beaten, and Pops got pounded so hard his legs were bruised for days. The violence took many forms and could break out at almost any time. After one particularly quiet week — no firefights, in other words — the tension got so unbearable that First Squad finally went after Weapons Squad with rocks. A rock fight ensued that got so heavy, I took cover behind some trees.

Men wound up bleeding and heated after these contests but never angry; the fights were a product of boredom, not conflict, so they always stayed just this side of real violence. Officers were left out of the full-on rumbles, and there were even a couple of enlisted guys who had just the right mix of cool and remove to stay clear of the violence. Sergeant Buno was one of those: he ran Third Squad and had Aztec-looking tattoos on his arms and a tattooed scorpion crawling up out the front of his pants. Buno almost never spoke but had a handsome, impassive face that you could read anything you wanted into. The men suspected he was Filipino but he never admitted to anything; he just wandered around listening to his iPod and saying strange, enigmatic things. The men nicknamed him Queequeg. He moved with the careful precision of a dancer or a martial artist, and that was true whether he was in a firefight or brushing his teeth. Once someone asked him where he'd been the previous night.

"Down in Babiyal," he answered, "killing werewolves."

2

I ARRIVE IN THE KORENGAL A WEEK AFTER
Vimoto was killed, flying into the KOP on a Chinook that pounds over the Abas Ghar and drops
fast onto a patch of crushed rock that serves as a
landing zone. I've planned five trips into the valley
to cover one platoon over the course of their fifteen-
month deployment. I've been in Afghanistan many
times before — starting in 1996, the year that Taliban fighters swept into Kabul — and it is a country
that I care about tremendously. This time, however,
I'm not interested in the Afghans and their endless,
terrible wars; I'm interested in the Americans. I'm
interested in what it's like to serve in a platoon of
combat infantry in the U.S. Army. The moral basis

of the war doesn't seem to interest soldiers much, and its long-term success or failure has a relevance of almost zero. Soldiers worry about those things about as much as farmhands worry about the global economy, which is to say, they recognize stupidity when it's right in front of them but they generally leave the big picture to others.

Journalistic convention holds that you can't write objectively about people you're close to, but you can't write objectively about people who are shooting at you either. Pure objectivity — difficult enough while covering a city council meeting — isn't remotely possible in a war; bonding with the men around you is the least of your problems. Objectivity and honesty are *not* the same thing, though, and it is entirely possible to write with honesty about the very personal and distorting experiences of war. I worked with a British photographer named Tim Hetherington, who had seen a huge amount of combat while covering the Liberian civil war in 2003 but had no experience with American soldiers. He undoubtedly thought that the level of combat in the Korengal would be nothing compared to the violence and chaos of West Africa. I'd briefly been "embedded" in Battle Company a couple of years earlier in Afghanistan's Zabul Province, but we'd gotten into contact only once, and very briefly.

Afghanistan had turned a corner since then, and Tim and I were utterly unprepared for the level of violence we were about to experience.

After the Chinooks lift off I shoulder my pack and walk up the slope to the operations building to meet Captain Kearney. He's six foot four and moves with a kind of solid purpose that I associate with athletes. Some part of him is always moving—usually a leg, which jams up and down so fast that it sends strange vibrations out across the bee-hut floor. He has dark eyes and a heavy brow and gives the impression that he'd barely fit inside a room, much less behind a desk. I ask him who is pushed the farthest out into the valley and he doesn't hesitate.

"Second Platoon," he says. "They're the tip of the spear. They're the main effort for the company, and the company is the main effort for the battalion, and the battalion is the main effort for the brigade. I put them down there against the enemy because I know they're going to get out there and they're not going to be afraid."

I tell Kearney those are the guys I want to be with.

Second Platoon is based at Firebase Phoenix, half a mile south into the valley. One hot summer night I bring my gear to the LZ and join a switch-out that is headed down there on foot. It's a half-hour walk on a dirt road that closely follows the contours of the hill. The base is a dusty scrap of steep ground surrounded by timber walls and sandbags, one of the smallest, most fragile capillaries in a vascular system that pumps American influence around the world. Two Americans have already lost their lives defending it. Rockets and ammo hang from pegs in the timber walls, and the men sleep on cots or in the dirt and an adopted Afghan dog sleeps in the dirt with them. The dog walks point and takes cover during firefights and sets to barking whenever anything moves outside the wire. The base hasn't been attacked in days, but there's intel that it will happen early the next morning. I lie down in my clothes and boots, and the last thing I hear before drifting off is Staff Sergeant Rice saying, "I hosey the .50 cal if we get hit tomorrow..."

We don't get hit but it happens soon enough. The men are coming out of Aliabad at dusk and suddenly there's a disorganized tapping sound in the distance that could be someone working on their car. The first tracer goes by the lieutenant's head and he turns around almost in annoyance, and then the rest of the burst comes in so tight everyone practically falls to the ground. The lieutenant's name is Matt Piosa, the first of three who will lead Second Platoon. We knew we were going to get hit — Prophet had already called us up with the news — but on some level it's always shocking that someone out there actually wants you dead. "Prophet" is the call sign for the American eavesdropping operation in the valley; they listen in on enemy radio communications and have Afghans translate them into English. That gets sent to commanders and rebroadcast across the company radio net. This can take place in minutes, seconds.

Piosa had gone to Aliabad to talk to the elders about a water pipe project. The project was left over from 10th Mountain Division's time in the valley and clearly isn't going to happen this year either, though no one dared admit that. Piosa broke off the meeting when Prophet called — the elders knew exactly what was going to happen; you could tell they couldn't wait to get out of there — and the men started bounding up the trail by squad. Bounding means one group runs while the next group covers them, then the first group covers while the second one runs. It's a way of making sure there's always someone in a position to shoot back. It's a way of making sure you don't lose the entire patrol all at once.

I'm carrying a video camera and running it continually so I won't have to think about turning it on when the shooting starts; it captures everything my memory doesn't. We're behind a rock wall that forms part of the village school when we get hit. "Contact," Piosa says, and a squad leader named Simon adds, "I'm pushing up here," but he never gets the chance. Rounds are coming straight down the line and there's nothing to do but flatten yourself against the wall and grit your teeth. The video jerks and yaws, and soldiers are popping up to empty magazines over the top of the wall and someone is screaming grid coordinates into a radio and a man next to me shouts for Buno. Buno doesn't answer.

Every man in the patrol is standing up and shooting, and later, on the video, I can see incoming rounds sparking off the top of the wall. I keep trying to stand up and shoot video but psychologically it's almost impossible; my head feels vulnerable as an eggshell. All I want to do is protect it. It's easier to stand up if I'm near someone, particularly if they're shooting, and I put myself next to Kim, and every time he pops up to shoot I pop up with him. He goes down, I go down. Below us is the Korengal River and across the valley is the dark face of the Abas Ghar. The enemy owns the Abas Ghar. Tracer fire is arcing out of American positions up and down the valley and converging on enemy positions along the ridge, and mortars are flashing silently on the hilltops, and then long afterward the boom goes galloping past us up the valley. Dusk is closing down the valley fast. O'Byrne is above us with his gun team, and tracer fire from their 240 streaks reassuringly overhead. Every fifth round is a tracer and there are so many that they form continual streams that waver and wobble across the valley and disappear into the dark maw of the mountains.

It's almost full night before we leave the safety of the wall, moving one by one at a run with the machine-gun fire continuing overhead. The men are laboring under the weight of their body armor and ammo and sweating like horses in the thick summer heat. The SAW gunners carry 120 pounds and the shortest runs leave them doubled over and gasping. One man shouts and stumbles and I think he's been hit—everyone does—but he's just twisted his ankle in the dark. He limps on. The last stretch is an absurdly steep climb through the village of Babiyal that the men call "the Stairmaster." Locals build their villages on the steepest hillsides so that everything else can be devoted to agriculture. Pathways are cut out of the rock like ladders, front doors give out onto neighbors' rooftops; in places you could literally fall to the bottom of town.

The men grind their way up the Stairmaster and file through the wire into Phoenix, dark shapes in the hot night staggering in circles, unlimbering their loads. Mortars are still thudding into the Abas Ghar and rivulets of white phosphorus burn their way down the slopes like lava. The fires they start will smolder for days. The men collect at the mortar pit to smoke cigarettes and go over what happened. After a while we see lights moving on the slopes of the Abas Ghar, almost certainly Taliban fighters gathering up their wounded and dead. A soldier radios that in and suggests dropping artillery on them. Battalion is worried the lights might be shepherds up in the high pastures and denies the request.

"Put the .50 all over it, we just had a fucking TIC, fuck those people," someone says.

A TIC means "troops in contact" — a firefight. The ".50" is a .50 caliber machine gun. After a while the lights go out; whoever it is has probably disappeared over the back side of the ridge. "Dude, that's it, they're leaving," someone says. A little while later a soldier walks up and tells me to hold out my hand. I do, and he drops something small and heavy into it: an AK round that smacked into a rock next to him during the fight.

"That," he says, "is how you know it was close."

FEAR

• • •

The enemy fighters were three or four hundred yards away, and the bullets they were shooting covered that distance in about half a second—roughly two thousand miles an hour. Sound doesn't travel nearly that fast, though, so the gunshots themselves arrived a full second after they were fired. Because light is virtually instantaneous, illuminated rounds—tracers—can be easily perceived as they drill toward you across the valley. A 240 gunner named Underwood told me that during the ambush he saw tracers coming at him from Hill 1705 but they were moving too fast to dodge. By the time he was setting his body into motion they were hitting the cedar log he was hiding behind. The brain requires around two-tenths of a second just to understand simple visual stimuli, and another two-tenths of a second to command muscles to react. That's almost exactly the amount of time it takes a high-velocity round to go from 1705 to Aliabad.

Reaction times have been studied extensively in controlled settings and have shown that men have faster reaction times than women and athletes have faster reaction times than nonathletes. Tests with soccer players have shown that the "point of no return" for a penalty kick—when the kicker can no longer change his mind about where to send the ball — is around a quarter of a second. In other words, if the goalkeeper waits until the kicker's foot is less than a quarter second from the ball and then dives in one direction, the kicker doesn't have enough time to adjust his kick. Given that quarter-second cutoff, the distance at which you might literally be able to "dodge a bullet" is around 800 yards. You'd need a quarter second to register the tracer coming toward you — at this point the bullet has traveled 200 yards — a quarter second to instruct your muscles to react — the bullet has now traveled 400 yards — and half a second to actually move out of the way. The bullet you dodge will pass you with a distinctive snap. That's the sound of a small object breaking the sound barrier inches from your head.

Humans evolved in a world where nothing moved two thousand miles an hour, so there was no reason for the *body* to be able to counter that threat, but the brain still had to stay ahead of the game. Neurological processes in one of the most primitive parts of the brain, the amygdala, happen so fast that one could say they compete with bullets. The amygdala can process an auditory signal in fifteen milliseconds — about the amount of time it takes a bullet to go thirty feet. The amygdala is fast but very limited; all it can do is trigger a reflex and wait for the conscious mind to catch up. That reaction is called the startle, and it is composed of protective moves that would be a good idea in almost any situation. When something scary and unexpected happens, every person does exactly the same thing: they blink, crouch, bend their arms, and clench their fists. The face also sets itself into what is known as a "fear grimace": the pupils dilate, the eyes widen, the brow goes up, and the mouth pulls back and down. Make that expression in front of a mirror and see not only how instantly recognizable it is, but also how it seems to actually produce a sense of fear. It's as if the neural pathways flow in both directions, so the expression triggers fear as well as being triggered by it.

The videotape I shot during the ambush in Aliabad shows every man dropping into a crouch at the distant popping sound. They don't do this in response to a loud sound — which presumably is what evolution has taught us — but in response to the quieter snap of the bullets going past. The amygdala requires only a single negative experience to decide that something is a threat, and after one firefight every man in the platoon would have learned to react to the snap of bullets and to ignore the much louder sound of men near them returning fire. In Aliabad the men crouched for a second or two and then straightened up and began shouting and taking cover. In those moments their higher brain functions decided that the threat required action rather than immobility and ramped everything up: pulse and blood pressure to heart-attack levels, epinephrine and norepinephrine levels through the roof, blood draining out of the organs and flooding the heart, brain, and major muscle groups.

"There's nothing like it, nothing in the world," Steiner told me about combat. "If it's negative twenty degrees outside, you're sweating. If it's a hundred and twenty, you're cold as shit. Ice cold. It's an adrenaline rush like you can't imagine."

The problem is that it's hard to aim a rifle when your heart is pounding, which points to an irony of modern combat: it does extraordinarily violent things to the human body but requires almost dead calm to execute well. Complex motor skills start to diminish at 145 beats per minute, which wouldn't matter much in a swordfight but could definitely ruin your aim with a rifle. At 170 beats per minute you start to experience tunnel vision, loss of depth perception, and restricted hearing. And at 180 beats per minute you enter a netherworld where rational thought decays, bowel and bladder control are lost, and you start to exhibit the crudest sorts of survival behaviors: freezing, fleeing, and submission.

To function effectively, the soldier must allow his vital signs to get fully ramped up without ruining his concentration and control. A study conducted by the Navy during the Vietnam War found that F-4 Phantom fighter pilots landing on aircraft carriers pegged higher heart rates than soldiers in combat and yet virtually never made mistakes (which tended to be fatal). To give an idea of the delicacy of the task, at one mile out the aircraft carrier is the size of a pencil eraser held at arm's length. The plane covers that distance in thirty-six seconds and must land on a section of flight deck measuring seven yards wide and forty-five yards long. The Navy study compared stress levels of the pilots to that of their radar intercept officers, who sat immediately behind them but had no control over the two-man aircraft. The experiment involved taking blood and urine samples of both men on no-mission days as well as immediately after carrier landings. The blood and urine were tested for a hormone called cortisol, which is secreted by the adrenal gland during times of stress to sharpen the mind and increase concentration. Radar intercept officers lived day-to-day with higher levels of stress—possibly due to the fact that their fate was in someone else's hands—but on mission days the pilots' stress levels were far higher. The huge responsibility borne by the pilots gave them an ease of mind on their days off that they paid for when actually landing the plane.

The study was duplicated in 1966 with a twelve-man Special Forces team in an isolated camp near the Cambodian border in South Vietnam. The camp was deep in enemy territory and situated to disrupt the flow of arms along the Ho Chi Minh Trail. An Army researcher took daily blood and urine samples from the men while they braced for an expected attack by an overwhelming force of Vietcong. There was a serious possibility that the base would be overrun, in which case it was generally accepted that it would be "every man for himself."

The two officers saw their cortisol levels climb steadily until the day of the expected attack and then diminish as it failed to materialize. Among the enlisted men, however, the stress levels were exactly the opposite: their cortisol levels *dropped* as the attack drew near, and then started to rise when it became clear that they weren't going to get hit. The only explanation the researchers could come up with was that the soldiers had such strong psychological defenses that the attack created a sense of "euphoric expectancy" among them. "The members of this Special Forces team demonstrated an overwhelming emphasis on self-reliance, often to the point of omnipotence," they wrote. "These subjects were action-oriented individuals who characteristically spent little time in introspection. Their response to any environmental threat was to engage in a furor of activity which rapidly dissipated the developing tension."

Specifically, the men strung C-wire and laid additional mines around the perimeter of the base. It was something they knew how to do and were good at, and the very act of doing it calmed their nerves. In a way that few civilians could understand, they were more at ease facing a known threat than languishing in the tropical heat facing an unknown one.

3

THE KOP DOMINATED THE CENTER OF THE valley, but halfway up the slopes of the Abas Ghar was a small firebase named Vegas. Its purpose was to control access to the Korengal from the east. Vegas was a five-hour walk from the KOP and almost never got into contact, so journalists only went out there if they could catch a resupply from the KOP. Vegas was manned by First Platoon and had a small HLZ—helicopter landing zone—but for a while lacked phone or Internet, and the men were stuck there for weeks at a time. "I guarantee you, half of First Platoon is going to be divorced by the time this is over," Kearney told me early on in the tour. The cook started talking to a finger puppet as a way of coping, but that unnerved the other men so much that one of them finally destroyed it.

I never went out to Vegas, but once in a while I'd get to know First Platoon guys who were rotating through the KOP for a hot shower and a call home. One was a sergeant named Hunter, who managed to be both very cynical about the Army and also a very good soldier. I was under fire with him once, he was leaning back against some sandbags saying things that made everyone laugh while sniper rounds went *schlaaack* over our heads. "We call him Single-Shot Freddy," his sniper rap went. "We believe he is a blind Afghan man between the ages of sixty-five and seventy…"

Hunter was known throughout the company for his pantomime of Single-Shot Freddy. He'd pretend to pull himself up a hillside along an imaginary guide rope, all the while muttering, *"Allahu Akhbar,"* and then unlimber the rifle from his shoulder and feel along the stock for the bolt. Sightless eyes turned heavenward, he'd jack the bolt back, chamber an imaginary round, and fire. *Allahu Akhbar!* He'd work the bolt and then fire again. I asked Hunter why he thought the sniper was blind. "Because he hasn't hit anyone yet," he replied.

A couple of months into the deployment Hunter came up with the phrase "Damn the Valley," which quickly became a kind of unofficial slogan for the company. It seemed to be shorthand not for the men's feelings about the war—those were way too complicated to sum up in three words—but for their understanding of what it was doing to them: killing their friends and making them jolt awake in the middle of the night in panic and taking away their girlfriends and wiping out a year—no, fifteen months—of their lives. Their third decade on the planet and a good chunk of it was going to be spent in a valley six miles long and six miles wide that they might not leave alive. Damn the Valley: you'd see it written on hooch walls and in latrines as far away as the air base at Jalalabad and tattooed onto men's arms, usually as "DTV."

Hunter was not from a military family, and he told me that his decision to join up left his parents proud but a little puzzled. It didn't matter, he was out here now and getting home alive was the only important issue. It was a weird irony of the war that once you were here—or your son was—the politics of the whole thing became completely irrelevant until very conservative families and very liberal ones—there were some—saw almost completely eye to eye. Misha Pemble-Belkin's father was a labor organizer who had protested every American war of the past forty years, yet he and his wife were wildly proud of their son. Pemble-Belkin wasn't allowed to have toy guns when he was young, even squirt guns, so he and his brother picked up crooked sticks and pretended to shoot those instead. The men of Second Platoon shortened Pemble-Belkin's name to "PB," which inevitably became "Peanut Butter" and then just "Butters." He spoke slowly and very softly, particularly on the platoon radio, and he played guitar and drew pictures of the valley on a sketch pad. He claimed it was the only thing he knew how to draw. Butters could easily have been an art major in college except that he was a paratrooper in the Korengal Valley. He joined the Army after spending a year living in his car, snowboarding.

For the first six months of the deployment, the men of Second Platoon squeezed into a tent and then a small brick-and-mortar building at the bottom of the KOP. There was a plywood bin full of two-quart water bottles outside the door and a broken office chair and some ammo crates to sit on, and the guys would collect there to smoke cigarettes and talk. The rest of the KOP was uphill from there—the landing zone and the mess tent and the latrines—and to get anywhere when there was shooting you had to thread your way through some trees and then climb past the burn pit and the motor pool. The only other route was across the LZ but that was wide open to both sides of the valley. The broken office chair had pretty good cover, though, and the men would sit there smoking even when the KOP was taking fire. The shooting had to get pretty intense before anyone went inside.

One afternoon I was sitting out there working on my notes when a soldier named Anderson walked up. He was a big blond kid who said he joined the military after a series of problems with the law (a lot of the men wound up here that way). Anderson's mother was a jazz singer, and Anderson had grown up playing saxophone in adult bands. There'd been a lot of fighting in the previous weeks and the men were under a lot of stress: Pemble kept dreaming that someone had rolled a hand grenade into the hooch, and when Steiner went home on leave, he instructed his mother to only wake him up by touching his ankle and saying his last name. That was how he got woken up for guard duty; anything else might mean they were getting overrun.

The fact was that the men got an enormous amount of psychiatric oversight from the battalion shrink—as well as periodic "vacations" at Camp Blessing or Firebase Michigan—but combat still took a toll. It was unrealistic to think it wouldn't. Anderson sat on an ammo crate and gave me one of those awkward grins that sometimes precede a confession. "I've only been here four months and I can't believe how messed up I already am," he said. "I went to the counselor and he asked if I smoked cigarettes and I told him no and he said, 'Well, you may want to think about starting.'"

He lit a cigarette and inhaled.

"I hate these fuckin' things," he said.

Battle Company was one of six companies in "The Rock," an 800-man battalion that was given its name after parachuting onto Corregidor Island in 1942. The Rock was part of the 173rd Airborne Brigade, an infamously tough unit that has been taking the brunt of the nation's combat since World War I. The men of the 173rd performed the only combat jump of the Vietnam War, fought their way through the Iron Triangle and the Cu Chi tunnels, and then assaulted Hill 875 during the battle of Dak To. They lost one-fifth of their combat strength in three weeks. By the end of the war, the 173rd had the highest casualty rate of any brigade in the U.S. Army.

The brigade was decommissioned after Vietnam and then activated again in 2000. They were dropped into Bashur, Iraq, to open a northern front that would draw Iraqi soldiers away from the southern defense of Baghdad. Two years later The Rock was sent to Zabul Province, in central Afghanistan, and saw limited but exceedingly intense combat in the wide-open moonscape around the newly paved Highway 1. The Taliban insurgency was just gaining traction that year, and the men of The Rock were surprised to find themselves in real combat in a war that was supposed to be more of a security operation. I was told that during one battle, a lieutenant colonel who was directing things from the air started throwing hand grenades out the bay door of his helicopter. When he ran out of grenades he supposedly switched to his 9 mil. A medic whose gun jammed during a firefight flipped it around and beat an attacker to death with the buttstock. I met him a few weeks later; on his helmet liner he'd drawn a skull for each of his confirmed kills. By the time the tour was over, half of Battle Company was supposedly on psychiatric meds.

The brigade was slated to go to Iraq for their next deployment, but a last-minute decision sent them back to Afghanistan instead. Insurgents were filing across the Pakistani border, in the northeastern part of the country, and infiltrating toward Kabul along the Pech and Kunar valleys. The Rock's job would be to occupy the main mobility corridors and try to stop them. Many of the Zabul veterans expected to see the same kind of wide-open terrain they had seen down south—terrain that favored airpower and armor—but instead they watched mountain peaks and knife-edge ridges slide past the windows of their Chinook. Even the privates knew this was bad.

The Rock inherited a string of bases and outposts throughout the Pech, Waygal, Shuryak, Chowkay, and Korengal valleys. The positions had been built by the Marines and the 10th Mountain Division that preceded them. It was some of the most beautiful and rugged terrain in Afghanistan and for centuries had served as a center of resistance against invaders. Alexander's armies ground to a halt in nearby Nuristan and stayed so long that the blond and red-haired locals are said to be descendants of his men. The Soviet army lost entire companies—200 men at a time—to ambushes along the Kunar River. ("They sent two divisions through here and left with a battalion through the Pech River Valley," The Rock's commander told me when I first arrived. "At least that's what the locals say.") The Americans didn't enter the area until 2003 and maintained no sizable presence there for another two or three years. There were rumors that 9/11 had been planned, in part, in the Korengal Valley. There were rumors that Osama bin Laden and Ayman al-Zawahiri passed through the area regularly on their way in and out of Pakistan.

Battalion headquarters was at Camp Blessing, in the upper Pech, and there were two howitzers there that could throw 155s all the way into the southern Korengal, ten miles away. Two more howitzers at the Special Forces camp in Asadabad covered just about everything else. Brigade headquarters was fifty miles west at Jalalabad Airfield, and the entire American effort was staged out of Bagram Airfield, thirty miles north of Kabul. Bagram is considered a forward operating base, or FOB, and grunts in places like the Korengal refer to soldiers on FOBs as Fobbits. Soldiers on those bases might go an entire tour without ever leaving the wire, much less firing a gun, and grunts look down on them almost as much as they look down on the press corps. Grunts claim that they're constantly getting yelled at by Fobbit officers for coming off the flight line dirty and unshaven and wandering around the base with their uniforms in shreds. ("We look like combat soldiers," as one guy put it. "We look like guys just getting out of the shit.") It's only on rear bases that you hear any belligerent talk about patriotism or religion and it's only on rear bases where, as a journalist, you might catch any flak for your profession. Once at Bagram I found myself getting screamed at by an 82nd Airborne soldier, a woman, who was beside herself because my shirt was covering my press pass. I'd just come out of two weeks in the Korengal; I just shrugged and walked away.

The U.S. military tends to divide problems into conceptual slices and then tackle each slice separately. Wars are fought on physical terrain — deserts, mountains, etc. — as well as on what they call "human terrain." Human terrain is essentially the social aspect of war, in all its messy and contradictory forms. The ability to navigate human terrain gives you better intelligence, better bomb-targeting data, and access to what is essentially a public relations campaign for the allegiance of the populace. The Taliban burned down a school in the Korengal, for example, and by accident also burned a box full of Korans. The villagers were outraged, and the Taliban lost a minor battle in the human terrain of the valley.

You can occupy a "hilltop" in human terrain much like you can in real terrain — hiring locals to work for you, for example — and that hilltop position may protect you from certain kinds of attack while exposing you to others. Human terrain and physical terrain interact in such complex ways that commanders have a hard time calculating the effect of their actions more than a few moves out.

FEAR

You can dominate the physical terrain by putting an outpost in a village, but if the presence of foreign men means that local women can't walk down certain paths to get to their fields in the morning, you have lost a small battle in the human terrain. Sometimes it's worth it, sometimes it isn't. Accidentally killing civilians is a sure way of losing the human terrain—this applies to both sides—and if you do that too many times, the locals will drive you out no matter how many hilltops you occupy. It has been suggested that one Taliban strategy is to lure NATO forces into accidentally killing so many civilians that they lose the fight for the human terrain. The physical terrain would inevitably follow.

The U.S. military depicts the human terrain with genealogical data and flowcharts of economic activity and maps of tribal or clan affiliation. That information is overlaid onto extremely detailed maps of the physical terrain, and a plan is developed to dominate both. Maps of the physical terrain are rendered from satellite data and show vegetation, population centers, and elevation contours. Superimposed on the maps is a one-kilometer grid, and the military measures progress on the physical terrain by what gridline they've gotten to. The Korengal Valley is ten kilometers long and ten kilometers wide—about half the size of Staten Island—and military control ends at Kilometer Sixty-two. The six-two gridline, as it is known, bisects the valley at Aliabad; north of there you're more or less safe, south of there you're almost guaranteed to get shot at. It's as if the enemy thought that the Americans would go for a de facto division of the valley, and that if they stayed out of the northern half, maybe the Americans would stay out of the south. They didn't.

The other major division is lengthwise, with the enemy more or less controlling the eastern side of the valley and the Americans controlling the west. The Americans, in other words, control about one-quarter of the Korengal. The six-two crosses the valley and climbs eastward right up the Abas Ghar, but if you follow it there with anything less than two platoons and dedicated air assets you risk getting shot to pieces. What the military calls "ratlines"—foot trails used by the enemy to bring in men and supplies—run eastward from the Abas Ghar through the Shuryak Valley to the Kunar, and then across the border to Pakistan. More ratlines run south into the Chowkay and north across the Pech. In the Korengal there is a high degree of correspondence between American control of the human terrain and control of the physical terrain. It's hard to control one without controlling the other. When the Americans gain access to a community and start delivering development projects, the locals tend to gravitate toward them and away from the insurgents. Entering a village requires a large military presence, however, and that offers a perfect target to insurgent gunners in the hills. Locals invariably blame the ensuing firefight on the Americans, regardless of who shot first.

Around the time Vimoto was killed, Third Platoon soldiers in the northern end of the valley shot into a truck full of young men who had refused to stop at a checkpoint, killing several. The soldiers said they thought they were about to be attacked; the survivors said they had been confused about what to do. Faced with the prospect of losing the tenuous support that American forces had earned in the northern half of the valley, the battalion commander arranged to address community leaders in person after the incident. Standing in the shade of some trees by the banks of the fast, violent Pech, Lieutenant Colonel William Ostlund explained that the deaths were the result of a tragic mistake and that he would do everything in his power to make it right. That included financial compensation for the grieving families. After several indignant speeches by various elders, one very old man stood up and spoke to the villagers around him.

"The Koran offers us two choices, revenge and forgiveness," he said. "But the Koran says that forgiveness is better, so we will forgive. We understand that it was a mistake, so we will forgive. The Americans are building schools and roads, and because of this, we will forgive."

The American rules of engagement generally forbid soldiers to target a house unless someone is shooting from it, and discourage them from targeting anything if civilians are nearby. They can shoot people who are shooting at them and they can shoot people who are carrying a weapon or a handheld radio. The Taliban know this and leave everything they need hidden in the hills; when they want to launch an attack they just walk out to their firing positions empty-handed and pick up their guns. They also make children stand near them when they use their radios. The Americans don't dare shoot because, other than the obvious moral issues involved, killing civilians simply makes the war harder. The Soviet military, which invaded Afghanistan in 1979, most emphatically did not understand this. They came in with a massive, heavily armored force, moved about in huge convoys, and bombed everything that moved. It was a textbook demonstration of exactly how *not* to fight an insurgency, and

7 percent of the prewar population was killed. A truly popular uprising eventually drove the Soviets out.

The Korengalis are originally from Nuristan, an enclave of mostly Persian- and Pashai-speaking tribesmen who practiced shamanism and believed that the rocks and trees and rivers around them had souls. The Nuristanis didn't convert to Islam until the armies of King Abdur Rahman Khan marched in and forced them to around 1896. The people who are now known as the Korengalis settled in their present location around the time of the great conversion, bringing with them both their newfound Islamic faith and their wild, clannish ways. They terraced the steep slopes of the valley into wheat fields and built stone houses that could withstand earthquakes (and, it turned out, 500-pound bombs) and set about cutting down the cedar forests of the upper ridges. The men dye their beards red and use kohl around their eyes, and the women go unveiled and wear colorful dresses that make them look like tropical birds in the fields. Most Korengalis have never left their village and have almost no understanding of the world beyond the mouth of the valley. That makes it a perfect place in which to base an insurgency dedicated to fighting outsiders. One old man in the valley thought the American soldiers were actually Russians who had simply stayed after the Soviet army pulled out in 1989.

The people aren't the only problem, however; the war also diverged from the textbooks because it was fought in such axle-breaking, helicopter-crashing, spirit-killing, mind-bending terrain that few military plans survive intact for even an hour. The mountains are sedimentary rock that was compressed into schist hundreds of millions of years ago and then thrust upward. Intrusions of hard white granite run though the schist like the ribs on an animal carcass. Even the trees are hard: knotted holly oaks with spiny leaves and branches that snag your clothing and won't let go. Holly forests extend up to around eight thousand feet and then give over to cedar trees that are so enormous, the mind compensates for their size by imagining them to be much closer than they are. A hilltop that looks a few hundred yards away can be a mile or more.

The locals cut the trees for export to Kabul and Pakistan, but the lumber is actually brokered by criminal groups that control their export. Korengali timber cutters are dependent on these groups to bribe police at border checkpoints and to connect them to buyers who are willing to violate the national ban on timber export. By some accounts, war came to the Korengal when timber traders from a northern faction of the Safi tribe allied themselves with the first U.S. Special Forces that came through the area in early 2002. When the Americans tried to enter the Korengal they met resistance from local timber cutters who realized that the northern Safis were poised to take over their operation.

Because of the timber ban there were stockpiles of logs throughout the valley that made perfect fighting positions for the insurgents. American soldiers can blow up enemy bunkers when they find them, but there's nothing they can do to squared-off cedar timbers that measure three or four feet across and are stacked by the dozen. The trees are felled on the upper slopes of the Abas Ghar and then skidded into the valley down luge runs made of other timbers greased with cooking oil. In the spring the logs get tipped into the river at flood stage and shepherded all the way down the valley to the Pech and then on to Asadabad. For sport, young men put themselves in the riverbed when the floodwaters come down and try to run fast enough to stay ahead of the logs. One soldier shot a video that shows a young man losing the race and simply disappearing into the logs. You never see him again.

The head of the Korengali timber cutters was

a man named Hajji Matin, who owned a fortified house in the town of Darbart, on the top of Hill 1705. Matin allied himself with an Egyptian named Abu Ikhlas, who had fought jihad against the Russians in that area during the 1980s and wound up marrying a local woman. It wasn't known for sure that Ikhlas was affiliated with Al Qaeda, but he might have fled on the assumption that the Americans wouldn't trouble themselves about the details. Around that time, the Americans allegedly bombed Hajji Matin's house and killed several members of his family. If true, that pretty much guaranteed war for as long as Matin remained alive. Fighting in the Korengal escalated further during the summer of 2005, when another local commander named Ahmad Shah arrested three men and accused them of being informers for the American military. Shah was a midlevel Taliban operative who ran a bomb-making cell in the area and was responsible for a number of attacks on American convoys. He was reported to have close ties with Al Qaeda leadership across the border in Pakistan and with the radical Islamic commander Gulbuddin Hekmatyar.

Shah executed the three men and waited for the Americans to arrive. It didn't take long: days later a four-man Navy SEAL team was dropped by helicopter onto the Abas Ghar. Their mission was to track the activity of Shah's men so that other American forces could keep them from disrupting upcoming elections. SEALs are the most highly trained commandos in the U.S. military, but nevertheless they were compromised eighteen hours later when a goatherd and two teenage boys walked past their position. The Americans agonized over whether to kill them or not and in the end decided to let them go. Marcus Luttrell, the only survivor of his team, later explained that it was his concern over the liberal American press that kept him from executing the three Afghans.

That wouldn't have saved them, however. The Taliban are well known to use shepherds as scouts, and on a mountain that big it was almost inconceivable that the shepherds stumbled onto the SEALs by accident. The Taliban knew exactly where the SEAL team was, in other words. And there were other, more serious problems. The radio barely worked but the SEALs did not use their satellite phone to abort the mission or call in reinforcements. No quick-reaction force had been put on standby at nearby American bases in Asadabad or Jalalabad, and insufficient intelligence had been gathered from inside the valley. No one knew that for the past eighteen hours an enemy force of several hundred fighters had been converging on four

SEALs who had no working radio, no body armor, and just enough water and ammo for a couple of hours of combat. It was not a fair fight, and some in the U.S. military questioned why the SEALs were even up there.

Luttrell and his men soon found themselves surrounded and catastrophically outnumbered by Shah's fighters. The battle went on all afternoon, spilling down off the upper ridges toward the Shuryak Valley east of the Korengal. The SEALs finally used their satellite phone to inform headquarters that they were in contact, and a Chinook helicopter with eight more SEALs and eight other commandos scrambled from Bagram Airfield and thundered off toward Kunar. Chinooks must always be escorted by Apache gunships that can provide covering fire if necessary, but for some reason this one came in on its own. It was immediately hit by a rocket-propelled grenade and crashed onto the upper ridges of the Abas Ghar. Everyone on board probably died on impact, but Shah's fighters allegedly put two bullets in the head of every American soldier just to make sure. They then picked through the wreckage and walked away with several "suppressed M4s"—that is, M4s with silencers—night vision goggles, helmets, GPS devices, hand grenades, and a military laptop. It would make the fight in the Korengal that much more difficult for those who were to follow.

Luttrell, meanwhile, had shot his way off the mountain and made it to the village of Sabray, where he was taken in by the locals. Everyone else on his team was dead; one man was found with twenty-one bullets in him. The people of Sabray were obligated to protect Luttrell under an honor code called *lokhay warkawal*, which holds that anyone who comes to your doorstep begging for help must be cared for no matter what the cost to the community. Taliban forces surrounded the village and threatened to kill everyone in it, but the villagers held out long enough for American forces to arrive.

The American response to the debacle on the Abas Ghar was swift and furious. B-52 bombers dropped two guided bombs on a residential compound in the village of Chichal, high above the Korengal Valley. They apparently missed Ahmad Shah by minutes but killed seventeen civilians in the compound, including women and children. Over the next twelve months American firebases were pushed deeper into the Pech River Valley and three miles into the Korengal itself. The Korengal was a safe haven from which insurgents could attack the Pech River corridor, and the Pech was the main access route to Nuristan, so a base in the Korengal made sense, but there was something else going on. The valley had enormous symbolic meaning because of the loss of nineteen American commandos there, and some soldiers suspected that their presence in the valley was the U.S. military's way of punishing locals for what had happened on the Abas Ghar. For both sides, the battle for the Korengal developed a logic of its own that sucked in more and more resources and lives until neither side could afford to walk away.

4
—

SUMMER GRINDS ON: A HUNDRED DEGREES
every day and tarantulas invading the living quarters to get out of the heat. Some of the men are terrified of them and can only sleep in mesh pup tents, and others pick them up with pliers and light them on fire. The timber bunkers at Phoenix are infested with fleas, and the men wear flea collars around their ankles but still scratch all day long. First Squad goes thirty-eight days without taking a shower or changing their clothes, and by the end their uniforms are so impregnated with salt that they can stand up by themselves. The men's sweat reeks of ammonia because they've long since burned off all their fat and are now breaking down muscle. There

are wolves up in the high peaks that howl at night and mountain lions that creep through the KOP looking for food and troops of monkeys that set to screeching from the crags around the base. One species of bird sounds exactly like incoming rocket-propelled grenades; the men call them "RPG birds" and can't keep themselves from flinching whenever they hear them.

One day I'm in the mess tent drinking coffee when three or four soldiers from Third Platoon walk in. It's early morning and they look like they've been up all night and are getting some breakfast before going to bed. "I jerked off at least every day for an entire CONOP," one guy says. A CONOP is a mission dedicated to a specific task. I sit there waiting to see where this is headed.

"That's nothing—I jerked off while pulling guard duty above Donga," another man answers.

Donga is an enemy town on the other side of the valley. "Illume is key," a squad leader weighs in, referring to the lunar cycle. "You know, you get that fifteen to twenty percent illume and it's so dark you can't see five feet in front of you. I did it in the tent with all the guys around, and afterward I thought, 'That's kind of fucked up.' But I asked the guys if they saw me and they said no, so I thought, 'That's cool.'"

FEAR

Someone raises the question of whether it's physiologically possible to masturbate during a firefight. That is, admittedly, the Mount Everest of masturbation, but the consensus is that it can't be done. Another man mentions a well-known bunker on the KOP and mimes a blur of hand movement while his head swivels back and forth, scanning for intruders. Someone finally notices me in the corner.

"Sorry, sir," he says. "We're like monkeys, only worse."

The attacks continue almost every day, everything from single shots that whistle over the men's heads to valley-wide firefights that start on the Abas Ghar and work their way around clockwise. In July, Sergeant Padilla is cooking Philly cheesesteaks for the men at Firebase Phoenix and has just yelled, "Come and get it before I get killed," when an RPG sails into the compound and takes off his arm. Pemble helps load him into a Humvee, and for weeks afterward he has dreams of Padilla standing in front of him with his arm missing. Battle Company is taking the most contact of the battalion, and the battalion is taking the most contact — by far — of any in the U.S. military. Nearly a fifth of the combat experienced by the 70,000 NATO troops in Afghanistan is being fought by the 150 men of Battle Company. Seventy percent of the bombs dropped in Afghanistan are dropped in and around the Korengal Valley. American soldiers in Iraq who have never been in a firefight start talking about trying to get to Afghanistan so that they can get their combat infantry badges.

In July, before switching over to First Squad, O'Byrne gets pinned down with the rest of his 240 team on the road above Loy Kalay. They're providing overwatch for a foot patrol that has gone down-valley when rounds suddenly start smacking in all around them. Reporters often think that taking cover from small-arms fire is the same as getting pinned down, but it's not. Getting pinned down means you literally can't move without getting killed. Once the enemy has you pinned down, they drop mortars or grenades on you. There's no way to hide from mortars or grenades; they come shrieking down out of the sky and after a couple of correction rounds you're dead.

"We picked a dumb spot, it was all our fucking fault," O'Byrne told me later. I'd asked him when was the first time he thought he was going to get hit. "We were fucking very dumb. We were in the wide open, you know, but we were laying down so we thought we were good. Seventeen-oh-five was right there, we were fucking idiots. We started getting shot at and me and Vandenberge didn't even pick up our weapons, they were shooting right at us, I mean the fucking rocks were kicking up right in front of us, this is in fractions of a second, you know? And we get behind this fucking log and I hear the fucking wood splintering, the wood pile is just crackling, the bullets hitting the wood and shit. They start closing in on us and there's a sniper and my squad leader raised his head and two or three inches above his head a fucking bullet hit the wood so Jackson throws him down says, 'Get down they're fucking shooting right above your head.' The only reason we're alive is the Apaches came in."

The enemy couldn't hope to inflict real damage on the Americans as long as they were in their bases, and the Americans couldn't hope to find the enemy and kill them *unless* they left their bases. As a result, a dangerous game started to evolve over the course of the summer in the Korengal Valley. Every few days the Americans would send out a patrol to talk to the locals and disrupt enemy activity, and they'd essentially walk until they got hit. Then they'd call in massive firepower and hope to kill as many of the enemy as possible. For a while during the summer of 2007 almost every major patrol in the Korengal Valley resulted in a firefight.

The trick for the Americans was to get behind

cover before the enemy gunners ranged in their rounds, which usually took a burst or two. The trick for the enemy was to inflict casualties before the Apaches and the A-10s arrived, which often took half an hour or more. Apaches have a 30 mm chain gun slaved to the pilot's helmet that points wherever he looks; if you shoot at an Apache, the pilot turns his head, spots you, and kills you. The A-10's weapons are worse yet: Gatling guns that unload armor-piercing rounds at the rate of nearly 4,000 per minute. The detonations come so close together that a gun run just sounds like one long belch from the heavens.

Pretty much everyone who died in this valley died when they least expected it, usually shot in the head or throat, so it could make the men weird about the most mundane tasks. Only once did I know beforehand that we were going to get hit, otherwise I was: about to take a sip of coffee, talking to someone, walking about a hundred meters outside the wire, and taking a nap. The men just never knew, which meant that anything they did was potentially the *last* thing they'd ever do. That gave rise to strange forms of magical thinking. One morning after four days of continuous fighting I said that things seemed "quiet," and I might as well have rolled a live hand grenade through the outpost;

every man there yelled at me to shut the fuck up. And then there were Charms: small fruit-flavored candies that often came in the prepackaged meals called MREs. The superstition was that eating Charms would bring on a firefight, so if you found a pack in your MRE, you were supposed to throw it off the back side of the ridge or burn it in the burn pit. One day Cortez got so bored that he ate a pack on purpose, hoping to bring on a firefight, but nothing happened. He never told the others what he'd done.

When a man is hit the first thing that usually happens is someone yells for a medic. Every soldier is trained in combat medicine—which can pretty much be defined as slowing the bleeding enough to get the man onto a MEDEVAC—and whoever is nearest to the casualty tries to administer first aid until the medic arrives. If it's a chest wound the lungs may have to be decompressed, which means shoving a fourteen-gauge angiocatheter into the chest cavity to let air escape. Otherwise, air can get sucked into the pleural cavity through the wound and collapse the lungs until the man suffocates. A man can survive a bullet to the abdomen but die in minutes from a leg or an arm wound if the round hits an artery. A man who is bleeding out will be pale and slow-speaking and awash in his own blood. A staggering amount of blood comes out of a human being.

A combat medic once told me what to do to save a man who's bleeding out. (He then gave me a combat medical pack—mainly, I suspect, so I wouldn't have to take one from another soldier if I ever got hit.) First you grind your knee into the limb, between the wound and the heart, to pinch off the artery and stop the blood flow. While you're doing that you're getting the tourniquet ready. You take pressure off the limb long enough to slide the tourniquet onto the limb and then you tighten it until the bleeding stops. If the medic still hasn't gotten there—maybe he's treating someone else or maybe he's wounded or dead—you pack the wound cavity with something called Kerlix and then bandage it and stick an intravenous drip into the man's arm. If you're wounded and there's no one else around, you have to do all this yourself. And you want to make sure you can do it all one-handed. When a soldier told me that, I unthinkingly asked him why. He didn't even bother answering.

The combat medic's first job is to get to the wounded as fast as possible, which often means running through gunfire while everyone else is taking cover. Medics are renowned for their bravery, but the ones I knew described it more as a terror of failing to save the lives of their friends. The only thing they're thinking about when they run forward to treat a casualty is getting there before the man bleeds out or suffocates; incoming bullets barely register. Each platoon has a medic, and when Second Platoon arrived in the valley, their medic was Juan Restrepo—O'Byrne's friend from their last trip to Rome. Restrepo was extremely well liked because he was brave under fire and absolutely committed to the men. If you got sick he would take your guard shift; if you were depressed he'd come to your hooch and play guitar. He took care of his men in every possible way.

On the afternoon of July 22 a foot patrol left Firebase Phoenix and moved south to the village of Aliabad under a light rain. Much of Second Platoon had already left for a month at Firebase Michigan, which saw so little combat that it practically qualified as summer camp, but there were still men left who had to conduct one last patrol. Restrepo was among them. On the way back they passed an open spot in the road just outside of the Aliabad cemetery and began to take fire. There were enemy gunners east of them above Donga and Marastanau and south of them on Honcho Hill and west of them at Table Rock. It was the first time the Americans had taken fire while inside a village—the enemy was usually too worried about civilian casualties — and the men took cover behind gravestones and holly trees and piles of timber stacked by the road.

Restrepo was the only man hit. He took two rounds to the face and fell to the ground, bleeding heavily. There was so much fire coming from so many different directions that at first no one even dared to run out to get him. When they finally pulled him to safety they didn't know what to do with such a bad wound, and he struggled to tell them how to save his life. Within minutes three Humvees roared out of the KOP and a MEDE-VAC flight lifted off from the air base in Asadabad, twenty miles away. A valley-wide firefight kicked off but they got Restrepo back to the KOP in less than twenty minutes. He was breathing but he was drifting in and out of consciousness, and they brought him to the aid station and ran an oxygen tube down his throat. Some of the oxygen went into his stomach, though, and made him throw up.

"It was the first time I'd seen one of ours like that," Sergeant Mac told me. "Besides Padilla, it was the first time I'd seen one of ours jacked up. When I helped get him into the truck I could see the life was gone. To move a body around that's just not moving was really odd. He was almost...foreign.

That kind of thing gets put someplace deep, to be dealt with later."

The MEDEVAC pilot had been circling the valley, unwilling to land while a firefight was still going on, but he finally put down at the KOP and Restrepo was loaded on.

The radio call came in three hours later. O'Byrne had already written in his journal that Restrepo was too good a man for God to let him die—wrote that despite the fact that he didn't even believe in God—and he and Mac were in the Second Platoon tent cleaning the blood off Restrepo's gear. They had to use baby wipes because the blood had combined with dirt to cement into the cracks of his M4. They also had to take all the bullets out of his magazines and wipe off the blood so that they could be distributed to the other men. They were almost done when a sergeant named Rentas stepped into the tent and grabbed O'Byrne by the shoulders. 'He didn't make it, man,' Rentas said. O'Byrne almost punched him for lying.

"For a long time I hated God," O'Byrne told me. "Second Platoon fought like animals after that."

The Black Hawk gunners bang out half a dozen rounds into the stone hillsides to clear their guns and we bank so hard that I can practically look out the bay door straight down to the ground below. Two Apaches trail us a quarter mile back, low-slung with weaponry and prowling from side to side like huge dark wasps. Neat green fields slide by a thousand feet beneath us, and here and there I can see men bathing in the river or washing pickup trucks that they've driven into the shallows like workhorses. One farmer waves at us as we pass by, which surprises me until I realize that maybe he's just trying to keep from getting shot. I waved at an Apache once; I was by myself on a hillside above the KOP and since I was not dressed like a soldier I was worried what this might look like from the air. The pilot had come down for a closer look and I thought I'd seen the .30 mm chain gun under the nose swing in my direction. It may have all been my imagination but it was not a nice feeling.

We pass the American base at Asadabad and swing west up the Pech. We're flying at ridgetop level and the valley has narrowed so that I can look straight out at Afghanistan's terrible geology. Everything is rock and falls off so steeply that even if you survived the crash your helicopter would just keep bouncing downhill until it reached the valley floor. Soldiers, as far as I can tell, don't think about such things. I've seen them fall asleep on Chinooks like they're on the Greyhound coming back from an all-nighter at Atlantic City. They don't even wake up when the helicopter gets spiked downward by the convection cells above the valleys.

We climb over a ridgeline, the rotors laboring like jackhammers, and then drop into the Korengal. From the air the KOP looks smaller than I remember and more vulnerable, a scattering of Hescos clinging to a hillside with camo net strung between some of them and a landing zone that looks way too small to land on. Red smoke is streaming off the ground, which means the KOP is taking fire, and we get off the bird fast and run for cover behind the Hescos. I find Kearney in the command center looking tired and ten years older than two months ago. He says that as bad as things had been earlier in the summer, they've fallen off a cliff since then. Last week Battle Company got into thirteen firefights in one day. Eighty percent of the combat for the entire brigade is now happening in the Korengal Valley. After firefights the outposts are ankle-deep in used brass. Restrepo was killed and Padilla lost his arm and Loza got hit in the shoulder and a Kellogg, Brown and Root contract worker was shot in the leg while taking a nap in his tent. "We built another outpost, though," Kearney says. "We named it Restrepo, after Doc Restrepo who was killed. It gets hit all the time, but it's taken the heat off Phoenix. The whole battle has shifted south."

In the dead of night a week earlier, Third Platoon walked up the spur above Table Rock and started digging. Second Platoon went as well to protect them. They set up fighting positions west of the new outpost and on the hillside above it and then all night long listened to the *dink, dink, dink* of pickaxes hitting shelf rock. Third Platoon was desperately digging in so that when dawn came they'd have some cover. The new outpost was on top of a position the enemy had used for months to shoot down into Firebase Phoenix and there were still piles of brass up there from their weapons. (Pemble found a round that had misfired and carried it for the rest of the deployment. He considered it good luck on the theory that, had it actually fired, it might have been the bullet that killed him.) From that hilltop the Americans controlled most of the high ground around Phoenix and the KOP, which meant that those bases could no longer be attacked effectively. It was, as Kearney told me, a huge middle finger pointed at the Taliban fighters in the valley.

Dawn brought fusillades of grenades and wave after wave of machine-gun fire. Third Platoon hacked away at the mountain and shoveled the results into sandbags that they could then pile up around them to provide more cover. The Taliban attacked every hour or so from every position they had all day long. The men of Third Platoon worked until the next firefight, rested while firing back, and then resumed work once it quieted down again. Second Platoon shot through so much ammunition that the guns started to jam. "Once I was shooting and I look over and bullets are fucking pinging all around Monroe and he's not firing," O'Byrne remembered. "I'm like, 'What the fuck, Monroe, get the fucking SAW fucking firing, why the fuck aren't you firing?'"

Monroe shouted that the weapon had jammed and then he methodically started taking it apart. Bullets were smacking the dirt all around him but he wouldn't be dissuaded. He wiped the weapon down and oiled it and reassembled it, and when he was done he slid an ammo belt into the feed tray and started returning fire.

After the initial build-out, Third Platoon walked back down to the KOP and Second Platoon took over. Temperatures over a hundred and the men working in full combat gear because they never knew when they were going to get hit. Some men swung pickaxes to break up the rock and other men shoveled the rubble into ammo cans and still others hoisted the cans over their heads and dumped them into an empty Hesco. Hescos are wire baskets with a moleskin lining that the U.S. military uses to build bases in remote areas. They measure eight feet cubed and can contain roughly twenty-five tons of rock or sand. It would take the men of Second Platoon an entire day to fill one to the top, and the plans called for thirty or so Hescos laid out in the shape of a big fishhook facing the enemy. Every time they filled a Hesco their world got a little bigger and every time they got into a firefight they realized where the next Hesco should go. They used plywood and sandbags to build a bunker for the .50 cal and ranged their cots against the southern wall because that was the only place that couldn't get hit. When it rained they stretched tarps over the cots or just got wet and when it was sunny they crouched in the coolness of the .50 cal pit smoking cigarettes and telling their endless grim soldier jokes.

I once asked O'Byrne to describe himself as he was then.

"Numb," he said. "Wasn't scared, wasn't happy, just fucking numb. Kept to myself, did what I had to do. It was a very weird, detached feeling those first few months."

"You weren't scared of dying?"

"No, I was too numb. I never let my brain go there. There were these boundaries in my brain, and I just never let myself go to that spot."

I walk out to Restrepo a couple of weeks after the outpost was started, climbing two hours up the hill with Captain Kearney and a guy from headquarters who keeps throwing up because he's not used to the heat. One soldier bets another twenty-five dollars that we'll get hit with machine-gun fire on the last stretch before the outpost, which is wide open to Taliban positions to the south. We take that part one by one at a sprint and the guy loses his bet. Restrepo sits on a ridge and rides up the mountainside like freighter on a huge wave, the bow in the air and the stern, filled with the bunkers and communications gear, sitting heavily in the trough. There is a wall of Hescos facing south and a burn-shitter enclosed by a supply-drop parachute and pallets of bottled water and MREs and of course stacks and stacks of ammunition: Javelin rockets and hand grenades and 203s and cases of linked rounds for the .50 and the 240 and the SAW. It seemed like there was enough ammo at Restrepo to keep every weapon rocking for an hour straight until the barrels have melted and the weapons have jammed and the men are deaf and every tree in the valley has been chopped down with lead.

When we arrive the men of Second Platoon are sitting on their cots behind the Hescos smoking cigarettes and slitting open pouches of MREs. There is no electricity at Restrepo, no running water, and no hot food, and the men will be up here for most of the next year. Propped above them is a plywood cutout of a man that Second Platoon uses to draw fire. The cutout is eight feet tall and has a phallus practically big enough to see from across the valley. The talk turns to an American base called Ranch House. Two weeks ago — right around the time Second Platoon was building Restrepo — eighty Taliban snipped the wires to the Claymores around the position, overran three guardposts, and were inside the wire practically before anyone knew what was happening. A platoon of Chosen Company soldiers was manning the base, and they'd gone through the first three months without getting into a single major firefight. They came spilling out of their hooches in their underwear throwing hand grenades and trying to put on their body armor. The Taliban were so close that the platoon mortarman had to shoot nearly straight up into the air to hit them; at one point he thought he'd miscalculated and mortared himself. A badly wounded specialist named Deloria found himself unarmed behind enemy lines and picked up a rock so that he could die fighting.

Video shot by a Taliban cameraman during the battle shows heavily armed fighters walking around the base as calmly as if they were organizing a game of cricket. The A-10s finally showed up and the platoon leader asked for a gun run straight through the base but the pilots balked. 'You might as well because we're all going to die anyway' — or something to that effect — the lieutenant yelled into the radio. The gun runs saved the base, but half the twenty American defenders were wounded in the fight, and the command started discussing how fast they could close the base down without having it look like a retreat. Word quickly got around that not only was the enemy unafraid to fight up close, they were willing to absorb enormous casualties in order to overrun an American position. There are small bases like Ranch House all over Afghanistan — they're a cornerstone of the American strategy of engaging with the populace — but most of them are manned by only a couple of squads. Tactically speaking, that is not an insurmountable obstacle to a Taliban commander who has a hundred men and is willing to lose half of them taking an American position. Restrepo was the most vulnerable base in the most hotly contested valley of the entire American sector. It seemed almost inevitable that, sooner or later, the enemy was going to make a serious try for it.

5

—

"GET HIS WAIST GET HIS WAIST!"

The workmanlike hammering of the 240, the terrible snap and buzz of bullets.

"UP ON THE FUCKIN' RIDGE!"

Everyone is yelling but I only hear the parts between the bursts. This is it, full-on contact from fifty meters outside the wire and my head is swiveling around like some kind of berserk robot. A Second Squad PFC named Gutierrez is down and no one knows if he took a round or broke his leg jumping off a Hesco; the medic is bent over him now and the outpost is working every gun it has. The .50 labors away inside the bunker and Toves is taking fire from the east and trying to unjam his SAW

91

and Olson is pouring fire into enemy positions to our south. Toves told me earlier that he joined the Army because he was tired of partying and living at his mother's house, and now he's behind sandbags on a hilltop in Afghanistan getting absolutely rocked. Shells arc out of the weapons and scatter into the dust and men scream information in their weird truncated war language and I'm more or less frozen behind a Hesco watching little gouts of dirt erupt from the ground in front of me. It takes me a moment to understand that those are incoming rounds and that I probably don't want to go there.

"HOW MANY ROUNDS YOU GOT?"

"HE'S IN THE DRAW!"

We're getting hit from the east and the south and the west and the guy to the west is putting rounds straight through the position. They've got another guy below us in the draw and Olson is trying to deal with that but the SAW won't angle low enough to hit him. "TOUGH LOVE!" one man shouts; I'm pretty sure another starts singing. My brain has sought refuge in some slow-motion default that doesn't allow for much decision-making, but after half a minute things regain their normal speed and I'm able to follow Kim as he sprints for the front gate. We stick close to the Hescos because incoming rounds are still doing their nasty thing to the air above our heads. Kim and Rudy lean out from the last Hesco, one high one low, shooting into the draw until Rice walks up with a sour expression on his face and unloads three or four bursts from his SAW. Rice is the head of Weapons Squad and once described himself to me as "one of those goofy guys who just loves combat." After he's done with the SAW he calls for a 203 and Kim hands him a loaded tube and he steps into the open and shoots one down into the draw. He turns away and steps back behind the Hescos before it has even exploded. The gunfire dies down except for the sound of mortars hitting the ridge. Whoever was shooting at us is either dead or out of ammo.

Gutierrez suffered complete fractures of both the tibia and fibula, offsetting his foot from his leg so badly that I found it hard to even look in his direction. He and a Third Squad PFC named Moreno were up on the Hescos dumping ammo cans of dirt when they were targeted by a Taliban gunner on the ridge. O'Byrne says that bullets sound like a rubber band being snapped against plastic when they pass close to you, and that's the sound both men heard all around them before throwing themselves off the Hesco. Moreno landed fine but Guttie caught a foot on the way down and hit with the full weight of his body plus thirty pounds of protective gear.

Moreno put his hands on him and started to pull him out of the gunfire. A Third Squad team leader named Hijar ran forward to help, and he and Moreno managed to drag Guttie behind cover before anyone got hit. By that time the medic, Doc Old, had gotten to them and was kneeling in the dirt trying to figure out how badly Guttie was hurt. Later I asked Hijar whether he had felt any hesitation before running out there. 'No,' Hijar said, 'he'd do that for me. Knowing that is the only thing that makes any of this possible.'

That's my memory of what he said, at any rate; I was still too amped to write anything down. It was our third firefight of the day and there was no reason to think they were done with us yet. Rice sends First Squad out to clear the draw but they come back without making contact and now they're busy reinforcing the position at the front gate with sandbags. Guttie's on his back in the bunker while Doc Old slides a needle into his arm. Guttie already has an IV drip in his arm, a cigarette in one side of his mouth, a fentanyl lollipop in the other side, and he's listening to music on his iPod. A moment later the morphine hits.

"Even my neighborhood dealer had better shit than this," Guttie says.

A soldier named Stichter walks past. He's a tall,

good-looking kid from Iowa who has "INFIDEL" tattooed across his chest and keeps a photo of his sister inside his helmet. (That way, he says, she's the last thing he sees before going out on patrol.) He looks down at Guttie and shakes his head. "Personally, I find it funny that an airborne-qualified soldier jumps five feet and breaks his ankle," he says.

The workday is over and the men start to gather in the bunker, joking and reading magazines and sneaking glances at Guttie. He's lying on a stretcher listening to music with his hands clasped across his chest and a beatific look on his face. He's not even here. I'm sitting on a cot next to Jones, the only black guy in the platoon and one of five in the entire company. He's from Reno, Nevada, but lived in Colorado for a while, where he says he had the highest PT score in the state. He benched 385 and burned the forty in 4.36 seconds. An athletic scholarship to the state university fell through and he wound up selling drugs in Reno before joining the Army to avoid getting killed or doing time. "I'd been shot at plenty back in the civilian world, so I already knew how I'd react under fire," he told me. "I mean I ain't stupid—I'll take cover—but there ain't no bitch in me, either."

Now he's morosely smoking a cigarette while other men joke and chatter around him. Solowski is flipping through a surfing magazine. Kim is in the bunker reading a Harry Potter book. The sun sits low in the west and has laid planks of light across the valley from the western ridges to the dark slopes of the Abas Ghar. I can hear animals—wolves? monkeys?—yapping from the crags above us. Patterson takes a radio call from headquarters and learns that Prophet has overheard the enemy talking about twenty hand grenades in the valley. Rice is standing next to him and says something quietly about Ranch House. "I know," Patterson answers. He walks out of the bunker and repeats the news to the men. No one responds.

"Those are for us," Jones finally mutters. The tip of his cigarette wobbles in the darkness as he speaks. "You don't get grenades to throw three hundred meters. They're going to try to breach this motherfucker."

I was to spend weeks at a time up on that hilltop, and it soon became clear that if I were to get killed over the course of the next year, Restrepo was almost certainly the place it would happen. It wasn't *likely* but it was possible, so I had the strange experience of knowing the location of my fate in advance. That made Restrepo an easy focus for all my fears, a place where the unimaginable had to be considered in detail. Once while leaning against some sandbags I was surprised to feel some dirt fly into my face. It didn't make any sense until I heard the gunshots a second later. How close was that round? Six inches? A foot? When the implications of that kind of thing finally sink in you start studying the place a little more carefully: the crows that ride the thermals off the back side of the ridge, the holly oaks shot to pieces first by the Americans and then by the enemy, and the C-wire and the sandbags and shantytown hooches clinging to the hillsides. It certainly isn't beautiful up there, but the fact that it might be the last place you'll ever see does give it a kind of glow.

For some reason my worry about dying took the form of planning the attack that would kill me—kill us all—in the most minute detail. Some of the men thought the place was impregnable, but I had other ideas. You'd want to hit Restrepo at four in the morning, I decided, while everyone was asleep or groggy from sleeping pills. (They took them to keep from jerking awake at night from imaginary gunfire.) First you'd hit the south-facing guard tower and take out the Mark 19, a belt-fed grenade machine gun that could stop almost any assault in its tracks. After that you'd rake the gun ports with small-arms fire from the south and west and send successive waves of men up the draw. The first wave would absorb the Claymores and the second probably wouldn't make it either, but by the third or fourth, you'd be inside the wire fighting hooch to hooch.

"It would start with RPGs and seventy-five to a hundred guys rushing the wire," Jones said when I asked him how it would go down. "And they don't take prisoners. The guys are killed next to you, you got to defend to the last man because nobody's gonna help you. The KOP is a thousand meters away but it might as well be in a different country because they're not getting to you. So you'd either have to make up your mind to fight until you die, or you'd just say, 'Okay, everyone is dead around me, I'm just gonna go, I'm just gonna leave this place.' And the problem is that all these weapons can be moved, we can set up the .50 and light up the KOP. Then you've got problems in the whole valley. And if they overran it they're gonna kill soldiers, so there's still gonna be bodies of soldiers up here. You wouldn't be able to recover those bodies if you dropped a bomb on it. For them to fully overrun us? It would *definitely* be a bad day."

That was Jones's take. At night I put my vest and helmet at my feet and kept my boots tied loosely so that I could jam my feet into them but not trip over the laces. Waking up to them doing a "Ranch House" on us was by far the most terrifying thing I could imagine, and arranging my things so that I could be out the door in thirty seconds was how I coped with those fears. It didn't work very well. I'd lie awake at night amazed by the idea that everything could change—could, in fact, end—at any moment. And even after I went to sleep those thoughts would just continue on as dreams, full-blown combat sequences that I wallowed through like a bad action movie. In those dreams the enemy was relentless and everywhere at once and I didn't have a chance.

As a civilian among soldiers I was aware that a failure of nerve by me could put other men at risk, and that idea was almost as mortifying as the very real dangers up there. The problem with fear, though, is that it isn't any one thing. Fear has a whole taxonomy—anxiety, dread, panic, foreboding—and you could be braced for one form and completely fall apart facing another. Before the firefights everyone got sort of edgy, glancing around with little half-smiles that seemed to say, "This is what we do—crazy, huh?" and those moments never really bothered me. I trusted the guys I was with and usually just concentrated on finding cover and getting the video camera ready. The fights themselves went by in a blur; if I remembered even half of what happened I was doing well. (I always watched the videotape afterward and was amazed by how much dropped out.) I truly froze only once when we got hit unexpectedly and very hard. I didn't have my body armor or camera near me—stupid, stupid—and endured thirty seconds of paralyzed incomprehension until Tim darted through fire to grab our gear and drag it back behind a Hesco.

Combat jammed so much adrenaline through your system that fear was rarely an issue; far more indicative of real courage was how you felt before the big operations, when the implications of losing your life really had a chance to sink in. My personal weakness wasn't fear so much as the anticipation of it. If I had any illusions about personal courage, they always dissolved in the days or hours before something big, dread accumulating in my blood like some kind of toxin until I felt too apathetic to even tie my boots properly. As far as I could tell everyone up there got scared from time to time, there was no stigma to it as long as you didn't allow it to affect the others, and journalists were no exception. Once I got completely unnerved when Second Platoon was standing by as a quick-reaction force for Firebase Vegas, which was about to get attacked. This was my last trip, I was days from leaving the Korengal forever, and there was a chance that in the next few hours a Chinook would drop us off in the middle of a massive firefight on the Abas Ghar. I was getting my gear ready for the experience — extra water, extra batteries, take the side plates off my vest to save weight — but I guess my face betrayed more anxiety than I realized. "It's okay to be scared," Moreno said to me, loud enough for everyone else to hear, "you just don't want to *show* it…"

There are different kinds of strength, and containing fear may be the most profound, the one without which armies couldn't function and wars couldn't be fought (God forbid). There are big, tough guys in the Army who are cowards and small, feral-looking dudes, like Monroe, who will methodically take apart a SAW while rounds are slapping the rocks all around them. The more literal forms of strength, like carrying 160 pounds up a mountain, depend more obviously on the size of your muscles, but muscles only do what you tell them, so it still keeps coming back to the human spirit. Wars are fought with very heavy machinery that works best on top of the biggest hill in the area and used against men who are lower down. That, in a nutshell, is military tactics, and it means that an enormous amount of war-fighting simply consists of carrying heavy loads uphill.

I was always amazed at the sheer variety of body shapes in the platoon, the radically different designs for accomplishing the same thing. Donoho was six-three and built like an ironing board but carried a full SAW kit, 120 pounds. Walker was an ample, good-natured kid who just sort of trudged along but was essentially unstoppable. (Once the guys quietly filled his ruck with an extra fifty pounds of canned food on top of the eighty he was already carrying; he just hoisted it onto his shoulders and walked to Restrepo without even commenting.) Bobby Wilson was a 240 gunner from Georgia with fingers like sausages and feet that were literally square: size 6, quadruple-E. He straight up described himself as fat but had some kind of crazy redneck strength that was more like hydraulics than musculature. He was known for not even bothering to duck punches when he got into bar fights, he just walked straight into whatever the other guy had for him until he got close enough to clinch. Once the platoon needed to get something called an LRAS down from Restrepo and there were no helicopters to sling it out. An LRAS is a thermal-optical device the size of a filing cabinet that weighs well over a hundred pounds. They just strapped it to Bobby and off he went with a bottle of water in one hand and his 9 mil in the other.

On and on the list went, scrawny guys like Monroe or Pemble carrying as much as big, rangy guys like Jones or the outright mules like Wilson or Walker. The only man who was truly in his own category was Vandenberge, a specialist in Weapons Squad who stood six foot five and arrived in the Korengal weighing three hundred pounds. His hands were so big I was told he could palm sandbags as if they were basketballs. He could pick up a SAW one-handed—twenty-three pounds plus ammo—and shoot it like a pistol. I saw him throw Kim over his shoulder, ford a stream, and then climb halfway up Honcho Hill without even seeming to notice. Once someone wondered aloud whether Vandenberge could ready-up the .50, meaning put it to his shoulder and fire it like a rifle. The .50 weighs almost a hundred pounds and is never fired off its tripod or carried by less than two men. Vandenberge wrapped his huge paws around it, brought it to his shoulder, and sighted down the barrel like he was shooting squirrels with a .22. He rarely spoke but had a shy smile that would emerge from time to time, particularly when men were talking about just how damn big he was. "Vandenberge you big bastard," someone said to him in passing once.

Vandenberge was sitting on a cot doing something. "My bad," he said without even looking up.

O'Byrne wasn't big but it was like he was made out of scrap metal, scars here and there, and nothing seemed to hurt him. Walking point on patrols he had to slow himself down so that he didn't outwalk the rest of the platoon. Once they were clawing their way up Table Rock after a twenty-hour operation and a man in another squad started falling out. "He *can't* be smoked here," I heard O'Byrne seethe to Sergeant Mac in the dark, "he doesn't have the *right* to be." The idea that you're not allowed to experience something as human as exhaustion is outrageous anywhere but in combat. Good leaders know that exhaustion is partly a state of mind, though, and that the men who succumb to it have on some level decided to put themselves above everyone else. If you're not prepared to walk for someone you're certainly not prepared to die for them, and that goes to the heart of whether you should even be in the platoon.

There was no way to overhear a comment like O'Byrne's without considering one's own obligation to keep up. You slow down a patrol, the enemy has time to get into position and then someone gets shot. Trying to imagine being the cause of that scenario was like trying to imagine crashing in a

Chinook: at some point my mind just refused to participate in the experiment. I reassured myself with the thought that I was twice the age of the soldiers but carried half the weight they did, so in some ways it was a fair fight. I also ran track and cross-country in college, and, twenty-five years later, I still remembered how to negotiate the long, horrible process of physical collapse. It starts with pain, of course, but that pain is at the edge of what I thought of as a deep, dark valley. At the bottom of the valley is true incapacitation, but it might take hours to get down there, working your way through strata of misery and dissociation until your muscles simply stop obeying and your mind can't even be trusted to give commands that make sense. The most valuable thing I knew from all that running was that when you start hurting you're not even *close* to the bottom of the valley, and that if you don't panic at the first agonies there's much, much more of yourself to give.

I wore a body armor vest like the soldiers did—they called it an "IBA"—and a helmet, which they called a "Kevlar." Together those weighed around thirty pounds. I had a five-pound video camera, five pounds of water in a CamelBak, and maybe another twenty pounds of food and clothing if we were going out overnight. I could walk all day with fifty or sixty pounds on my back but I couldn't run more than a hundred yards at a time—no one could—and few people could run uphill more than a few steps. I carried my camera on a strap but it got destroyed swinging into rocks on a nighttime operation, so I hooked the new one onto a carabiner that hung off my left shoulder. That way it swung less and was easier to put my hands on quickly. I had extra batteries and tapes in my vest as well as a medical kit, and on patrols I strapped a CamelBak directly to it so that I could ditch my pack and still be okay. I had my blood type, "O POS," written on my boots, helmet, and vest, and I had my press pass buttoned into a pants pocket along with a headlamp, a folding knife, and notebook and pens. Everything I needed was on me pretty much all the time.

Patrols on hot days came down to water versus distance: you didn't want to go dry, but neither did you want to carry ten extra pounds if you were going to have to run anywhere. I'd try to have drunk three-quarters of my water by the turn-around point of a patrol, and then at the bottom of the steep climb to Restrepo I'd sip at it steadily so I was light and hydrated when we were most likely to get hit. I'd find myself doing a body check all the way up: "Legs okay, breathing labored, mouth dry but not too bad," various internal levels that had been calibrated during races in college and never forgotten. (It didn't matter how badly off I was as long as some other soldier was worse; I just didn't want to be the one holding things up.) I never went on a patrol that hurt more than an even moderately hard college race, and I've never run a race that held anything close to the implications of the most mundane task a hundred meters outside the wire.

Giving in to fear or exhaustion were the ways in which a soldier could fail his platoon, but there were ways a reporter could screw things up as well. Tim broke his ankle on a nighttime operation on the Abas Ghar, but the medic told him it was only sprained so that, mentally, Tim would think he could walk on it. And he did. There was no other way to get him out of there, and if the platoon were still on the mountain at dawn they were going to get hammered. He walked all night on a fractured fibula with only Motrin as a painkiller, and they didn't tell him it was broken until he got to the KOP. They put a steel plate and a bunch of screws into his leg and a few months later he was back in business.

Several years earlier in Zabul I had asked the battalion commander how discreet I had to be on my satellite phone when calling home, and he just said, "Big-boy rules, I hope I don't have to explain what that means." Tim was playing by big-boy rules up there, which essentially means making your interests secondary to those of the group no matter how much it costs you.

"There are guys in the platoon who straight up *hate* each other," O'Byrne told me one morning. We were sitting in ambush above the village of Bandeleek listening to mortars shriek over our heads, and there wasn't much to do but flinch and talk about the platoon. "But they would also die for each other. So you kind of have to ask, 'How much could I really hate the guy?'"

Around midmorning a squad of Scouts comes walking in through the wire, uniforms plastered to their bodies and sweat running off the ends of their noses. Second Platoon has been hacking away at the hillside all morning and the men pause at their shovels and pickaxes to greet them. Guttie was MEDEVACed last night without incident and it has been quiet all morning, which may simply mean the enemy is out of ammunition. The Scouts have a different vibe from the regular line soldiers, leaner and quieter, and they seem to carry a little less gear. Their job is to patrol beyond anywhere line infantry would go and then report back what they see. Sometimes they'll set in for days at a time and just watch. They're not supposed to get into firefights, and when they do engage, it's often just a single shot from a sniper rifle.

The squad leader is a short, strong-looking man with dark eyes and jet-black hair named Larry Rougle. Rougle has done six combat tours in six years and is known in Battle Company as a legendary badass and some kind of ultimate soldier. Once Phoenix got hit and Rougle and his men grabbed their weapons at the KOP and ran down there so fast that Piosa was still on the radio calling in the attack when they walked in the wire. You couldn't even get there that fast in a Humvee. Rougle talks to Piosa in the bunker while his men pour bottled water down their throats and half an hour later they form up and Tim and I grab our packs and follow them out of the wire. We contour around the draw until we reach OP 1, which sits on a promontory west of the KOP. It's only manned by four men at a time and it's almost impossible to attack, so there's nothing for the men to do up there but wave away the flies and think about how many months they have left. When we arrive Rougle stands on a bunker and looks eastward toward the Abas Ghar.

"Everything you can see," he says to me, "I've walked on."

6

DAWN AT THE KOP: ONE LAST PLANET LIKE
a pinhole in the sky, crows rising on the valley thermals. The sun about to crack open the day from
beyond the Abas Ghar. I'm sitting on the broken
office chair outside the hooch waiting to see what
will happen. Kearney has ordered stand-to at zero
hundred hours—4:30 a.m. local—because there's
intel the enemy may attack the KOP and try to
breach the wire. Men are shuffling around, fum-
bling for their weapons. Stand-to means you get
dressed and geared up and if you don't get attacked
you can go back to sleep. The men sleep as much
as they can, every chance they get, far beyond the
needs of the human body. "If you sleep twelve hours

111

a day it's only a seven-month deployment," one soldier explained.

The day broadens and no attack comes. I walk
up to the operations center to talk to Kearney, who
is half asleep at his desk. Third Platoon will be
going onto the Abas Ghar in a couple of days and
Tim and I are going with them. (Jones: "Personally, I wouldn't follow them into a Dairy Queen.")
Around midafternoon a sniper on the ridge above
Restrepo starts shooting into the KOP; it's not
the attack that was expected but it's enough to get
everyone's attention. When the men move around
the base they sprint the open sections until, *ka-
SHAAH*, another round cracks past and they stop
behind a Hesco. (Soldiers spend a good deal of time
trying to figure out how to reproduce the sound of
gunfire verbally, and "ka-SHAAH" was the word
Second Platoon seemed to have settled on.) I'm sitting in the broken office chair outside the hooch,
which has pretty good cover, watching Tim make
his way to the burn-shitters. He runs to a tree, lurks
there for a moment, and then runs to the next tree.
If you didn't know about the sniper you'd think he
was doing some comic routine of an Englishman
gone completely mad in the noonday sun.

Snipers have the power to make even silence
unnerving, so their effectiveness is way out of

proportion to the number of rounds they shoot. The KOP's mortars eventually start up, great explosions that crash through the base and then rumble back to us from the mountaintops. They may have killed the guy, but I doubt it, and in the end it doesn't even matter; it's just one man with a rifle and ten dollars' worth of ammunition. He doesn't even *need* to hit anyone to be effective: helicopters aren't flying into the valley and thirty or forty men spend the afternoon behind sandbags trying to figure out whether they're getting shot at by a Russian-made Dragunov or an old Enfield .308. Once I was at the operations center when single shots started coming in, and First Sergeant Caldwell headed for the door to deal with it. On his way out I asked him what was going on. "Some jackass wastin' our time," he said.

That jackass was probably a local teenager who was paid by one of the insurgent groups to fire off a magazine's worth of ammo at the KOP. The going rate was five dollars a day. He could fire at the base until mortars started coming back at him and then he could drop off the back side of the ridge and be home in twenty minutes. Mobility has always been the default choice of guerrilla fighters because they don't have access to the kinds of heavy weapons that would slow them down. The fact that networks of highly mobile amateurs can confound—even defeat—a professional army is the only thing that has prevented empires from completely determining the course of history. Whether that is a good thing or not depends on what amateurs you're talking about—or what empires—but it *does* mean that you can't predict the outcome of a war simply by looking at the numbers.

For every technological advantage held by the Americans, the Taliban seemed to have an equivalent or a countermeasure. Apache helicopters have thermal imaging that reveals body heat on the mountainside, so Taliban fighters disappear by covering themselves in a blanket on a warm rock. The Americans use unmanned drones to pinpoint the enemy, but the Taliban can do the same thing by watching the flocks of crows that circle American soldiers, looking for scraps of food. The Americans have virtually unlimited firepower, so the Taliban send only one guy to take on an entire firebase. Whether or not he gets killed, he will have succeeded in gumming up the machine for yet one more day. "Everything in war is simple, but the simplest thing is difficult," the military theorist Carl von Clausewitz wrote in the 1820s. "The difficulties accumulate and end by producing a kind of *friction*."

That friction is the entire goal of the enemy in the valley; in some ways it works even better than killing. Three days later we're in the mechanics' bay waiting for the Pech resupply to come in, two Chinooks that run a slow route through the northeast every four days picking up men and dropping off food and ammo. Tim and I are leaving the valley, and the Pech is our way out. The men are on edge because the sniper has been at it all morning, and when the first Chinook comes in, it immediately takes fire from across the valley. A bullet goes up the gunner's sleeve without breaking his skin and exits through the fuel tank. It was supposedly his first combat mission. After a while a Black Hawk makes it in and drops off the battalion commander, Colonel Ostlund, who strides across the LZ flanked by several officers and two Al Jazeera journalists in powder-blue ballistic vests. One of the officers sees us crouched behind the Hescos and realizes that something must be up. "DO WE HAVE A SITUATION HERE?" he shouts over the rotor noise.

Once again, a couple of guys with rifles have managed to jam up an entire company's worth of infantry. Ostlund and his staff get back on the Black Hawk and head across the valley for Firebase Vegas. I'm standing next to a tall Marine named Cannon who tells me that the war here is way more intense than most people understand. While we're talking the shooting starts up again, a staccato hammering that I now recognize as the .50 out at Vegas. Cannon is wearing a radio and gets a communication on the company net that I can't quite understand.

"Vegas is in a TIC," he says.

The mortars start firing and an A-10 tilts into its dive and starts working the Abas Ghar with its chain guns. A minute later Cannon's radio squawks again. "One wounded at Vegas," he repeats for me, and then, "The platoon sergeant was shot in the neck, he's not breathing."

Hunter, who is standing near us, overhears this and walks away. He's a team leader in First Platoon and knows the sergeant well. His name is Matt Blaskowski, and he's already received a Silver Star for dragging a wounded comrade to safety during a six-hour firefight in Zabul. A while later Cannon gets another radio update.

"He died on the MEDEVAC bird," he says.

Neither of us could know this, of course, but Cannon himself would be dead in a couple of weeks, shot through the chest during an ambush outside Aliabad. I was already in New York when I heard the news, and I know this is a stupid point, and obvious, but for some reason that was when I realized how easy it was to go from the living to the dead: one day you hear about some guy getting killed out at Vegas and the next day you're that same guy for someone else.

Apaches finally come in and clear the upper ridges. Two days later I'm at the Delhi airport waiting for a flight home.

BOOK TWO

KILLING

We sleep soundly in our beds because rough men stand ready in the night to visit violence on those who would do us harm.

— Winston Churchill (or George Orwell)

1
—

SQUAD AND PLATOON LEADERS GATHER IN AN
unfinished brick-and-mortar at the top of the KOP,
tense and quiet in the hours before the operation.
It's called Rock Avalanche—a play on the battalion nickname—and will probably be the biggest operation of the deployment. The men will
be going into some of the most dangerous places
in the valley looking for weapons caches and infiltration routes, and what happens over the course
of the next week could well determine the level of
combat in the valley for the coming year. The men
sit on a low bench next to an orange Atika cement
mixer under steel rafters that do not yet have a roof
and wait for Kearney to begin the meeting. In the

front row is Rougle, the Scout leader, and then Stichter and Patterson and Rice and McDonough and Buno, all from Second Platoon. Men from the other two platoons stand and squat along the walls. They're in their body armor and most of them have wads of chew under their lower lip. They're so clean and well-shaven, they could almost pass for rear-base infantry.

Kearney stands before them with a rake in one hand and a sheaf of papers in the other and reading glasses jammed crookedly under the rim of his helmet. At his feet is a sandbox that has been sculpted into a rough three-dimensional model of the Korengal. Cardboard cutouts of Chinooks dangle from strings where the air assaults will go in. The first phase of the operation is a sweep of Yaka Chine, one of the centers of armed resistance in the Korengal. Much of the weaponry that comes into the valley passes through Yaka Chine, as do most of the local commanders, and there is every reason for the men of Battle Company to think they'll wind up in the fight of their lives. Second Platoon will get dropped off at a landing zone code-named Toucans and move in from the south. First Platoon will get dropped east of town and hook up with Second Platoon near a building complex nicknamed the "Chinese Restaurant." From a distance, through binoculars, the building's cornices are ornate and seem to curve upward in a way that suggests the Far East. It's supposed to be the location of a major weapons depot.

"The other area we're going to have to focus some of our efforts on is going to be the lumberyard," Kearney says, pointing with his rake. "The lumberyard is where we believe that there is a lot of the caches, and it's kind of the battle handover spot for the guys coming from the Chowkay Valley into the Korengal and then pushin' it through Yaka Chine, where they end up divvying it up to the different subcommanders."

Piosa comes forward and explains what Second Platoon's task and purpose will be, then calls on Rice and McDonough and Buno to go into more detail for each squad. Rougle stands up and walks around to the top of the sandbox and points where the Scouts will come in and what their role will be in the operation. The radio call sign for the Scouts is "Wildcat," and Rougle tells the rest of the company what the Wildcat element will be doing: "We'll be occupying somewhere in this vicinity," he says, gesturing with a pointer. "We'll find a good place where we can set up the Barrett and the twenty-five. We'll also be holding overwatch on the lumberyard."

The Yaka Chine operation is expected to take

twenty-four hours, and then the men will be picked up by helicopter and dropped on the upper slopes of the Abas Ghar and an intersecting ridge called the Sawtalo Sar. There's intel about cave complexes up there and weapons caches and supply routes that cross over to the Shuryak and then on into Pakistan. The largest cave is supposed to have electricity and finished walls and a boulder at the entrance that can be moved into position with a car jack. When the fighters want to disappear, they supposedly jack the boulder into place from the inside and wait until the danger has passed. Chosen Company will be blocking enemy movement in the Shuryak Valley, to the east, and Destined will be in the Chowkay, to the south. The men of Battle Company will be on unfamiliar terrain with enormous loads on their backs chasing a fluid and agile enemy, and almost every advantage enjoyed by a modern army will be negated on the steep, heavily timbered slopes of the Abas Ghar.

Caldwell tells the men that if there's no air they'll be walking, but no one laughs because they're not sure it's a joke. Could the Army be dumb enough to make them walk the entire valley and then climb the Abas Ghar with 120 pounds on their backs? Each man will carry enough food, water, and ammo for a day or two, and after that they'll be resupplied by "speedball": body bags of supplies thrown out of moving helicopters. There will be two full platoons on the mountain as well as Kearney and his entire headquarters element, a squad of scouts, and a couple of platoons of ANA. There will be long-range bombers and F-15s and -16s from Diego Garcia, in the Indian Ocean, as well as Apache helicopters flying out of JAF and A-10 Warthogs and an AC-130 Spectre gunship based at Bagram. It's a huge, weeklong operation, and it's virtually certain that some men who are alive at this moment will be dead or injured by the time it's over. Even without an enemy it's hard to move that many men and aircraft around a steep mountain range and not have something bad happen.

The men spend the last hours of daylight packing their gear and making sure their ammo racks are correctly rigged. Chuck Berry is playing on someone's laptop inside the brick-and-mortar. Donoho helps Rice adjust his rack, cinching it down in the back until it's balanced and snug. Rice's assault pack weighs seventy pounds and his weapon, ammo, and body armor will be at least another forty or fifty on top of that. Buno has a pack that looks so heavy, Rueda can't resist coming over and trying to lift it. Moreno bets Hijar ten bucks that Hoyt can't do twenty pull-ups on one of the steel girders in their barracks. He does, barely. The men paint their faces with greasepaint but Patterson makes them wipe it off and then they just sit and talk and go through the slow, tense countdown until the birds arrive. Some men listen to music. Some just lie on their cots staring at the ceiling. In some ways the anticipation feels worse than whatever may be waiting for them down in Yaka Chine or up on the Abas Ghar, and every man gets through it in his own quietly miserable way.

Shortly after eight o'clock the first Chinooks come clattering into the KOP from the north, rotors ablaze with sparks from the dust that they kick up as they land. First Platoon hustles on with their gear and the huge machines lift off and make the run south with their Apache escorts and then they come back to the KOP for the next load. At 8:41 p.m. the men of Second Platoon file into the back of their Chinook and sit facing each other on web seats with their night vision scopes down. The infrared strobes on the outside of the aircraft pump light out into the night in a long slow heartbeat. The aircraft fights its way up into the sky and tilts south and puts down ten minutes later at LZ Toucans. The men move out, grabbing their packs as they go, and a minute later they're on the mountainside listening to the wind in the trees and the occasional squelp of the radios. Yaka Chine is three or four clicks away. The men fall into line and start walking north.

Kearney has signal intelligence teams scattered around the valley, three LRAS devices watching the town, and surveillance drones circling overhead. He is directing everything by radio from the summit of Divpat, a flat-topped mountain to the east. Almost immediately, drones spot two fighters moving toward Kearney's position and a Spectre gunship, circling counterclockwise overhead, drills them with 20 mm rounds. That begins a game of cat-and-mouse where American airpower tries to prevent fighters from crossing open ground and gaining the protection of the houses in town. Later that night a group of fighters make it to a house outside Yaka Chine, and Kearney is granted permission by the brigade commander to destroy it with cannon fire from a Spectre gunship. Later, a B-1 bomber drops 2,000 pounds of high explosive on a ridgeline, where more insurgents had been observed positioning themselves for an attack.

The men of Second Platoon walk most of the night to the rip and boom of ordnance farther up the valley, and at dawn they find themselves close enough to human habitation to hear roosters crowing. A surveillance drone motors endlessly overhead.

WAR

The men move slowly and awkwardly along the hillsides under their heavy loads but eventually come out onto a corduroy road built of squared-off timbers that serves as a skidway for the enormous trees that get cut on the upper ridges. The walking is easy but they're wide open and after a while they leave the road and climb a brutally steep hillside to a grassy upland plateau. First Platoon comes into contact from a farm complex above town and they return fire, and then Second Platoon clears the buildings and waits in the bright fall sunlight while chickens peck past them in the dirt and cows groan from the alleyways.

Eventually a delegation of village elders tracks down Piosa and his men and leads them to a house with three children with blackened faces and a woman lying stunned and mute on the floor. Five corpses lie on wooden pallets covered by white cloth outside the house, all casualties from the airstrikes the night before. Medics start treating the wounded while Piosa's men continue sweeping the village for weapons. They find eight RPG rounds and a shotgun and an old German pistol and some ammo and a pair of binoculars and an old Henri-Martin rifle—all contraband, but not the huge cache they were expecting. Prophet picks up radio traffic of one Taliban fighter asking another, "Have they found it, have they found it?" Obviously, they have not.

The civilian casualties are a serious matter and will require diplomacy and compensation. Second Platoon spends the night at a hilltop compound overlooking Yaka Chine, and the next morning Apaches come in to look around and then a Black Hawk lands on a rooftop inside the village. Ostlund jumps out like a strange camouflaged god and climbs down a wooden ladder to the ground. With him is a member of the provincial government—the first time a representative of any government, past or present, has made it past the mouth of the valley. Kearney arrives with Ostlund and quickly moves to the front of twenty or thirty locals with the weapons arrayed at his feet. There are old men with their beards dyed orange and eyes like small black holes and young men who don't smile or talk and are clearly here to see, up close, the men they're trying to kill from a distance, and young boys who dart around the edges, seemingly unmindful of the seriousness of things. Kearney is unshaven and shadowed with dirt from two nights on Divpat. The Americans are by far the dirtiest men there.

The locals sit with their backs against a stone wall and Kearney crouches in front of them to speak but soon stands back up. "I'm here to tell you guys why

I did what I did. I'm Captain Kearney, the U.S. commander for the Korengal," he says, and waits for the translator to finish. "When I come into villages and I find RPGs and weapons that are shot at myself and at the ANA, that indicates that there's bad people in here. Good people don't carry these weapons."

Every few sentences Kearney stops to let the translator catch up, and spends the time pacing back and forth, getting more and more heated. "I can walk into Aliabad and not get shot at and not find any weapons...and I come into your village and I find RPGs." He picks one up and waves it at the elders. "I bet I could give this RPG to any one of these younger kids and they'd know how to fire it— and they probably don't even know how to read."

He points to a young man seated in front of him. "You know how to shoot this thing?"

The kid shakes his head.

"Yeah, right."

Kearney looks around. "You guys have insurgents here that are against myself and against the ANA and against the government. And they're going to cause you guys to be hurt if you don't help me out. I was able to pinpoint fifty insurgents that were in and around your village. The first building I engaged, the next morning when I get there I find five RPGs in it. So I know there's not only good people in the building, there's also bad people."

Hajji Zalwar Khan, the wealthy and dignified leader of the valley, sits cross-legged on the ground directly in front of Kearney. He's got a white beard and a handsome face and a narrow, aquiline nose that would easily pass for French at a Paris café. Kearney finishes by asking him point-blank for help: he wants Zalwar Khan to bring representatives from Yaka Chine to the weekly *shura* at the KOP. The old man says that Kearney will have to supply the fuel for the trip, and Kearney is about to agree but catches himself.

"I already told you: one Dishka and I'll pay for your fuel," he says. "When you tell me where a Dishka is, I'll give you fuel for every single Friday for as long as I'm here."

Zalwar Khan laughs. Kearney pinches the bridge of his nose and shakes his head.

"Hajji, I trust you," he says. "I trust you."

Ostlund is up next. He stands there bareheaded and clean-shaven, looking more like a handsome actor in a war movie than a real commander in the worst valley in Afghanistan. His style is respectful and earnest and he appeals to the men before him as husbands and fathers rather than as potential enemies.

"We came here with a charter from the U.S. government with direction from the Afghan government and the Afghan national security forces," he says. The translator delivers the sentence in Pashto and then stops and looks over. "And we were asked to bring progress to every corner of Afghanistan. Somehow miscreants have convinced some of your population that we want to come here and challenge Islam and desecrate mosques and oppress Afghan people. All of those are lies. Our country supports all religions."

The translator catches up. None of the expressions change.

"All of my officers are trained and educated enough that they could teach at a university," Ostlund goes on. "I challenge you elders to put them to work; put them to work building your country, fixing your valley. That's what they're supposed to do — that's what I *want* them to do — but they can't until you help us with security."

The translator is good; he delivers Ostlund's points with nuance and feeling and looks around at the old men like he's delivering a sermon. They stare back unmoved. They've seen the Soviets and they've seen the Taliban, and no one has made it in Yaka Chine more than a day or two. The name means "cool waterfall," and it's a truly lovely place where you're never far from the gurgle of water or the quiet shade of the oak trees, but it's no place for empires.

"You can be poisoned by miscreants and they can tell you that America is bad, that the government's bad, but I ask you this: what have the people who run around with this stuff"—Ostlund waves a hand at the weapons—"done for your families? Have they provided you an education? Have they provided you a hospital? I don't think so. I would say, shame on you, if you follow foreign leaders that leave their beautiful homes in Pakistan and come here and talk you into fighting against your own country, and they do nothing for you."

He stops so that the translator will get every word, then goes on:

"The ACM that comes in and gives you five dollars to carry this stuff around the mountains and tells you you're doing a jihad, is doin' nothing for you except making you a slave for five dollars. These foreigners won't fight my soldiers; they hide on a mountain in a cave under a rock and talk on the radio and pay *your* sons a small amount of money to go ahead and shoot at my soldiers. And my soldiers end up killing your sons."

ACM means "Anti-Coalition Militia"—essentially, the Taliban. It's a good speech and delivered with the force of conviction. That night a dozen or so fighters are spotted moving toward Kearney's position on Divpat, and an unmanned drone fires a Hellfire missile at them. They scatter, but the Apaches won't finish them off because they can't determine with certainty that the men are carrying weapons. The Americans fly out of Yaka Chine, and valley elders meet among themselves to decide what to do. Five people are dead in Yaka Chine, along with ten wounded, and the elders declare jihad against every American in the valley.

2

DAWN ON THE ABAS GHAR, SOLDIERS CURLED on the ground wrapped in poncho liners or zipped into sleeping bags. The platoon has made a cold camp in a forest of small spruce after walking most of the night chasing heat signatures on the upper ridges. The signatures turned out to be embers that were still burning from artillery strikes days earlier. When the men kick out of their bags the sun is already over the eastern ridge and the Afghans have started a twig fire in a patch of bare open ground to warm their hands. There are stumps of huge trees cut down years earlier and hillsides of chest-high brush now blaze-yellow in the late season and dirt trails packed so hard they'll barely take a footprint.

WAR

The men change their socks and lace up their boots and smoke the day's first cigarette and line up with their rifles balanced sideways on their ammo racks. Then they move out.

The men walk slowly and deliberately under their heavy loads, stopping when the line accordions and then starting up again without a word. Walking point is a four-man team from Mac's First Squad, and their job is to clear the terrain ahead of the main group and trip any ambushes. First Squad is the lead element for the platoon, which is spearheading the effort for the entire company, which represents the main thrust of the battalion. It's a significant honor and a huge responsibility. The men are sweating now and moving uphill toward the rising sun through burned-over logging slash and quiet dense stands of spruce and fir. Off to the south the mountains are still smoking from the airstrikes above Yaka Chine. Around midmorning Piosa calls a halt because Prophet has picked up enemy fighters discussing American troop movements, and then a possible bunker is spotted on a ridge to the southwest. Rougle's sniper puts three rounds into it but nothing happens, so Piosa sends First Squad to clear the structure and get a grid coordinate, and then they move on.

It's as if they're alone on the mountain, but they're

almost certainly not. Prophet picks up radio chatter that insurgents have caught an Afghan soldier and are going to cut his head off. The Americans conduct a furious personnel count and determine that it's just a bit of psychological warfare to throw them off their game. Kearney finally calls mortars down on a ridgeline to the south—a suspected enemy position—but even that fails to stir anything up. At one point, a shepherd wanders through the position with a herd of goats; later, Prophet picks up radio traffic of men whispering. The insurgents have never whispered on their radios before and no one gives it any thought until much later, when the reasons are all too clear.

The second night is spent again in thick spruce forests high up on a spur of the Abas Ghar called the Sawtalo Sar. Second Platoon orients themselves toward the north, with the ANA to the south, headquarters to the west, and Rougle and his Wildcat element to the east. Rice and his gun team—Jackson, Solowski, and Vandenberge—are up there with Wildcat as well, on a hill that has been designated 2435, for its altitude in meters. From their positions some of the men can see the remains of the Chinook that was shot down in 2005. That night the shadow people arrive, weird hallucinations that occur after too many nights without sleep. The men have slept a total of eight or ten hours in the past hundred and their judgment couldn't be more impaired if they were piss-drunk. Trees turn into people and bushes shift around on the ridgelines as if preparing to attack; it's all the men on guard can do to keep from opening fire.

Dawn of the second day: a raw wind sawing across the ridgetops and the ground frozen like rock. On a trail above the camp the men line up and eat MREs while waiting for orders to move out. "We eat our boredom," Jones says while watching Stichter put cheese spread on a chocolate energy bar. They've got four days' growth on their chins and their faces are dark with dirt and it's so cold that everyone is wearing ski caps under their helmets. Enemy fighters are still whispering on their radios, but they haven't fired a shot since Yaka Chine and the men are just starting to think this isn't going to happen. Chosen Company will be clearing villages in the Shuryak, and Battle's job is to support them by making sure no fighters cross the Abas Ghar in either direction. They'll spend another night in this area and then probably start their exfil the following day.

That's more or less what the men are thinking about when the first smattering of gunfire comes in.

At first no one knows where it's coming from,

and then bullets start clipping branches over people's heads and smacking the tree trunks next to them. The men jump off the trail into a steeply sloped spruce forest and Jones gets his 240 going and Donoho starts popping 203s across the draw to their south. They're taking heavy, accurate fire from an adjacent ridgeline and it's so effective that much of Second Platoon is having trouble even getting their guns up. It's during these first few minutes of confusion that Buno comes sprinting down the line with a strange look on his face. It occurs to Hijar that he's never seen Buno look scared before.

'An American position is getting overrun,' Buno tells him.

Hijar grabs a LAW rocket and starts running up the line with the rest of his fire team. Piosa is on the radio to Kearney and Stichter is calculating grid coordinates for mortars and the men are crawling around in the forest trying to find cover. Pemble is behind a tree stump and he looks to his right and sees rounds chopping the branches off a tree next to him. 'Shit, it's really close,' he thinks. Bullets are coming from so many directions that there's no way to take cover from everything. Upslope toward Wildcat someone starts screaming for a medic and Pemble passes word down the line, but nothing comes back up so he and Cortez start running up there. They sprint through heavy fire, keeping to the treeline as long as they can and then breaking across an open patch right below Wildcat's position. The first man they see is Vandenberge, who's sitting on the ground holding his arm. Blood is welling out between his fingers. 'I'm bleeding out, you gotta save me,' he says. 'I'm dying.'

He's been hit in the artery and will be dead in minutes without medical help. Pemble kneels down and starts unpacking his medical kit, and while he's doing that he asks Vandenberge where the enemy is.

'The last guy I saw was about twenty feet away,' Vandenberge says.

Pemble starts stuffing the wound with Kerlix until he's knuckle-deep in Vandenberge's huge arm. Vandenberge is soaked with blood from his boots to his collar and soon Pemble is too, and when he cuts the sleeve off Vandenberge's uniform another two or three cups of blood spill out. "You could see it in his face that he's slowly dying," Pemble said. "He was turning really ghost-looking. His eyes started sinking into his head, he started to get real brown around his eyes. And he kept saying, 'I'm getting really dizzy, I want to go to sleep.' That's some rough shit to hear, coming from one of your best friends and you're watching him die right in front of you, that's some fucking shit. All I did was block everything he was saying out except what I needed to hear, like where the Taliban was at and checking for all his wounds."

Jackson shows up with nothing but a rifle in his hand—no helmet or vest. He'd been pushed off the hilltop along with Solowski, who'd emptied a whole magazine at the enemy and then fallen back under continuous heavy fire. By now Cortez has made it to Rice, who's sitting in some brush holding his gut. He's taken a bullet through the back of his shoulder that ricocheted strangely inside him and came out his abdomen, just below the ballistic plate of his vest. The last thing he remembers was a Taliban fighter aiming an RPG at him from forty yards away. He had time to think that it was the last thing he'd ever see, but now Cortez is kneeling in front of him asking where he's wounded. He's already done a quick assessment on himself—which more or less consists of realizing that if he hasn't died yet he probably isn't going to—and he knows the enemy has just overrun a critical hill in the middle of the American line. If they get set in up there they can shred any Americans coming to help.

'Just take back the hill,' he says.

Cortez, Jackson, and Walker assault up the hill but the enemy has already retreated and there's no one to fight, no one to kill. Cortez goes to one knee behind cover with his rifle up and glances to the right and sees a body lying facedown—an American. Walker runs to him and shakes him to see if he's all right and finally rolls him over. It's Staff Sergeant Rougle, shot through the forehead and his face purple with trauma. "I wanted to cry but I didn't—I was shocked," Cortez said. "I just wanted to kill everything that came up that wasn't American. I actually didn't care who came up—man, woman, child, I still would've done something."

They're joined by Hijar, Hoyt, and Donoho. Someone has thrown a poncho liner over Rougle, but it's clear from the boots protruding at the bottom that it's an American soldier. Rougle was hit multiple times on one side of his body in a way that made Kearney think he was caught midstride and had turned to meet a sudden threat from behind. Cortez worried that Rougle was still alive when the enemy overran the position and that they had executed him where he lay, but there was no evidence to support that. Nevertheless, the thought was to torment Cortez in the coming months. Every night he'd dream he was back on the mountain trying to run fast enough to make things turn out differently. They never would. "I'd prefer to not sleep and not dream about it," Cortez said, "than sleep with that picture in my head."

Rougle's men arrive minutes later. Shortly before the attack Rougle left their position to talk to Staff Sergeant Rice and his men have no idea what happened to him. There was so much gunfire that they thought they were about to get overrun, so a Scout named Raeon broke down the Barrett sniper rifle and scattered the pieces around the position so the enemy couldn't use it against American forces. Now the Scouts come running forward looking for their commander and all they find is blood and gear all over the hilltop and a body covered by a poncho liner. Next to the body is an empty MRE packet and a water bottle. "Is Rougle and them up?" a Scout named Clinard asks. Hoyt glances at him and looks away.

"What?" Clinard says. No one says anything and Hoyt walks over to him and just cups his hand on the back of Clinard's neck.

"Who's over there?" Clinard says, voice rising in panic.

"It's Rougle," Hoyt says quietly.

A strange animal noise starts coming up out of Clinard and he breaks away from Hoyt and backs up in horror. Solowski comes up and asks if Rice is alive. He's crying as well.

"Yeah, he's good," Hoyt says.

"He's alive?"

"He's gonna make it, dude."

The men are taking cover and aiming their weapons southward off the top of the hill and Clinard is roaming around the position shrieking with grief. He finally comes to a stop near Hijar and sits down, sobbing. Hijar is behind a tree stump scanning the draw. "We got friendlies over there we tried to push through and they lit us the fuck up," Clinard says, trying to explain why they didn't get to Rougle faster.

"Let's go brother, come on," Hoyt says, beckoning Clinard with one hand. Clinard just sits there shaking his head. "That ain't Sergeant Rougle—you're lyin' right, man?" he says.

"I ain't lyin'—why would I lie about something like that?"

Clinard gets up but stays stooped with grief. "Where'd he get hit?—I got to see."

"Don't look at him."

"Is it bad?"

"It was quick."

Clinard stays bent double as if he's just finished a race and moans again in his strange animal way. He says something about how Rougle's death was their fault. The men around him are prepping hand grenades and getting ready to repel another attack and Piosa finally makes it up to the hilltop with

Donoho as his radioman. Donoho's eyes are wide and he's swallowing hard. "Battle Six Romeo this is Two-Six, I've pushed to the site of the KIA, break," Piosa says into the radio. (Battle Six refers to Kearney and Two-Six refers to Piosa himself. "Six" generally follows the unit name and means "leader" or "commander.") "Right now we have the hilltop, we're going to move the wounded-in-action, there's two of them, up to LZ Eagles. I'm also going get my KIA there, break."

Mortars start hitting the enemy ridge with a sound like a huge oak door slamming shut. Rougle lies alone under the poncho liner off in the brush and finally two of his men and an Afghan soldier bend over him and start stripping the ammo out of his rack. When they're done, six Afghan soldiers put him on a poncho and start carrying him downhill toward the landing zone, but they're not carrying him well and he keeps touching the ground. The Scouts scream at them to stop, and Raeon puts Rougle over his shoulder in a fireman's carry but that doesn't work either. Finally the Scouts zip him into a body bag and carry him down that way. The sight is particularly upsetting to Donoho, who is still coping with what he saw when Vimoto was shot in the head. Rice and Vandenberge are making their way down the hill as well, having both decided that they're too big for anyone to try to carry. Stichter and the medic got an IV into Vandenberge's arm just in time—a few minutes later and he'd have been dead—and now he's stumbling white-faced down the mountain with a soldier supporting him under each arm. Rice walks unaided with his shirtfront covered in blood and a fentanyl lollipop in his mouth for the pain.

They walk half a mile through a blasted landscape of burned-over tree stumps and powdery dust and arrive at the LZ to find Kearney waiting for them. He tells them about Rougle and then the MEDEVAC comes in and they climb on board. "There was still fighting going on—guys were still being engaged throughout our positions," Rice told me later. "Part of you doesn't want to leave the fight, but then just a kind of overwhelming joy came across both me and Specialist Vandenberge because, you know, he was in pretty rough shape and just kind of knowing that we're okay now. I remember laying there on my back and the flight medic asked something and I remember kind of reaching over and me and Vandenberge grabbed hands. We've been through the tough part, we're gonna get help, and we're gonna make it out of this alive."

Kearney climbs from the LZ to the site of Rougle's death and arrives so winded he can barely speak. From there one can look across the valley to OP Restrepo—at this distance just another nameless ridgeline in the tumble of mountains falling off toward the west. Kearney leans on his M4 and gulps water from a plastic bottle while Piosa briefs him. He points to where they took fire from and how the enemy came out of a compound farther down the mountain and outflanked them from an unexpected direction. "Okay, where's this fucking compound I want destroyed?" Kearney asks Stichter. He spits and doesn't wait for an answer. "Stichter, destroy it now."

As fire support officer, Stichter is in charge of calling in artillery and air attacks, and he rushes off to direct a bomb strike on the compound. The most serious problem is that after the enemy overran Rice's position they grabbed American weapons and gear. They made off with Vandenberge's 240, two assault packs, Rice's M14 sniper rifle, Rougle's M4—equipped with a silencer—and two sets of night vision gear. They also grabbed ammunition for all the weapons. Not only is that dangerous equipment for them to have, but it makes for excellent propaganda. They could show off a suppressed M4 or an assault pack with a dead American's nametag on it and claim that the Americans are getting slaughtered in Kunar. Operation Rock Avalanche abruptly goes from a search-and-destroy mission to a desperate attempt to get the gear back.

"Battle Base this is Battle Six, break," Kearney says into his radio. He has to yell because an Apache is making slow passes overhead looking for enemy movement. "Right now I believe the enemy exfilled to the vicinity of Kilo Echo 2236 and 2237. I'd like to get Gunmetal to engage or push off-station so that I can drop 120s down there and prevent these guys from getting back into the village of Landigal, break. I'm looking at a plan so I can go into Landigal and clear it and find weapons and NODS, break. We will consolidate our forces on the Sawtalo Sar spur and focus our efforts on Landigal."

Gunmetal is the radio call sign for Apache helicopters. Kearney wants the Apaches to chew up the mountains above Landigal to keep the enemy penned in or to get out of the way so his own mortars can do it. The terrain is extremely steep there, and dropping mortars onto the known routes off the mountain might slow the enemy down enough that they can be trapped and killed. If the fighters get into Landigal they'll be able to hide the weapons and disappear into the populace. Anyone moving on the mountain south of the American position now has a shoot-to-kill classification unless they're clearly civilian.

The men immediately start comparing impressions of the attack and putting together an idea of how the enemy pulled it off. Between Rice's and Wildcat's positions is a low hill with a cliff that faces south. When the Americans first saw it they considered the cliff to be "impassable terrain," so they didn't incorporate it into their defensive positions. The enemy fighters that overran Rice's team must have spent the previous twenty-four hours creeping through the woods to the base of the cliff and then waited until their comrades attacked from the south. They were whispering on their radios because they were so close that otherwise the Americans would have heard them. They must have climbed the cliff with their weapons over their shoulders and then started pouring heavy fire into Rice's and Wildcat's positions; they were only fifty yards away, so their fire was deadly accurate. Once they had the Americans suppressed they overran Rice's men and turned Vandenberge's 240 around and started using it against the other American positions. The hilltop was sprinkled with American brass. Once they'd stripped Rougle of his weapon and gear they fled the hilltop before the Americans could counterattack.

Rice was sitting down when he got hit and the force of the bullet sent him face-forward down the hill. Moments later he looked up and saw an enemy fighter shoot an RPG at him, which exploded very close and sent shrapnel throughout his body. He kept rolling downhill into some brush and then just lay there trying to figure out what had happened. He put his hand to his stomach and when he took it away it was covered with blood, so he knew he was wounded, but he was far more concerned about his men. He had no idea what had happened to them or whether they were even alive. Vandenberge had been hit in the left arm, and he stumbled off the hilltop away from his gun and into the cover of some rocks. Solowski took cover as well and then circled around the hill and tried to move up the far side. He came face-to-face with an enemy fighter who dropped out of sight off the back side of the hill. The experience left him in such a state of shock, and so pale, that when Raeon saw him a few minutes later he thought Solowski had been hit.

Vandenberge knew he was dying and started calling for a medic even though enemy fighters were only forty or fifty yards away; Cortez and Pemble may well have arrived in time to prevent the enemy from walking down the hill and finishing him off. Rougle probably started running back toward his men when he heard gunfire. His Scouts tried to assault the hill the enemy had just taken because they knew their squad leader was in that area, but the volume of fire was so intense that they were repeatedly pushed back. It's likely that the enemy simply dropped back off the hilltop once they'd grabbed all the weapons they could carry.

Within an hour or so artillery starts working the far ridgeline where Wildcat thinks they see enemy movement. Kearney lies prone on the hill making marks on his map and calling in artillery strikes along enemy escape routes. He wants helicopters to pick up First Platoon and drop them along the five-nine gridline south of Landigal so that they can block enemy movement into the inaccessible southern end of the valley. Meanwhile, Second Platoon will push down from the north. While Kearney is on the radio Hijar yells that he's found an enemy blood trail coming off the hilltop. "After we get the KIA out of here I want Gunmetal to search directly to my west," Kearney shouts to Stichter. "Hijar believes he has a blood trail, it's likely that where we find this son of a bitch, we'll find everybody else."

The Apaches come in and start rocketing the next ridge over and then working it with gun runs. The rounds explode in the treetops with sharp flashes and they come so close together that the detonations sound like one long crackle. The men watch the Apaches do their work and then scrutinize the area through their rifle scopes, looking for enemy fighters trying to flee. Raeon has a suppressed M14 sniper rifle and he sits with his knees up and sweeps it across the ridgelines searching for the men who killed his commander. He is covered in Rougle's blood from his trouser cuff to his collar as if he rolled in red paint. After a while he puts the rifle down and lights a cigarette.

"He was a good dude, man," Raeon says. Stichter is kneeling next to him under a pine tree looking west into the draw. His hands are caked in Vandenberge's blood.

"Sergeant Rougle?"

Raeon nods.

"You want a real cigarette?"

"Yeah."

Stichter hands him a Marlboro.

"I worry about the rest of the guys," Raeon says. "Some of them are takin' it real bad, kind of blamin' it on themselves because we couldn't push over the top. But the thing they got to understand is he was dead instantly—there's just nothin' you could do right there."

Raeon lights his cigarette and exhales.

"I go on leave in like two weeks," he says. "It's not how I wanted to go, though."

3

THAT NIGHT THE MEN SLEEP WITH A HAND grenade in one hand and their 9 mil in the other. Instead of one man pulling guard while two men sleep, it's the other way around, two-and-one. All night long enemy fighters have been observed walking from Yaka Chine to Landigal and then on up the mountain, and Kearney finally requests a bomb drop. The request is denied, and Kearney radios back, 'The other night we let eight guys get away, and now we have one dead and two wounded. If we don't drop now, I *guarantee* more will die.' Brigade gives permission, and a B-1 comes in and drops a bomb on a house where the fighters have taken shelter. The bomb misses, but Apaches come in to clean up the "squirters"—survivors who are trying to get away.

The next morning everyone wakes up tense and exhausted. Prophet starts picking up radio chatter that the enemy is closing in again, and around mid-morning several fighters are spotted moving along a nearby ridge. The entire American line opens up on them: mortars, 240s, LAWs, even First Sergeant Caldwell on his M4. Pemble alone shoots forty grenades out of his 203. The enemy fighters duck over the far side of the ridge and Apaches come in to do gun runs up and down the mountainside trying to catch them as they flee. Radio chatter indicates that fifteen are killed. All day long bombs and 155s crump into the mountainsides and the men sit behind cover on Rougle's hill waiting for the enemy to come at them again. By midafternoon it's clear they're not going to and the men get a little rest and then move out around midnight. Second Platoon works their way down the mountainside toward Landigal on terrain so steep that they take much of it by simply sliding downhill on their asses. Their pants are shredded by the time they get to the bottom.

First Platoon had already returned to the KOP the previous night, and the next day at dusk they head back out with half of Third Platoon. There

is intel that the enemy is planning to attack either
Phoenix or Restrepo — the bases were left with
only a dozen or so American soldiers during the
operation — but the valley remains quiet except for
the buzz of surveillance drones overhead and the
occasional bump and thud of mortars. First Lieutenant Brad Winn leads First Platoon past Phoenix
and Aliabad and then across the Korengal River
and up a series of terraces to the top of the Gatigal spur. To their north is a pretty little valley with
Landigal nestled into it and to their south is the
rest of the Korengal — wild, unknown country so
thick with fighters that it would take a whole battalion to get in and out of there safely. Winn sets
his men up along the Gatigal and overwatches Second Platoon as they clear through the town looking for weapons. Kearney, Caldwell, and the rest of
company headquarters are to the north and men at
OP Restrepo watch from the west.

Winn and his men spend a long day on the
ridgetop overwatching Landigal while Ostlund, a
lieutenant colonel from the Afghan National Army,
and the governor of Kunar fly in by Black Hawk to
talk to the elders. It is the first time that a governor
from *any* government has ever stood in the southern
Korengal. One of their primary aims is to recover
the weapons that were taken the day before, but the

talks don't progress very far. Around nine o'clock that night, Winn gets word that Second Platoon has moved out of Landigal, and First Platoon gets ready to move out themselves. There's been radio chatter all day long about an attack on the Americans— one Taliban commander even said, 'If they're not leaving by helicopter they're in trouble'—but no one pays much attention. Kearney has so many air assets flying around the valley—surveillance drones, two Apaches, a B-1 bomber, and even a Spectre gunship—that an enemy attack would seem to be an act of suicide.

The soldiers walk single file along the crest of the spur spaced ten or fifteen yards apart. The terrain falls off steeply on both sides into holly forests and shale scree. The moon is so bright that they're not even using night vision gear. Unknown to Winn and his men, three enemy fighters are arrayed across the crest of the ridge below them, waiting with AK-47s. Parallel to the trail are ten more fighters with belt-fed machine guns and RPGs. In the U.S. military, this is known as an "L-shaped ambush." Correctly done, a handful of men can wipe out an entire platoon. Walking point is Sergeant Josh Brennan, an alpha team leader. He's followed by a SAW gunner named Eckrode and then Staff Sergeant Erick Gallardo and then Specialist Sal Giunta, bravo team leader. Giunta is from Iowa and joined the Army after hearing a radio commercial while working at a Subway sandwich shop in his hometown.

"Out of nothing — out of taking your next step — just rows of tracers, RPGs, everything happening out of nowhere with no real idea of how it just fucking happened — but it happened," Giunta told me. "Everything kind of slowed down and I did everything I thought I could do, nothing more and nothing less."

The Apache pilots watch this unfold below them but are powerless to help because the combatants are too close together. At the bottom of the hill, Second Platoon hears an enormous firefight erupt, but they too just hold their fire and hope it turns out well. At first, the sheer volume of firepower directed at Brennan's squad negates any conceivable tactical response. A dozen Taliban fighters with rockets and belt-fed machine guns are shooting from behind cover at a distance of fifteen or twenty feet; First Platoon is essentially inside a shooting gallery. Within seconds, every man in the lead squad takes a bullet. Brennan goes down immediately, wounded in eight places. Eckrode takes rounds through his thigh and calf and falls back to lay down suppressive fire with his SAW. Gallardo takes a round in his helmet and falls down but gets back up. Doc Mendoza, farther down the line, takes a round through the femur and immediately starts bleeding out.

After months of fighting an enemy that stayed hundreds of yards away, the shock of facing them at a distance of twenty feet cannot be overstated. Giunta gets hit in his front plate and in his assault pack and he barely notices except that the rounds came from a strange direction. Sheets of tracers are coming from his left, but the rounds that hit him seemed to come from dead ahead. He's down in a small washout along the trail where the lip of packed earth should have protected him, but it didn't. "That's when I kind of noticed something was wrong," Giunta said. "The rounds came right down the draw and there are three people—all friends—in the same vicinity. It happened so fast, you don't think too hard about it, but it's something to keep in mind."

Much later, a military investigation will determine that the enemy was trying to throw up a "wall of lead" between the first few men and the rest of the unit so that they could be overrun and captured. Gallardo understands this instinctively and tries to push through the gunfire to link up with his alpha team, Brennan and Eckrode. Twenty or thirty RPGs come sailing into their position and explode among the trees. When Gallardo goes

down with a bullet to the helmet, Giunta runs over
to him to drag him behind cover, but Gallardo
gets back on his feet immediately. They're quickly
joined by Giunta's SAW gunner, PFC Casey, and
the three men start pushing forward by throwing
hand grenades and sprinting between the blasts.
Even enemy who are not hit are so disoriented by
the concussion that they have trouble functioning
for a second or two. The group quickly makes it to
Eckrode, who's wounded and desperately trying to
fix an ammo jam in his SAW, and Gallardo and
Casey stay with him while Giunta continues on his
own. He throws his last grenade and then sprints
the remaining ground to where Brennan should
be. The Gatigal spur is awash in moonlight, and
in the silvery shadows of the holly forests he sees
two enemy fighters dragging Josh Brennan down
the hillside. He empties his M4 magazine at them
and starts running toward his friend.

The Army has a certain interest in understanding
what was going through Giunta's mind during all of
this, because whatever was going through his mind
helped save the entire unit from getting killed. A
year or so later, several squads of American soldiers
conducted an identical L-shaped ambush at night on

the Abas Ghar and wiped out a column of Taliban fighters—nearly twenty men. The reason First Platoon did not get wiped out had nothing to do with the Apaches flying overhead or the 155s at Blessing; it was because the men reacted not as individuals but as a unit. Stripped to its essence, combat is a series of quick decisions and rather precise actions carried out in concert with ten or twelve other men. In that sense it's much more like football than, say, like a gang fight. The unit that choreographs their actions best usually wins. They might take casualties, but they win.

That choreography—*you lay down fire while I run forward, then I cover you while you move your team up*—is so powerful that it can overcome enormous tactical deficits. There is choreography for storming Omaha Beach, for taking out a pill-box bunker, and for surviving an L-shaped ambush at night on the Gatigal. The choreography always requires that each man make decisions based not on what's best for *him*, but on what's best for the group. If everyone does that, most of the group survives. If no one does, most of the group dies. That, in essence, is combat.

Most firefights go by so fast that acts of bravery or cowardice are more or less spontaneous. Soldiers might live the rest of their lives regretting a decision that they don't even remember making; they might receive a medal for doing something that was over before they even knew they were doing it. When Congressional Medal of Honor recipient Audie Murphy was asked why he took on an entire company of German infantry by himself, he replied famously, "They were killing my friends." Wars are won or lost because of the aggregate effect of thousands of decisions like that during firefights that often last only minutes or seconds. Giunta estimates that not more than ten or fifteen seconds elapsed between the initial attack and his own counterattack. An untrained civilian would have experienced those ten or fifteen seconds as a disorienting barrage of light and noise and probably have spent most of it curled up on the ground. An entire platoon of men who react that way would undoubtedly die to the last man.

Giunta, on the other hand, used those fifteen seconds to assign rates and sectors of fire to his team, run to Gallardo's assistance, assess the direction of a round that hit him in the chest, and then throw three hand grenades while assaulting an enemy position. Every man in the platoon — even the ones who were wounded — acted as purposefully and efficiently as Giunta did. For obvious reasons, the Army has tried very hard to understand why some men respond effectively in combat and others just freeze. "I did what I did because that's what I was trained to do," Giunta told me. "There was a task that had to be done, and the part that I was gonna do was to link alpha and bravo teams. I didn't run through fire to save a buddy—I ran through fire to see what was going on with him and maybe we could hide behind the same rock and shoot together. I didn't run through fire to do anything heroic or brave. I did what I believe *anyone* would have done."

During World War II, the British and American militaries conducted a series of studies to identify what makes men capable of overcoming their fears. A psychiatrist named Herbert Spiegel, who accompanied American troops on the Tunisia campaign, called it the "X-factor": "Whether this factor was conscious or unconscious is debatable," he wrote for a military journal in 1944, "but this is not so important. The important thing was that it is influenced greatly by devotion to their group or unit, by regard for their leader and by conviction for their cause. In the average soldier, which most of them were, this factor...enabled men to control their fear and combat their fatigue to a degree that they themselves did not believe possible."

The U.S. military found that, to a great degree,

fearfulness was something they couldn't do much about. A fearful man is likely to remain that way no matter what kind of training he undergoes. During one experiment, completely untrained airborne candidates were told to jump off a thirty-four-foot tower. They jumped in a harness that allowed them to fall about twelve feet and then ride a 400-foot cable to the ground. As easy as it sounds, more than half of a group of qualified paratroopers said that jumping off the tower was more frightening than jumping out of a real airplane. The military tested roughly thirteen hundred candidates on the tower and then tracked their success through airborne school. They found that the men who were "slow" to jump off the tower were more than twice as likely to fail out of the program as "fast" jumpers, and those who refused to jump at all were almost guaranteed to fail.

One of the most puzzling things about fear is that it is only loosely related to the level of danger. During World War II, several airborne units that experienced some of the fiercest fighting of the war also reported some of the lowest psychiatric casualty rates in the U.S. military. Combat units typically suffer one psychiatric casualty for every physical one, and during Israel's Yom Kippur War of 1973, frontline casualty rates were roughly consistent with that ratio. But Israeli logistics units, which were subject to far less danger, suffered *three* psychiatric cases for every physical one. And even frontline troops showed enormous variation in their rate of psychological breakdown. Because many Israeli officers literally led from the front, they were four times more likely to be killed or wounded than their men were—and yet they suffered one-fifth the rate of psychological collapse. The primary factor determining breakdown in combat does not appear to be the objective level of danger so much as the feeling—even the illusion—of control. Highly trained men in extraordinarily dangerous circumstances are less likely to break down than untrained men in little danger.

The division between those who feel in control of their fate and those who don't can occur even within the same close-knit group. During World War II, British and American bomber crews experienced casualty rates as high as 70 percent over the course of their tour; they effectively flew missions until they were killed. On those planes, pilots reported experiencing less fear than their turret gunners, who were crucial to operations but had no direct control over the aircraft. Fighter pilots, who suffered casualty rates almost as high as bomber crews, nevertheless reported extremely low levels of fear. They were both highly trained and entirely in control of their own fate, and that allowed them to ignore the statistical reality that they had only a fifty-fifty chance of surviving their tour.

Among men who are dependent on one another for their safety—all combat soldiers, essentially—there is often an unspoken agreement to stick together no matter what. The reassurance that you will never be abandoned seems to help men act in ways that serve the whole unit rather than just themselves. Sometimes, however, it effectively amounts to a suicide pact. During the air war of 1944, a four-man combat crew on a B-17 bomber took a vow to never abandon one another no matter how desperate the situation. (A fifth team member, the top turret gunner, was not part of the pact.) The aircraft was hit by flak during a mission and went into a terminal dive, and the pilot ordered everyone to bail out. The top turret gunner obeyed the order, but the ball turret gunner discovered that a piece of flak had jammed his turret and he could not get out. The other three men in his pact could have bailed out with parachutes, but they stayed with him until the plane hit the ground and exploded. They all died.

• • •

One of the Taliban fighters falls to the ground, dead, and the other releases Brennan and escapes downhill through the trees. Giunta jams a new magazine into his gun and yells for a medic. Brennan is lying badly wounded in the open and Giunta grabs him by the vest and drags him behind a little bit of cover. He cuts the ammo rack off his chest and pulls the rip cord on his ballistic vest to extricate him from that and then cuts his clothing off to look for wounds. Brennan's been hit multiple times in the legs and has a huge shrapnel wound in his side and has been shot in the lower half of his face. He's still conscious and keeps complaining that there's something in his mouth. It's his teeth, though Giunta doesn't tell him that.

The B-1 flying overhead drops two bombs on Hill 1705, and that stuns the enemy enough that the Americans are able to consolidate their position. The Third Platoon medic arrives and gives Brennan a tracheotomy so he can breathe better, and then they get him ready for the MEDEVAC. A Spectre gunship and a couple of Apaches are finally able to distinguish Americans from the enemy and start lighting up the hillsides with cannon and gunfire, and half an hour later the MEDEVAC comes in and they start hoisting casualties off the ridge. When they're done, the rest of First Platoon shoulder their gear and resume walking home.

"We waited for First Platoon for hours," Hijar told me about that night, "and once we linked up with them it was still two and a half hours' walk back to the KOP. You could just tell on the guys' faces, it wasn't the right time to ask. You already knew what the answer was going to be. Some of them were walking around with bullet holes in their helmets."

Brennan doesn't survive surgery. Mendoza is dead before he even leaves the ridge. Five more men are wounded. Then there's Rougle from the day before, as well as Rice and Vandenberge. It's been a costly week. It's been the kind of week that makes people back home think that maybe we're losing the war.

4
—

O'BYRNE MISSED ROCK AVALANCHE BECAUSE
his younger sister, Courtney, had been badly burned
in a house fire and he rushed home to be with her.
He left the Korengal with the understanding that
she would probably not survive. He arrived in Syracuse, New York, and found the rest of his family
in the hospital waiting room. He said he wanted to
see her alone and then walked into her room and
sat down by her bed. Courtney was semiconscious
and had a tube down her throat and was hooked up
to a respirator that had swelled her belly with air.
The sight was too much for O'Byrne, and he broke
down and started crying. He squeezed her hand
and said, 'Courtney, I love you, squeeze my hand

171

if you can hear me.' And she squeezed his hand back. And he said, 'Squeeze my hand three times if you love me back,' and she squeezed his hand once, twice, three times.

Her lungs were badly damaged by the fire and the doctors told the family that if she didn't improve by a certain date she was almost certainly going to die. O'Byrne visited her in the hospital every day and tried to let the days tick by without going crazy. It was during that awful time that he got a call from a friend that something bad had happened on Rock Avalanche. It took some digging but he finally found out that Rougle, Brennan, and Mendoza were dead. Courtney was being treated at the VA hospital at the University of Syracuse, and he wandered around campus until he found a bar and then he sat down and started drinking. Someone asked him why he was getting drunk and he said, 'I have a few friends who need a drink,' and then he drank a pitcher of beer for each man who had died.

He headed back to the Korengal about a week later. Courtney was out of immediate danger, but it tormented O'Byrne that if he got killed, her last memory of him would be from a hospital bed. He passed through New York, and on a whim he called me from a bar where he was having dinner with two friends. It was strange to see him in civilian clothes and without a gun, and when I walked up he stood and shook my hand and then gave me a hug. He was wearing a blue T-shirt and a blue ghetto-style cap sideways and couldn't focus his eyes.

"My boys got messed up," he said. "Brennan got killed. Rougle got killed."

We sat down and he asked me to tell him everything. All he knew were the names of the dead, and I asked him what kind of detail he wanted this in.

"Everything," O'Byrne said. "Tell me everything you know."

O'Byrne was most of the way through a bottle of red wine and his friends were drinking beers and shots of tequila. I apologized to them for taking the conversation back to the war and they said please, go ahead, and I told O'Byrne about how the enemy had opened up from one ridgeline and then snuck up another side and overran the hilltop. I told him about Rice and Vandenberge and how First Platoon had walked straight into an ambush on the Gatigal spur. It took O'Byrne a while to absorb this.

"And Mendoza's a fuckin' hero, right?" he said. "He's an American hero, right?"

"Yeah, he's a hero."

"And Brennan was dead, right?" O'Byrne said. "I mean, they weren't dragging him off alive, were they?"

I wasn't sure what to say. Soldiers can seem pretty accepting of the idea that they might die in combat, but being taken alive is a different matter. "No, he didn't die until later," I said. "He was alive at the time."

O'Byrne looked around the room. I tried to think what I should do if he started crying. He concentrated and gathered himself and finally asked how many enemy fighters were killed.

"They killed a lot," I told him. "Like fifty. Thirty of them were Arabs. The A-10s really messed them up."

"Yeah, kill those fuckers," O'Byrne said. He repeated that a few times and took another drink. I asked him how he felt about going back.

"I got to get back there," he said. "Those are my boys. Those are the best friends I'll ever have."

He was gripping my arm and trying to look at me, but his eyes kept needing to refocus. They never got it quite right. I got up to go, and O'Byrne stood up as well and hugged me several times. I wished him luck and told him I'd see him back out there in a month or two. On the way out I told Addie, the bar manager, that I'd like to pick up their check.

Later she told me she had to shut them off after the next drink because O'Byrne fell out of his chair and the girl could hardly talk.

"He was so polite, though," Addie said. "I mean, drunk as he was, he still took off his hat whenever I walked up."

5

FORWARD OPERATING BASES ARE A SPECIAL kind of hell, none of the excitement of real war but all the ugliness: rows of plywood bee huts and weapons everywhere and Apaches jolting you awake at all hours running the flight line ten feet off the ground. Journalists usually moved around the theater on scheduled resupply flights, but even minor problems can ripple outward through the logistics web and leave you stuck at a FOB for days. At least Bagram had decent food and a huge PX; Jalalabad had absolutely nothing. In winter the wind drove you mad with the rattling of tent flaps and in summer it got so hot—130 in the shade—that you almost couldn't make it across the parade ground without drinking water. I stayed in the VIP tent, all the journalists did, and one afternoon I tried to escape the flamethrower heat by lying down on my bunk and going to sleep. I woke up so disoriented from dehydration that someone had to help me to another tent with better air-conditioning. There was nothing to do at JAF but hit your mealtimes and pray that if the enemy somehow mustered the nerve to attack it would be while you were stuck there and could report on it.

In the Korengal the soldiers never talked about the wider war—or cared—so it was hard to get a sense of how the country as a whole was faring. And the big bases had the opposite problem: since there was almost no combat, everyone had a kind of reflexive optimism that never got tested by the reality outside the wire. The public affairs guys on those bases offered the press a certain vision of the war, and that vision wasn't *wrong*, it just seemed amazingly incomplete. There was real progress in the country, and there was real appreciation among the Afghans for what America was trying to do, but the country was also coming apart at the seams, and press officers didn't talk about that much. During the year that I was in the Korengal, the Taliban almost assassinated Afghan president Hamid Karzai, blew up the fanciest hotel in Kabul, fought to the outskirts of Kandahar, and then attacked the city prison and sprang scores of fellow insurgents from captivity. More American soldiers were killed that year than in any year previous, but if you pointed that out, you were simply told that it was because we were now "taking the fight to the enemy." That may well have been true, but it lacked any acknowledgment that the enemy was *definitely* getting their shit together.

I thought of those as "Vietnam moments." A Vietnam moment was one in which you weren't so much getting misled as getting asked to participate in a kind of collective wishful thinking. Toward the end of my year, for example, the Taliban attacked an American base north of the Pech and killed nine American soldiers and wounded half the survivors. When I asked American commanders about it, their responses were usually along the lines of how it was actually an American *victory* because forty or fifty enemy fighters had also died in the fight. Since the Army had already admitted that this was not a war of attrition, using enemy casualties as a definition of success struck me as a tricky business.

And we reporters had our own issues. Vietnam was *our* paradigm as well, *our* template for how not to get hoodwinked by the U.S. military, and it exerted such a powerful influence that anything short of implacable cynicism sometimes felt like a sellout. Most journalists wanted to cover combat—as opposed to humanitarian operations—so they got embedded with combat units and wound up painting a picture of a country engulfed in war. In fact, most areas of the country were relatively stable; you had to get pretty lucky to find yourself in anything even vaguely resembling a firefight. When you did, of course, other journalists looked at you with a kind of rueful envy and asked how they could get in with that unit. Once at a dinner party back home I was asked, with a kind of knowing wink, how much the military had "censored" my reporting. I answered that I'd never been censored at all, and that once I'd asked a public affairs officer to help me fact-check an article and he'd answered, "Sure, but you can't actually *show* it to me—that would be illegal."

That wasn't a story anyone really wanted to hear, and I almost felt like a bit of a patsy for telling it. Vietnam was considered a morally dubious war that was fought by draftees while the rest of the nation was dropping acid and listening to Jimi Hendrix. Afghanistan, on the other hand, was being fought by volunteers who more or less respected their commanders and had the gratitude of the vast majority of Americans back home. If you imagined that your job, as a reporter, was to buddy up to the troops and tell the "real" story of how they were dying in a senseless war, you were in for a surprise. The commanders would realize you were operating off a particular kind of cultural programming and would try to change your mind, but the men wouldn't bother. They'd just refuse to talk to you until you left their base.

Once in a while you'd meet a soldier who didn't fit into any clear category, though. These were men who believed in the war but also recognized the American military's capacity for self-delusion. "We're not going to win the war until we admit we're losing it," one of these guys told me in the spring of 2008. He was in a position of moderate influence in the U.S. military, and his pessimism was so refreshing that it actually made me weirdly optimistic. And then there was the sergeant from Third Platoon whom I recognized at the Bagram air terminal while waiting for a flight. I said something vague about the progress in the valley and he didn't even bother masking his disgust. "What are you talking about, it's a fucking quagmire," he said. "There's no progress with the locals, it's just not happening, and I don't even trust the S-2—he's full of shit. I was at an intel briefing and the S-2 was talking about how the Iranians were funding

the Taliban. I asked about all the money coming from Wahhabis in Saudi Arabia, and he said
that those are private donations that are harder to
trace. *Harder to trace than money sent by the Iranian
government?"*

S-2 is the designation for a military intelligence
officer. There were a lot of soldiers around us,
mostly new recruits who had just arrived in country, and by the time the sergeant got to the part
about the Iranians they were giving us some pretty
hard stares. Sometimes it was the new guys, the
guys who'd never seen combat, who were the most
hostile to any questioning of the war, the most belligerent about a supposed American prerogative.
To change the subject I asked the sergeant how he
would fight the U.S. military if he was an insurgent in the Korengal. He'd clearly given it some
thought:

"I'd put a shooter above Vegas with a low MOA
rifle and I'd take single shots to the groin," he said.
"MOA means 'minute of angle'—the bullet doesn't
drop more than an inch per hundred yards. Every
shot sends a guy home in a helicopter. We'd get so
frustrated we'd just charge up the hill. So you'd
have a couple of guys to the side with machine
guns. The guy with the rifle keeps shooting, and
the machine guns wipe us out."

KILLING

• • •

The battalion commander was an insanely fit lieutenant colonel of Cherokee descent named Bill
Ostlund who graduated from the Fletcher School
of Law and Diplomacy and wrote a thesis on
the Soviet military's defeats in Afghanistan and
Chechnya. Ostlund would look you straight in
the eye while crushing the bones of your hand in
a handshake and launch straight into, say, the lat-
est about the new trade school in Asadabad. He
had such full-on enthusiasm for what he was doing
that when I was around him I sometimes caught
myself feeling bad that there wasn't an endeavor of
equivalent magnitude in my own life. It wasn't the
war, per se, that he was so fired up about so much
as the whole idea—a truly radical one when you
thought about it—that America was actually over
here trying to put a country like this back together.
Not many nations have the resources to attempt a
project on this scale or the inclination to try. And
Ostlund was exactly the kind of guy you'd want to
have do it: seemingly immune to heartbreak, way
more knowledgeable than most of the press corps
that came through and capable of working eighteen
hours a day for fifteen months straight.

Ostlund often referred to the Taliban as "miscreants" and spoke of them in the singular, as in, "We cornered the enemy and destroyed him." The third-person singular lent the war a vaguely gentle-manly feel, as if there were no hard feelings and all this was just an extraordinarily violent lawn sport. In fact, I don't think Ostlund felt any particular animosity toward the men he was fighting, and I know for a fact that he made repeated offers to grant temporary immunity to any Taliban leaders who would meet with him at a local shura. ("If they put together a meeting with all my close friends, I promise they will not be detained and that I will respect the tradition that shuras are not deceitful," he told me.) As far as I know none of them took him up on it, but I always liked that he operated that way. He was the highest-ranking officer to spend the night at Restrepo, and the men told me that instead of taking an empty bunk he just curled up on the ground and went to sleep. They said he didn't even take off his body armor.

Ostlund's base was Camp Blessing, which overlooked the Pech River Valley just a few miles west of the Korengal. It was a random conglomeration of brick-and-mortar buildings that climbed unevenly up a mountainside, the newest buildings at the top and still smelling of fresh cement. The market town of Nagalam was a mile to the east and boasted a "men's club," whatever that meant; at night something akin to Christmas lights flashed weirdly over the rooftops. Blessing was the stopping-off point for supply convoys going into the Korengal because that way they could make it in and out in a single day. (Spending a night at the KOP was suicide: there was only one road out of the valley, which gave the enemy a whole night to dig in bombs.) The convoys were called CLPs and were the responsibility of Fusion Company, which made the run up the Pech every few weeks and got attacked almost every time. A CLP was usually composed of a dozen armored Humvees and twenty or so local "jingle" trucks driven by Afghans. The road to Blessing was newly paved, which meant the convoys moved too fast to be ambushed, but the last few miles into the Korengal were dirt and considered to be the most dangerous stretch of road in the country. Army mechanics bolted a .50 cal to the top of the wrecking truck because even the salvage and repair guys were expected to return fire. I was told it was the only armed wrecking truck in the entire U.S. Army.

I manage to avoid CLPs until halfway through the tour, when a series of winter storms grounds flights for a couple of weeks. We roll out of the base on a miserable January day with high-level clouds filtering out a weak sun and the wind shrieking down off the Hindu Kush completely unchecked. The night before, Able Company had spotted twenty or thirty fighters in the Watapor Valley and wiped them out with artillery and airpower, and most of the dead turned out to be Korengalis. The morning we head out a public affairs officer takes me aside and tells me he has information that a Taliban cell in the valley knows that our convoy is coming and is going to attack it. It's the kind of news that journalists are eager to hear as long as everything turns out okay. Of course, there's no way to know that except to take a deep breath and find out.

I have a spot in the second Humvee of the convoy with Captain John Thyng, the commander of Fusion Company. Thyng had been hit by a roadside bomb in Iraq and seemed more or less resigned to that happening in Afghanistan as well. He sits next to the driver and I sit diagonally across from him in the back, and then there's another soldier next to me and a gunner up in the turret with a .50 cal. I've been told that it will be up to me to pass him more ammo if he needs it. As soon as our wheels cross the wire the gunner racks his weapon and we grind slowly through Jalalabad and then head north on new black pavement that ribbons smoothly along the river. There are rice paddies along the flood-plain and, here and there, clusters of jagged slate gravestones shoved into the ground like spades. Green prayer flags toil around them in the wind. The winter sun glances off the wide braidings of the river and makes the water look dull and heavy as mercury, and beyond that, rank after rank of mountains fall off toward the east: Pakistan. An old man stands in a field of stones watching us go by.

"The thing about the military is, every unit thinks they're the coolest," Thyng says as we roar past. We're all wearing headsets so we can hear each other over the engine and communicate with the other trucks. "I mean, the BSB guys think they're cool, but they're obviously not. And they don't even *know* it, which is the most tragic thing about that situation."

The old man is well behind us now and we're coming up on a police checkpoint that has been shot to pieces by previous Taliban attacks. Behind it on the river, two men paddle a crude inner-tube raft toward our shore, stroking hard into the current. Thyng grabs a pair of binoculars and glasses them as we go by.

"But in their hearts I think they know," he adds after a while.

We reach the Korengal the morning of the

following day. We'd spent the night at Blessing listening to the apocalyptic thunder of the 155s calibrating new rounds and left just after dawn so the convoy could make it out of the valley before dark. "I think we're going to get hit today," the driver of my Humvee says as he climbs into his seat. We jolt through Nagalam and then cross the Pech on a narrow bridge and enter the mouth of the Korengal. The road is excruciatingly narrow and if you look out the window you can see straight down to the bottom of the canyon several hundred feet below. It's easier to just look straight ahead and think about something else. After half an hour Thyng points to a ridge up ahead and says that after we pass that, things are going to get interesting.

"All right, keep it good right now," Thyng tells the gunner as we roll into a draw on the far side of the ridge. Creeks run down the creases of the draws, and where the road passes there, the dirt is always moist and easy to dig into. And some of the draws are too deep to observe from any of the American outposts in the valley, so they are a natural spot for an ambush. "Once we get into that lip I want you to scan high, all right?" Thyng continues telling the gunner. "The first thing that will come in on this bitch will be fuckin' RPGs, okay?"

"Roger," the gunner says.

"If that happens they're going to miss, so just look where they came from and fuck it up, all right?"

"Roger."

I concentrate on running the camera. That is the easiest way to avoid thinking about the fact that what you're filming could kill you.

"All right, you stay in there," Captain Thyng tells the gunner. "We're going to pull up around that corner—"

And that's as far as he gets.

The idea that there are rules in warfare and that combatants kill each other according to basic concepts of fairness probably ended for good with the machine gun. A man with a machine gun can conceivably hold off a whole battalion, at least for a while, which changes the whole equation of what it means to be brave in battle. In World War I, when automatic weapons came into general use, heavy machine gunners were routinely executed if their position was overrun because they caused so much death. (Regular infantry, who were thought to be "fighting fairly," were often spared.) Machine guns forced infantry to disperse, to camouflage themselves, and to fight in small independent units. All that promoted stealth over honor and squad loyalty over blind obedience.

In a war of that nature soldiers gravitate toward whatever works best with the least risk. At that point combat stops being a grand chess game between generals and becomes a no-holds-barred experiment in pure killing. As a result, much of modern military tactics is geared toward maneuvering the enemy into a position where they can essentially be massacred from safety. It sounds dishonorable only if you imagine that modern war is about honor; it's not. It's about winning, which means killing the enemy on the most unequal terms possible. Anything less simply results in the loss of more of your own men.

There are two ways to tilt the odds in an otherwise fair fight: ambush the enemy with overwhelming force or use weapons that cannot be countered. The best, of course, is to do both. I had a lot of combat nightmares at Restrepo — I think everyone did — and they were invariably about being helpless: guns were jamming, the enemy was everywhere, and no one knew what was going on. In military terms, that's a perfect ambush. Once I watched an Apache helicopter corner a Taliban fighter named Hayatullah on an open hillside and kill him. He had nowhere to run and on the second burst he was hit by a 30 mm round and exploded. There was nothing fair about it, but Hayatullah was the leader of a cell that detonated roadside bombs in the valley, and one could argue there wasn't much fair about his line of work either. I later asked O'Byrne if he could imagine what it must feel like to be targeted by an Apache, and he just shook his head. We were talking about combat trauma, and I said that anyone who survived something like that had to have some pretty horrific nightmares. "I goddamn hope so," O'Byrne said.

Taliban fighters in the Korengal switched to roadside bombs because they were losing too many men in firefights. And it was also creating problems with the locals: when Taliban fighters first started attacking American patrols, the Americans didn't necessarily know where to shoot back. By the end of the summer, locals were pointing enemy positions out to the Americans just so they would aim in the right direction. Roadside bombs avoided those problems. They were cheap, low-risk, and didn't get civilians killed. I doubt many villagers actually *wanted* Americans to get blown up, but few of them cared enough to walk up to the KOP and tell the soldiers where bombs had been dug in. This fight was between the Taliban and the Americans and the villagers more or less stayed out of it.

WAR

The first major bomb strike in the Korengal came two days after Christmas. Destined Company had mounted units scattered throughout the battalion firebases, and four of these trucks had taken up positions to support a foot patrol that had come down from Restrepo. One of the Humvees was in the middle of a three-point turn when an antitank mine detonated beneath it and blew the turret gunner, Jesse Murphree, so far down the hill that at first no one even realized he was gone. The rest of the crew suffered concussions and broken bones. The Humvee was immediately swallowed by flames, and while they tried to put it out Hijar and Buno and Richardson of Second Platoon climbed downslope to look for Murphree. They found him several hundred feet away, semiconscious and both his legs turned to jelly. They put tourniquets on him so he wouldn't bleed out and helped carry him up to the road and slide him into a Humvee. Murphree knew he was badly hurt but didn't yet realize his legs were gone. He kept asking his squad leader, Staff Sergeant Alcantara, if he could still go to the Alcantaras' wedding after they all got back to Italy.

The enemy now had a weapon that unnerved the Americans more than small-arms fire ever could: random luck. Every time you drove down the road you were engaged in a twisted existential exercise where each moment was the only proof you'd ever have that you hadn't been blown up the moment before. And if you *were* blown up, you'd probably never know it and certainly wouldn't be able to affect the outcome. Good soldiers died just as easily as sloppy ones, which is pretty much how soldiers define unfair tactics in war. Halfway through the deployment, Battle Company took over Destined's trucks and ran mounted patrols out of the KOP in support of their own men. It was a sensible way to do it, but it put men who were used to foot patrols into cramped steel boxes where there wasn't much to do during firefights except scream at the turret gunner and pray. The trucks reduced war to a kind of grim dice game that was impossible to learn from or get good at; you just had to hope your luck lasted until it was time to go home.

The guy who blows us up is a hundred feet away behind a rock. He touches two wires to a double-A battery and sends an electrical charge to a pressure cooker filled with fertilizer and diesel that has been buried in the road the night before. His timing is off by ten feet or so and the bomb detonates under the engine block rather than directly beneath us, which saves us from being wounded or killed. The explosion looks like a sheet of flame and then a sudden darkening. The darkening is from dirt that lands on the windshield and blocks the sun. The gunner drops out of his turret and sits next to me, stunned. Someone comes up over the net saying, "WE JUST HIT AN IED, OVER!" That is followed by another man screaming for the convoy to keep moving.

Now it's gray and muffled inside the Humvee, and for a moment my mind makes the odd association of being home during a blizzard when I was young. The power would go out and the windows would drift over with snow and produce a similar quiet darkness. That doesn't last long. "GET ON THAT GUN!" Thyng starts yelling at the gunner. "GET ON THAT GUN AND START FIRING INTO THAT FUCKIN' DRAW!"

The gunner is either too frightened or too disoriented to function, but a Humvee behind us opens up with a grenade machine gun — *blap-kachunk, blap-kachunk* — and Thyng yells, "WHO THE FUCK IS THAT?" I tell him it's ours, not theirs, and our gunner finally stands up in the turret and starts returning fire toward the east and then toward the west. Big, hot .50 cal shells clatter into the interior of the Humvee. *Shot, eight o'clock,* a computer voice in the cabin informs us. The detection system is picking up gunfire from other vehicles in our convoy and reporting it as if it were coming from the enemy.

There's a lot of shooting out there and I'm not looking forward to running through it, but the cabin is filling with toxic gray smoke and I know we're going to have to bail out eventually. I keep waiting for something like fear to take hold of me but it never does, I have a kind of flatlined functionality that barely raises my heart rate. I could do math problems in my head. It occurs to me that maybe I've been injured—often you don't know right away—and I pat my way down both legs until I reach my feet, but everything is there. I get my gear in order and find the door lever with my hand and wait. There is a small black skeleton hanging from the rearview mirror and I notice that it's still rocking from the force of the blast. I just sit there watching it. Finally Thyng gives the order and we all throw ourselves into the fresh cool morning air and start to run.

War is a lot of things and it's useless to pretend that exciting isn't one of them. It's insanely exciting. The machinery of war and the sound it makes and the urgency of its use and the consequences of almost everything about it are the most exciting things anyone engaged in war will ever know. Soldiers discuss that fact with each other and eventually with their chaplains and their shrinks and maybe even their spouses, but the public will never hear about it. It's just not something that many people want acknowledged. War is supposed to feel bad because undeniably bad things happen in it, but for a nineteen-year-old at the working end of a .50 cal during a firefight that everyone comes out of okay, war is life multiplied by some number that no one has ever heard of. In some ways twenty minutes of combat is more life than you could scrape together in a lifetime of doing something else. Combat isn't where you might die — though that does happen — it's where you find out whether you get to keep on living. Don't underestimate the power of that revelation. Don't underestimate the things young men will wager in order to play that game one more time.

The core psychological experiences of war are so primal and unadulterated, however, that they eclipse subtler feelings, like sorrow or remorse, that can gut you quietly for years. Once in Paris I caught sight of two men carrying a mattress across the street and went straight into full-blown panic: eyes wide, heart pounding, hands gripping my chair. I'd just come out of Liberia, where I'd seen a lot of dead and wounded people carried that way, and at the time I'd had no reaction at all, zero. I was too terrified by the violence around me, and too amped by the magnitude of the story I was covering, to pay much attention to anything else. Then a sagging mattress in Paris triggered a three-week backlog of trauma and shame.

We drive into the KOP late that afternoon, our destroyed Humvee chained to the one ahead of us and getting dragged through the mud like some kind of stubborn farm animal. The place has changed since I was last here, the men are cleaner and less wild-eyed and don't have to wear body armor all the time. It's strange to see them walking around as if this were just any old place in the world and the hills weren't crawling with enemy fighters who wanted them all to die. There's a new brick-and-mortar for the command center and there are shower curtains on the shitter doors and there are seven or eight new laptops with a high-speed satellite Internet connection. I'm told to sleep in one of the new buildings, so I carry my gear up and drop it on an empty cot. There's only one other man in the room, a Third Platoon soldier named Loza who's been in Italy for three months recovering from a shoulder wound. He sits quietly on a cot listening to music on his laptop and rigging out his gear. He ties his night vision scope to his helmet with green "550 cord" and attaches a nylon sling to his rifle and tries on his new boots and then puts them, heels together, against the cement wall.

Loza was shot up at Restrepo on the second day and his return to the KOP was mildly controversial because he still can't lift his arm higher than his shoulder. He wanted to come back to be with his friends and someone behind a desk basically did him a favor. He pulls an X-ray out of his pack and shows it to me and at first I don't even understand what I'm looking at. It looks like a black-and-white photo of a suspension bridge in the fog, until I realize that the spans and cables are actually pieces of metal screwed into his bone. I ask him if it hurt to get shot.

"No," he said. "I just thought I'd been slapped."

I've been on some kind of high-amplitude ride all day since the bomb went off, peaks where I can't sit still and valleys that make me want to catch the next resupply out of here. Not because I'm scared but because I'm used to war being exciting and suddenly it's not. Suddenly it seems weak and sad, a collective moral failure that has tricked me — tricked us all — into falling for the sheer drama of it. Young men in their terrible new roles with their terrible new machinery arrayed against equally strong young men on the other side of the valley, all dedicated to a kind of canceling out of each other until replacements arrive. Then it starts all over again. There's so much human energy involved — so much courage, so much honor, so much blood — you could easily go a year here without questioning whether any of this needs to be happening in the first place. Nothing could convince *this* many people to work *this* hard at something that wasn't necessary — right? — you'd catch yourself thinking.

That night I rewind the videotape of the explosion and try to watch it. My pulse gets so weird in the moments before we get hit that I almost have to look away. I can't stop thinking about the ten feet or so that put that bomb beneath the engine block rather than beneath us. That night I have a dream. I'm watching a titanic battle between my older brother and the monsters of the underworld, and my brother is killing one after another with a huge shotgun. The monsters are cartoonlike and murderous and it doesn't matter how many he kills because there's an endless supply of them.

Eventually he'll just run out of ammo, I realize. Eventually the monsters will win.

6

I don't leave the valley, I stay, and after a few days the war becomes normal again. We go on patrol and I focus on the fact that one foot goes in front of the other. We get ambushed and the only thing I'm interested in is what kind of cover we've got. It's all very simple and straightforward, and it's around this time that killing begins to make a kind of sense to me. It's tempting to view killing as a political act because that's where the repercussions play out, but that misses the point: a man behind a rock touched two wires to a battery and tried to kill me—to kill *us*. There are other ways to understand what he did, but none of them overrides the raw fact that this man wanted to

negate everything I'd ever done in my life or might
ever do. It felt malicious and personal in a way that
combat didn't. Combat theoretically gives you the
chance to react well and survive; bombs don't allow
for anything. The pressure cooker was probably
bought in Kandigal, the market town we passed
through half an hour earlier. The bomber built a
campfire in the draw to keep himself warm that
night while waiting for us. We could see his foot-
prints in the sand. The relationship between him
and me couldn't be clearer, and if I'd somehow had
a chance to kill him before he touched the wires
together I'm sure I would have. As a civilian, that's
not a pretty thought to have in your head. That's
not a thought that just sits there quietly and reas-
sures you about things.

It was the ten feet that got me; I kept thinking about Murphree and then looking down at my
legs. The idea that so much could be determined
by so little was sort of intolerable. It made all of
life look terrifying; it made the walk to the chow
hall potentially as bad as a night patrol to Karingal.
(The American contract worker who got shot at the
KOP took a bullet to the leg instead of the head
only because he happened to change directions on
his cot that day.) The only way to calm your nerves
in that environment was to marvel at the insane

amount of firepower available to the Americans and hope that that changed the equation somehow. They have a huge shoulder-fired rocket called a Javelin, for example, that can be steered into the window of a speeding car half a mile away. Each Javelin round costs $80,000, and the idea that it's fired by a guy who doesn't make that in a year at a guy who doesn't make that in a lifetime is somehow so outrageous it almost makes the war seem winnable. And the roar of a full-on firefight could be so reassuring that you wanted to run around hugging people afterward. That roar was what was keeping you alive, and it created an appreciation for firepower so profound that it bordered on the perverse.

"Oh, yeah, everyone's got their favorite weapon," Jones told me. "There are Mark guys and .50 guys. Walker's a Mark guy. The Mark is an automatic grenade launcher that shoots a 40 mike-mike round that explodes on impact. I'm a .50 guy. I don't know if it's true, but they say the round only has to come within eighteen inches of you to sear flesh. That's badass. It doesn't have to hit you and it can still tear you open. It's just a sexy weapon. It's the ultimate machine gun. It has the ability to shoot through walls. It's fun to shoot during a test fire but it's twice as fun during a firefight."

The one absolute impossibility at Restrepo—

you could even get booze if you wanted—was sex with a woman, and the one absolute impossibility back home was combat. Whether the men realized it or not, they had made a rough trade where one risked becoming a stand-in for the other. The potential for humor was enormous, but even when no one was joking, things could still sound awfully funny. "It doesn't need much oil but if you give it too much it'll rock that much more," I overheard O'Byrne telling Vaughn about the .50 cal. "If your shit gets sluggish in a firefight just pour oil all over the bolt and it'll pick right back up."

If you're nineteen and haven't gotten laid in a year, a sentence like that—meant in all sincerity about a very serious matter—can resonate through your psyche in ways you don't even understand. (There was a hill across the valley that the men referred to as "Nipple Rock," and all I can say is that you'd have to have spent a goddamn long time in the valley to see a woman's nipple in that thing.) There was so much sexual energy up at Restrepo that it might as well have been a Miami nightclub, except that the only outlet for it was combat, so that's what the men spent their time thinking about. Once a firefight kicked off and I watched Hoyt and Alcantara race into the east bunker to claim the .50. Hoyt had the lead but Alcantara threw him out of the way and got there first and started firing. They took turns on the gun until the firefight died down and then they settled back in the bunker with cigarettes. They'd shot through so much ammo that the barrel was smoking and they had to pour oil on it to cool it down. Suddenly another burst came in. "*Yes!*" Hoyt whooped as he got back on the gun. "I *knew* this shit wasn't over yet..."

Most of the fighting was at four or five hundred yards, so no one ever got to see—or had to deal with—the effects of all that firepower on the human body. There were exceptions, though. One day Prophet called in saying they'd overheard enemy fighters discussing how they wouldn't shoot at the Americans unless a patrol crossed to the east side of the valley. Soon afterward, Afghan soldiers at OP 3 spotted armed men in the riverbed and started shooting at them. The men fled up the flanks of the Abas Ghar and Third Platoon sent a patrol out of the KOP to give chase. The Americans took contact as soon as they crossed the river and found themselves badly pinned down behind a rock wall, and within seconds every American position in the valley opened up on the guys who were shooting at them. The KOP started dropping mortars and OP 3 engaged with a .50 cal and a Barrett sniper rifle, and the trucks opened up from above Babiyal, and

Restrepo swung its 240s around and poured gunfire across the valley for almost an hour.

It was a hot day and there hadn't been much fighting lately, so when the men jumped on the guns most of them were only wearing flip-flops and shorts. They joked and laughed and called for cigarettes between bursts. Once in a while a round would crack past us, but mostly it was just a turkey shoot at a wide-open mountainside where the enemy had nowhere to hide. Hot brass was filling up the fighting positions and more was cascading down out of the weapons every second. At one point I watched a shell drop into Pemble's untied shoe and he slipped it off, wiggled the shell out, and then slipped his shoe back on without ever stopping firing. The lieutenant was shirtless on the ammo hooch calling coordinates into the KOP and some of the Afghans were firing from the hip even though they didn't stand a chance of hitting anything that way and Jackson was up on the guard position unloading one of the SAWs. Restrepo alone had to be putting out a thousand rounds a minute and the Abas Ghar was sparkling with bullet strikes even though it was broad daylight. Finally Hog showed up — Hog was the radio call sign for the A-10s — and dropped a couple of bombs on the mountain for good measure.

KILLING

At some point a call came in over the radio that the Scouts were watching a guy crawl around on the mountainside without a leg. They watched until he stopped moving and then they called in that he'd died. Everyone at Restrepo cheered. That night I couldn't sleep and I crept out of my bunk and went and sat on the roof of the ammo hooch. It was a nice place to watch the heat lightning out along the Pech or to lie back on the sandbags and look up at the stars. I couldn't stop thinking about that cheer; in some ways it was more troubling than all the killing that was going on. Stripped of all politics, the fact of the matter was that the man had died alone on a mountainside trying to find his leg. He must have been crazed with thirst and bewildered by the sheer amount of gunfire stitching back and forth across the ground looking for him. At one point or another every man in the platoon had been pinned down long enough to think they were going to die—bullets hitting around them, bodies braced for impact—and that's with just one or two guns. Imagine a whole company's worth of firepower directed at you. I got the necessity for it but I didn't get the joy. It seemed like I either had to radically reunderstand the men on this hilltop or I had to acknowledge the power of a place like this to change them.

"You're thinking that this guy could have murdered your friend," Steiner explained to me later. "The cheering comes from knowing that that's someone we'll never have to fight again. Fighting another human being is not as hard as you think when they're trying to kill you. People think we were cheering because we just shot someone, but we were cheering because we just stopped someone from killing us. That person will no longer shoot at us anymore. That's where the fiesta comes in."

Combat was a game that the United States had asked Second Platoon to become very good at, and once they had, the United States had put them on a hilltop without women, hot food, running water, communication with the outside world, or any kind of entertainment for over a year. Not that the men were complaining, but that sort of thing has consequences. Society can give its young men almost any job and they'll figure how to do it. They'll suffer for it and die for it and watch their friends die for it, but in the end, it *will* get done. That only means that society should be careful about what it asks for. In a very crude sense the job of young men is to undertake the work that their fathers are too old for, and the current generation of American fathers has decided that a certain six-mile-long valley in Kunar Province needs to be brought under military control. Nearly fifty American soldiers have died carrying out those orders. I'm not saying that's a lot or a little, but the cost does need to be acknowledged. Soldiers themselves are reluctant to evaluate the costs of war (for some reason, the closer you are to combat the less inclined you are to question it), but someone must. That evaluation, ongoing and unadulterated by politics, may be the one thing a country absolutely owes the soldiers who defend its borders.

There are other costs to war as well—vaguer ones that don't lend themselves to conventional math. One American soldier has died for every hundred yards of forward progress in the valley, but what about the survivors? Is that territory worth the psychological cost of learning to cheer someone's death? It's an impossible question to answer but one that should keep getting asked. Ultimately, the problem is that they're normal young men with normal emotional needs that have to be met within the very narrow options available on that hilltop. Young men need mentors, and mentors are usually a generation or so older. That isn't possible at Restrepo, so a twenty-two-year-old team leader effectively becomes a father figure for a nineteen-year-old private. Up at Restrepo a twenty-seven-year-old is considered an old man, an effeminate

Afghan soldier is seen as a woman, and new privates are called "cherries" and virtually thought of as children. Men form friendships that are not at all sexual but contain much of the devotion and intensity of a romance. Almost every relationship that occurs in open society exists in some compressed form at Restrepo, and almost every human need from back home gets fulfilled in some truncated, jury-rigged way. The men are good at constructing what they need from what they have. They are experts at making do.

As for a sense of purpose, combat is it—the only game in town. Almost none of the things that make life feel worth living back home are present at Restrepo, so the entire range of a young man's self-worth has to be found within the ragged choreography of a firefight. The men talk about it and dream about it and rehearse for it and analyze it afterward but never plumb its depths enough to lose interest. It's the ultimate test, and some of the men worry they'll never again be satisfied with a "normal life"—whatever that is—after the amount of combat they've been in. They worry that they may have been ruined for anything else.

"I like the firefights," O'Byrne admitted to me once. We'd been talking about going home and whether he was going to get bored. "I know," he added, probably realizing how that sounded. "Saddest thing in the world."

We walk the steep hill from the KOP up to OP 1 at the end of the day, kicking through patches of crusty snow near the top and sweating heavily in our winter clothes. I'm with Lieutenant Steve Gillespie, the former leader of Third Platoon who has been switched to Second Platoon after a group of his soldiers were caught drinking at the KOP. (Family members were sending them care packages with bottles of mouthwash filled with vodka.) The switch wasn't punishment so much as an attempt to shake things up. The men at the outpost are dirty and unshaved and have been freezing up there quietly since they ran out of heating oil a week ago. In summer the post is overrun with camel spiders and scorpions but now it's just cold and silent and lifeless, four men with nothing to do but stare at the mountains and recalculate how much of the deployment they still have left.

A patrol comes in from Obenau with a detainee who is dressed in nothing but a thin cotton shalwar kameez. He's shaking with cold but for some reason keeps looking around and laughing. Maybe he can't believe how rough the Americans are living.

The patrol takes him on down to the KOP and we continue on the high trail to Restrepo with the wind picking up at the end of the day and monkeys screaming their outrage from the peaks. We don't bother running the last stretch of road because there hasn't been any shooting in the valley in weeks, and with snow-covered mountains all around us it's hard not to think we're just on some weird camping trip. Restrepo now has plywood bee huts fastened crookedly to the mountainside and a guard tower with a Mark 19 in it and a tiny two-man outpost a hundred yards outside the wire. The outpost is called Columbus and covers the draw below Restrepo. An all-out attack would probably take Columbus without difficulty, but the position would buy the men at Restrepo enough time to grab their guns and roll out the door.

We walk into Restrepo and drop our packs in a pile. The sun has fired the Abas Ghar with a red glow and a few of the brighter planets are already infiltrating the afternoon sky. The men are standing around in dirty fleeces and their pants unbelted smoking cigarettes and watching another day come to an end. They're dirty in their pores and under their nails and their skin has burnished to a kind of sheen at the wrists and neck where the uniforms rub. Dirt collects in the creases of the skin and shows up as strange webs at the corners of the eyes and their lifelines run black and unmistakable across the palms of their hands. It's a camp of homeless men or hunters who have not reckoned with a woman in months and long since abandoned the niceties. They belch and fart and blow their noses on their sleeves and wipe their mouths on their shirtfronts and pack every sentence with enough profanity to last most civilians a week. After the fighting ended last fall they got so bored that they started prying boulders out of the hillside and rolling them into the valley. They were trying to get one inside the wire at Firebase Phoenix just to keep Third Platoon on their toes. Caldwell finally told them to knock it off.

Gillespie takes command immediately. Patterson, the platoon sergeant, delivers a short, sharp speech making it clear that the problems with Third Platoon are no reflection on Gillespie and then hands it over to him. Everything about Gillespie is long: his torso, his legs, his neck, and he's slightly pigeon-toed in a way that belies how tough he really is. Now he stands that way, lanky and awkward, in the dying gray light, taking command of arguably the most combat-intensive outpost in the entire U.S. military. "I've been down there with Third Platoon for the past five months so you guys have probably been seeing me around," he says. "Pretty laid-back guy, like Sergeant Patterson says. I'll watch you guys and we'll go from there. You guys got any questions for me?"

Jones raises his hand. There's a strange expectation in the air, the men seem to be trying to not catch each other's eyes. Gillespie has his hands jammed into his pockets so there's nothing he could possibly do about what's about to happen. "You ever seen the movie *Blood In Blood Out*, sir?" Jones asks.

Pause.

"Get him!" someone yells, and First Lieutenant Steve Gillespie disappears beneath a scrum of enlisted men. They quickly rack him out on the ground, pull up his shirt, and take turns smacking his abdomen as hard as they can. Donoho spits on his palm first so it will hurt more. Every man takes a turn and Patterson is offered a hit, though he declines, and then they help Gillespie back to his feet. Glasses askew, he slaps the dirt off himself and shakes his head, trying to laugh. I've just watched an officer in the U.S. military get overpowered and beaten by his men at a remote outpost in Afghanistan, and it occurs to me that not only is this not happening in other armies, it probably isn't even happening at other *outposts*. The previous fall, O'Byrne and Sergeant Mac were trying to figure out how to welcome someone back after leave and the only thing they could think of was to beat the shit out of him, which is what they did. That started a tradition that even other platoons in Battle Company weren't interested in emulating. "The guys I love the most I beat the worst," O'Byrne explained. "It's a sign of affection in the weirdest possible way. It's the *hard* way, that's what it is. They beat Lieutenant Piosa down so badly his face looked like he was getting tortured."

Gillespie was taking command of Second Platoon and it prompted a lot of talk up on the hill; it was serious business up here and the men knew a bad leader could easily get them killed. They weren't that familiar with Gillespie beyond the fact that he bore a passing resemblance to Napoleon Dynamite, and a collective decision was made that fell so far outside of Army protocol no one even wanted to claim ownership of it. "Third Platoon wasn't doing so hot," O'Byrne told me months later, "so we had our doubts already—you know? So we said, 'We're going to beat the shit out of him and if he doesn't take it, well fuck it—then we just won't listen to the motherfucker. If he can't take a beating then he's not part of Second Platoon anyway. He's not part of what we're about.'"

It was a lot of tough talk but the truth was that

the men respected Gillespie enormously, and roughing him up was their way of demonstrating that. A lesser officer would never have rolled with that situation, and lesser troops would never have even thought of it. It was about brotherhood, not discipline, and the command was smart enough to understand that and stay out of the way. "Man's natural instinct is to survive," Kearney said about Second Platoon. (Tim had just asked him whether they had "demons.") "The boys don't go out there and fight for freedom, they don't fight for patriotism — they fight because they know that if they go out there alone and walk into Aliabad they're going to get killed."

Margins were so small and errors potentially so catastrophic that every soldier had a kind of de facto authority to reprimand others — in some cases even officers. And because combat can hinge on the most absurd details, there was virtually nothing in a soldier's daily routine that fell outside the group's purview. Whether you tied your shoes or cleaned your weapon or drank enough water or secured your night vision gear were all matters of public concern and so were open to public scrutiny. Once I watched a private accost another private whose bootlaces were trailing on the ground. Not that he cared what it looked like, but if something happened suddenly—and out there, everything happened suddenly—the guy with the loose laces couldn't be counted on to keep his feet at a crucial moment. It was the *other* man's life he was risking, not just his own. Another time a couple of squads were lying in ambush outside Karingal and a man rolled to the side to urinate. You could smell it ten feet away, which meant he wasn't well hydrated, and when Patterson caught a whiff he chewed the man out in an irritated growl. If you're not hydrated you're that much closer to being a heat casualty, and that could slow a patrol down long enough to get cornered and overrun. There was no such thing as *personal* safety out there; what happened to you happened to everyone.

The attention to detail at a base like Restrepo forced a kind of clarity on absolutely everything a soldier did until I came to think of it as a kind of Zen practice: the Zen of not fucking up. It required a high mindfulness because potentially everything had consequences. Once I attended a shura at the KOP with a cast-off Army shirt that Anderson had given me, and when I left the building I forgot to take it with me. A few hours later I realized I couldn't find it and went into a controlled panic: if one of the elders picked it up and gave it to an enemy fighter, that man would be able to use it to pass himself off as an American soldier. Potentially someone could get killed. Eventually I found the shirt, but it was clear from the looks I was getting that I'd fucked up pretty badly and that it had better not happen again.

Frontline soldiers have policed their own behavior at least since World War II and probably a lot longer than that. In a study of bravery conducted by the U.S. military in the forties, the author, Samuel Stouffer, had this to say about personal responsibility: "Any individual's action which had conceivable bearing on the safety of others became a matter of public concern for the group as a whole. Isolated as he was from contact with the rest of the world, the combat man was thrown back on his outfit to meet the various affectional needs . . . that he would normally satisfy with his family and friends. The group was thus in a favored position to enforce its standards on the individual."

In the civilian world almost nothing has lasting consequences, so you can blunder through life in a kind of daze. You never have to take inventory of the things in your possession and you never have to calculate the ways in which mundane circumstances can play out — can, in fact, kill you. As a result, you lose a sense of the importance of things, the gravity of things. Back home mundane details also have the power to destroy you, but the cause and effect are often spread so far apart that you don't even make the connection; at Restrepo, that connection was impossible to ignore. It was tedious but it gave the stuff of one's existence — the shoelaces and the water and the lost shirt — a riveting importance. Frankly, after you got used to living that way it was hard to go home.

There was carelessness and then there were real mistakes, and once it crossed that line, discipline came down from above and was relentless. Once I woke up in the middle of the night to grunts and shouting and went outside to find Staff Sergeant Alcantara smoking his entire squad. Whoever was on guard duty had let the batteries run down on a thermal sight called a PAS-13 that allowed them to scan the hillsides at night. On a dark night the PAS-13 was the only way they could see if the enemy was creeping close for a surprise attack, and dead batteries could literally put the base at risk of getting overrun. The best way to ensure that no one fucked up was to inflict collective punishment on the entire squad, because that meant everyone would be watching everyone else. Al had them out there in stress positions lifting sandbags and essentially eating dirt for so long that I finally just went back inside and went to sleep. The next morning I asked him if the punishment had wiped the slate clean — or was there some residual stigma that would take longer to erase?

"There are no hard feelings after everyone gets smoked," he said. "They're more pissed that they all let each other down. Once it's over it's over."

With dark the cold comes down like some kind of court sentence and the men drift inside to sit around the diesel stoves until it's time to go to sleep. Each squad built their own hooch from plywood and two-by-fours slung in by Chinook and the construction is straight ghetto: uninsulated plywood and gaps in the walls and strange patchwork solutions to elementary problems. Some colonel upstream decided that Restrepo would be an "outpost" rather than a "base," so Second Platoon was restricted to using tools and materials that would barely have been adequate for a ten-year-old making a tree fort. They cut their wood with a four-inch folding Gerber saw and pulled nails out of old pieces of wood to reuse on new pieces of wood and leveled floors by guess and plumbed walls by eye. Third Squad didn't dig out the hillside enough, so their hooch, nicknamed "the Submarine," wound up so narrow that there was no room for the stove. It was stuck in a drafty alcove and barely raised the inside temperature above freezing. Weapons Squad built their hooch on an angle and then overcompensated with the angle of the bunks, which in turn were angled differently from the shelving and the roof. The result was an optical illusion that left you disoriented and not entirely sure where the horizon line was. You could put a marble on one of the bunks and swear to God it was rolling upward.

I'm staying with O'Byrne and the rest of First Squad. The bunks are plywood and stacked two high and the aisle between them is just wide enough for two men to pass turning sideways. Lying on your bunk you could reach out and touch three other men without much trouble. Weapons and full ammo racks hang from nails pounded into the walls and socks dry on "550 cord" that has been strung between rafters, and combat packs and boots and packages from home are stuffed under the bunks. Most of the men have photographs of women nailed to the walls — magazine photos, not personal ones; you wouldn't really want to subject your girlfriend to that kind of scrutiny — and a few have blankets nailed over their bunk for privacy. Others simply escape with sleeping pills.

I take a lower bunk near the stove and unpack my gear. Around me the men are eating MREs and talking about their plans in the military, about the troubles in Third Platoon, about how everything fell apart once the fighting stopped. Friends started arguing and a sour discontent crept through the company that was almost as threatening to their mission as the enemy. The lull was much harder on group dynamics than combat and caught everyone by surprise, even the commanders. Prophet recently picked up radio chatter that a hundred men had come into the valley with the intention of overrunning Restrepo, but that almost seemed too good to be true.

"I hope they try it," one guy told me; it was a common sentiment. "I hope they try it because if they do, they're all going to die."

One day a patrol goes down to Loy Kalay, searches the bazaar, and returns without even generating radio chatter. A squad-plus sets in an ambush on a south-facing hill just outside the wire but all they see are women collecting firewood. Another patrol turns up wires running to a 107 mm rocket hidden in a wood pile and an explosives team comes in by helicopter to blow it up. The men at Restrepo work slowly at odd jobs around the base and lift weights while the sun is still high and then break at the end of the day to sit on the ammo hooch smoking. At eight o'clock the generator cuts out and everyone goes to their bunks; after that, the only men awake are the ones at the guardposts. Sometimes it would occur to me how incredible — how very close to the experience of childhood — it is to be watched over by others while you slowly float off into sleep.

One evening Steiner and I are sitting around the heater and he's telling me about his efforts to understand women. He wants to understand them so that he can sleep with them more easily. He has read everything he can on the topic, including books on feminism, and he favors what he calls the "cocky-funny" routine when talking to them, which is explained in one of his books. Steiner was a wrestler in high school and has sandy blond hair and a big wide-open smile and looks like he could easily carry a kitchen sink up a mountain. "He's too pretty for himself," was how First Sergeant Caldwell described him to me once. Steiner arrived in the Korengal a few months late, having spent the beginning of the deployment as a driver for the battalion sergeant major. He and I discuss women for a while and eventually Lambert shuffles in and looks around. Lambert's new to the platoon and is from the South and has a slight stammer that he claims women fall for. He says he killed his first deer at age ten, and his father made him gut it and then take a bite of the raw heart ("—and I've been stuttering ever since," someone else jokingly finished the story for him).

Lambert says he's going to start a landscaping business when he gets home and then he's going to buy a backhoe and dig graves in cemeteries. "It's guaranteed work because people die every day," he says. "People die and it's, like, five hundred dollars a grave and you can dig five or six graves in a day."

I watch Steiner frown and consider this plan. It seems like there should be a catch but maybe there's not; maybe earning a living really is that simple. Steiner is still thinking about it when Jackson and Monroe walk in. The first nickname Jackson got in the platoon was "Jacko," but that was quickly changed to "Wacko." Wacko made an impression early on by completing a twelve-mile road march on blisters that were so bad his boots filled with blood. Monroe's nickname is "Money." Money will barely speak for days at a time but looks around in ways that suggest he knows something no one else has figured out yet. Maybe he has. He's lean and a little feral-looking and very tough. He makes a kind of bleating sound from time to time, a cross between a goat and a machine gun, and for a while he was hiding behind things at Restrepo and jumping out at unsuspecting men screaming, "WHAT'S UP MOTHERFUCKER?" The sudden boredom after fighting season ended affected everyone differently.

Lambert is still talking about gravedigging when O'Byrne walks in. He has his cap pulled low over his eyes and a quilted parka liner buttoned with just the top button and his face is smudged with dirt and his pants are ripped in three different places. O'Byrne arrived in the Army with a mustache and a full head of hair but by the time he got to the Korengal he'd shaved both off. During his two years in the service much of his hair had disappeared anyway. ("The Army stole my hair," he liked to say. "But who needs fucking hair?") He leans against one of the bunks and announces that he's going to write a book about his life one day. Someone asks him why.

"Because of all the interesting shit that's happened," he says.

"Like what?"

"Like for starters, I was shot by my father."

No one says a word.

"When I was a kid me and my dad liked to drink a lot," O'Byrne continues, and someone laughs. O'Byrne's head swivels around.

"That's just not a sentence you hear very often," Steiner explains.

That seems to satisfy O'Byrne, who goes on to

explain how his father came to shoot him. "But everything happens for a reason, I surely do believe that," he concludes. "If my dad hadn't shot me I wouldn't have joined the Army—and wouldn't be where I am right now."

He says this without a trace of irony. There is a complicated silence in the room.

"Well, I'm not buyin' your fuckin' book," Money finally says.

Months later, O'Byrne told me the whole terrible story. I already knew he'd grown up in a small town, and I asked if he'd ever hunted as a kid. He said once he killed a salamander and felt so guilty he never killed anything again.

"But I've always had guns...my dad always had guns," O'Byrne said. "He raised me—which is fucking weird, but we'll get to that—he raised me to respect weapons and never point them at anybody. Both of us failed *that* fucking miserably. I was a bad kid in high school, I was a fucking punk—I did *not* know how to be a nice kid. My dad just drank and drank and drank. So one night, for my buddy's birthday, this girl came over and we got a gallon of vodka. Vodka is not good for me, it makes me violent as shit. I drank probably half a gallon, I was fucking obliterated, I was smashed. I get home and the first thing I see is my dad. I walk through the door and he's fucking screaming at me. He swings. I swing. We start fighting. This fight goes on and on—I mean we fought for a long time. All my friends were trying to hold me back. Someone hit me with a two-by-four just trying to calm me down."

The fight eventually broke up and O'Byrne went to his room. After a while he heard his father yelling again, so he went back downstairs and started walking back and forth in front of his father's bedroom door, screaming at him. Suddenly his hip gave out and the next thing he knew he was lying in the hallway and his leg didn't work. He didn't hear gunshots or feel any pain and he thought he'd somehow dislocated his hip. Then his father came out of the bedroom and pointed a rifle at his head. It was O'Byrne's favorite gun, a semiautomatic Ruger with a folding stock, and O'Byrne said, 'So you're going to shoot me when I'm down?' and his father said, 'I already did.'

"I was too drunk to realize what was going on, so I go upstairs, I walk up two flights of stairs and I start playing video games and then I go lay down because I'm losing blood. I'm crying now because I realize what's going on and I'm in some fucking trouble now, I have two fucking bullets in me. This is not good. This is not a good situation."

An ambulance finally arrived and O'Byrne was taken to a hospital in Scranton. He had one bullet in his hip and another in the small of his back less than an inch from his spinal column. After doctors finished operating on him a cop showed up and asked for a statement. O'Byrne thought about it: whatever his father's problems, he'd always held down a job and provided for the family, and if he went to prison, there'd be no one to take care of the family. That would compound an already terrible situation. 'It was my fault,' O'Byrne told the cop. 'He did it in self-defense.'

"My father wouldn't have made it through jail—he's not a violent person. The *situation* was violent but he's not. So I was three days in the hospital and then they sent me to lockup—no rehab, nothing. I was charged with simple assault. I was a pussy in there, man, like, I didn't try to fight *anyone*. It was the best thing—but the worst thing—that ever happened to me. My father and I put ourselves in that position to be fucking evil to each other. It's a tough story but it's a good one, too. How dare I hit my father—even if he hit me? If he popped me in my nose right now I'd look at him and I'd be like, 'All right, I'm going downstairs and I'll give you time to cool off.' I'll never hit that man again. *That* was my fault—you know? I didn't have the respect. It's a story of triumph. It's a story of going through some hard shit and making out really good. I know bullets can't stop me now. Fucking bullets are okay."

7

I GO TO SLEEP ONE NIGHT MENTALLY PREPARED for a twenty-four-hour operation called Dark City, but at three in the morning Donoho comes through the hooch announcing that it's been canceled because of the weather. Third Platoon was going to cross over to the far side of the valley, and Second Platoon was going to support them from Table Rock with a lot of firepower. We all roll over and go back to sleep and the next time I wake up it's full light and Jones is sitting on a bunk eating an MRE. Jones ordinarily sleeps in the Submarine, but last night was so cold that he moved in with us. He's picking the mushrooms out of his Thai Chicken and muttering to no one in particular, "Not a big fan of mushrooms. Only people you ever see eating mushrooms are white folks. 'What you want on your pizza, sir?' 'Mushrooms.' 'What else do you want on your pizza?' 'More mushrooms.'"

The door opens and O'Byrne walks in. He's looking for Money, who's still asleep in his bunk. O'Byrne sits next to him and puts him in a headlock. "I just don't understand," he says. "If you were Hajj, why would you want to wake up in the morning and shoot at us?"

Money doesn't answer. He's not interested in this conversation. "Money, why would Hajj want to do that? Why would he climb up onto the hilltops to start shooting at us?"

The immediate answer was that we built a firebase in their backyard, but there was more to the question than that. Once in a while you'd forget to think of the enemy as *the enemy* and would see them for what they were: teenagers up on a hill who got tired and cold just like the Americans and missed their families and slept poorly before the big operations and probably had nightmares about them afterward. Once you thought about them on those terms it was hard not to wonder whether the men themselves—not the American and Taliban commanders but the actual guys behind the guns—couldn't somehow sit down together and work this out. I'm pretty sure the Taliban had a healthy respect for Second Platoon, at least as fighters, and once in a while I'd hear someone in Second Platoon mumble a kind of grudging approval of the Taliban as well: they move like ghosts around the mountains and can fight all day on a swallow of water and a handful of nuts and are holding their own against a brigade of U.S. airborne infantry. As a military feat that's nothing to sneeze at. The sheer weirdness of this war—of any war—can never entirely be contained and breaks through at odd moments:

"I went out to use the piss tubes one night," O'Byrne admitted to me once, "and I was like, 'What am I doing in Afghanistan?' I mean literally, *What am I doing here?*' I'm trying to kill people and they're trying to kill me. It's crazy..."

The enemy had to have their piss-tube moments as well—how could they not? In January, Prophet overheard two Taliban commanders discussing the American presence in the valley by radio. One of them was making the point that if the Americans were willing to build roads and clinics in the valley, maybe they shouldn't be attacked. The other guy didn't quite agree, but at least someone was asking the question. The number of firefights in the battalion area of operation had dropped from five a day to one a day, the number of shuras with local leaders had quadrupled, and the Americans hadn't been shot at from inside a village in the Korengal since the end of October. That was an important gauge of local sentiment because it meant that the villagers were telling the fighters to take their insurgency elsewhere. There was even a story going around that one of the valley elders had slapped a Taliban commander across the face for refusing to leave the area, and the commander didn't dare retaliate. The human terrain in the Pech and the Korengal was changing so fast that Colonel Ostlund felt confident a little more development money would allow NATO forces and the Afghan government to absolutely "overrun" the area. "The arguments I've heard against the American presence here are all economically based," he told me. "Which is the good news, because economic arguments are arguments we can win."

Kearney is convinced that in the spring the fight is going to move northward, out of the Korengal and into the Pech, which would allow him to create a little breathing room for the incoming unit. As far as he knows that will be Viper Company of the First Infantry Division, which is a mechanized unit, and the new soldiers will probably be out of shape and used to riding in trucks. They'll be faced with foot patrols on some of the steepest terrain in the entire war, and Kearney wants to make sure that at least the northern half of the valley has bought into the idea of government control. He's going to build another outpost, called Dallas, more or less at the spot where Murphree lost his legs last month. That will extend American firepower deep into the central Korengal and prevent the enemy from digging bombs into a crucial section of road. He's going to put Third Platoon down at Dallas and hand Phoenix over to the Afghan National Army, which is coming into the valley with two full companies—300 men. The idea is to have the ANA start conducting their own patrols in the safer villages, like Babiyal and Aliabad, which would free up the Americans to push farther down-valley.

"We're still gonna take casualties, unfortunately," Kearney says. "We'll probably lose another soldier, if not more, but I think the kinetic activity will drop. The people of the valley will hopefully start seeing some changes, and we'll hopefully have a food distribution center set up. That way I can bring the local villagers in and empower *them* rather than the elders, who are working with the Taliban."

Kearney wants to start issuing identity cards so that locals can come to the KOP and pick up food and other types of humanitarian aid. Until now those supplies have been distributed through village elders who make huge profits by taking most of it for themselves. Identity cards will also enable the S-2, the intelligence officer, to conduct a crude census of the valley, and the food pickups will give locals an opportunity to tip the Americans off to upcoming attacks without the Taliban knowing about it. Kearney also wants to buy three or four jingle trucks, put benches in the back, and start running a bus service up and down the valley. Right now it costs around a hundred dollars in fuel to drive a truck from Babiyal, at the center of the valley, up to the nearest market town and back. A bus service would allow commerce to start flowing more freely into and out of the valley, which would take control out of the hands of the village elders and put it into the hands of ordinary people.

"The villagers are almost like indentured servants," Kearney says. "I got to bring these people up so they're not reliant on the elders, so they're taking some ownership of themselves and their families. Right now the elders are the only ones getting out to Asadabad, they own gas stations on the A-bad-J-bad road. They don't let the people out because then they'll lose their free labor."

As the most exposed base in the Korengal,

KILLING

Restrepo is exquisitely attuned to social changes in the valley. If the price of wheat goes up because of a bad harvest, the amount of fighting drops because the fighters have less money to spend on ammo. Second Platoon hasn't been shot at in weeks, they can walk into Loy Kalay without any problem, and old men are stopping patrols to tip them off about Taliban movements. Everything is starting to shift. One night I find O'Byrne sitting on one of the lower bunks framed in blinking Christmas lights slowly picking out "Paint It Black" on his guitar. He says he's trying to imagine Restrepo as some kind of ski lodge and health spa. The locals could be ski instructors — it would pay better than fighting the Americans. Hijar and Underwood could run the gym. They could shoot blank rounds over the outpost once in a while, just so people would get a feel for what it was like during the war. You could make it down to Phoenix on a snowboard in about sixty seconds and take a ski lift back up.

I ask O'Byrne if he'll get bored without any fighting this spring and he stops playing guitar and looks upward, searching for how to put this. "All right, this is how it goes," he says. "This is the thought process in my head: if we never get shot at again, I won't mind. But if we do." He gives me a look. "*I...won't...mind.* Ha-ha-ha!"

WAR

• • •

It's early morning and I'm down at Phoenix with Anderson and the rest of Third Squad. Operation Dark City is finally under way but I've passed on the chance to go out on it. (An all-night walk with Third Platoon and almost no chance of contact—even Second Platoon guys were telling me it wasn't worth the night's sleep.) The sun is warm and I'm up at the guardpost scanning the ridgelines with binoculars. After a while I can pick out Third Platoon on Honcho Hill and a squad from Second Platoon at Table Rock. Near me, Anderson and a medic named LeFave talk down the morning. They have a two-hour guard shift and then they can go back to sleep. Anderson wants to know whether LeFave would sew his finger back on if it got shot off. LeFave doesn't even look up.

"You can't just sew a finger back on, you have to reattach all the nerves and shit."

"Well, if my finger gets shot off I want you to try to save it," Anderson says. He's a saxophone player so his request makes sense.

"If your finger gets shot off, I'll find it and put it in your cargo pouch."

"Suppose I don't want it in my cargo pouch?"

"I'll put it anywhere you want."

Silence for five or ten minutes. "Maybe it would be cool to be a homicide detective," Anderson finally says.

"Why?"

"Well, it's not like we haven't seen enough dead bodies out here."

"Yeah, but you have to be all creepy and shit," LeFave answers. "You'd have to think like a killer."

"Well," Anderson says, "that sure as hell wouldn't be hard."

Daylight only lasts six or seven hours but there's so little work at Restrepo that even that feels endless. The men fill up their time as best they can. One morning Gillespie conducts a "law of war" class in which he goes over what is and isn't legal in terms of killing people. ("As much as you hate the Taliban and Al Qaeda, they're still people. Napalm? If you can get away without using it, so much the better.") There are a lot of squad brawls, and one man clears his hooch instantly by pulling out a hand grenade and waving it around. Steiner, Lambert, and Donoho put on "Touch Me," by Gunther and the Sunshine Girls, and briefly turn the First Squad hooch into a gay disco. Mace toboggans through the outpost on a flexible Skedco litter after a particularly heavy snowfall. O'Byrne receives a random care package from a high school girl that contains two hundred toothbrushes—more than enough for an entire company. She also sent pink plastic soap dishes. ("Are you serious? We make fun of each other out here enough as it is.") One morning O'Byrne walks past me muttering, "Fuckin' pervert," about a platoonmate he accidentally caught committing a private act in his bunk. Jones wanders around the outpost wearing a fake afro with a purple plastic pick jammed in the back. He says he's going on patrol that way, helmet balanced on the top of all that hair, until O'Byrne points out it'll only aggravate the local rednecks.

The guys are experts, of a sort, at being funny, and they seem to go out of their way to be. Maybe it's the only way to stay sane up there. Not because of the combat—you're never saner than when your survival is in question—but because of the unbelievable, screaming boredom. "Okay, who's going to die today?" was a standard one-liner before patrols. ("Hey, Anderson, what do you want on your tombstone?" I heard someone ask before we all headed down to Karingal. "Now *that's* fucked up," Anderson muttered as he put on his helmet.) Before patrols, guys promised their laptops to each other or their new boots or their iPods. One pair of friends had a serious agreement that if one of them should die, the other would erase all the porn on his laptop before the Army could ship it back to his mom. Mothers were an irresistible source of humor. "If I start bangin' your mom when we get home, will that mean I'm your dad?" — or some version of that — was pretty much boilerplate humor at Restrepo. Once I watched O'Byrne grab someone's ass and give it a good, deep squeeze. When the man demanded an explanation O'Byrne said, "Just trying to get an idea what your mom's ass is gonna feel like when we get home." Only wives and girlfriends are off-limits because the men are already so riddled with anxiety over what's going on back home that almost nothing you could say would be funny. Anything else — mothers, sisters, retarded nephews — is fair game.

Not all the humor involved gutting your best friend's personal dignity. Donoho would pretend to see obstacles on night patrols and climb over them so he could watch the next guy in line try to do the same thing. Money ate a two-pound bag of tuna in one sitting just to see what would happen. O'Byrne and Sergeant Al fashioned a tarantula out of pipe cleaners to slip into my sleeping bag. (They giggled like schoolgirls while they were making it so I knew something was up.) Some of the men were deeply, intentionally funny, others—like Money—were inadvertently funny, and a few seemed to act as fulcrums for a sick hilarity that could well up from almost anywhere. Jones was one of those. He was the only black guy in the platoon, and that alone made him an irresistible source of humor. That was also true of Kim, the only Asian, and Rueda, who looked awfully Indian. (He had no idea whether he really was or not, but O'Byrne called him "Apache" anyway.)

Not only was Jones the only black guy in the platoon, he was one of only five in the entire company and he'd clearly given the matter some thought. "Black people don't jump out of planes," he told me when I asked him why there weren't more blacks in the unit. The platoon was on ambush west of Restrepo and we had a lot of time to kill. "Black people don't want to come out here and get shot at. It's not what they do. Most times black folks join the Army because they're trying to get a skill set to do something else with their life. I get plenty of shit around here for being the only black dude, but ninety-eight percent of the time it's all in good fun. You're gonna run across some guys out there who don't like me, I guaran-god-damn-tee it, but at the same time I bet there's not one of 'em that would say, 'I wouldn't take him in a firefight.' And that's what I'm looking for. I don't need you to like me, but I need you to respect me. I need you to want to go to war with me."

Jones had a kind of rangy muscularity that made him seem capable of going to the Olympics in virtually anything. He roamed Restrepo like some kind of alpha predator, and if you caught his attention, you didn't know whether he was going to jump you, look right through you, or drape an arm over your shoulder and ask how you were doing. He exuded a strange, sullen anger that never quite came to the surface but instead wound up getting slid between your ribs as a casual observation that was devastating because it was so accurate. He dubbed one officer "Chinless the Fearless" and probably wouldn't have even bothered except that the guy really *was* fearless. He was fond of giving someone a dismissive look and saying, "Just a *mess*. A soup sandwich. Just a goddamn mess." I liked him tremendously. I think it took most of the year for him to say more than two words to me.

"Personally, I don't give a fuck, you know what I mean?" he went on to tell me about his life before the Army. "I'll tell anyone who will listen: I smoked a lot of weed, I sold a lot of drugs, I don't care who knows it, it's the way it was. I never got caught, my choice was pretty much on the streets dead, or in jail. I didn't want either so I joined the Army. And now it's dead or back home, but I guess the jail thing is out of the fucking equation. My mom raised me better than that, plain and simple. She just raised me better than to be selling drugs. She was the realest person in my life."

If humor wasn't enough to get you through the week you could always talk about the exploits of the men on leave. By mid-tour there was a steady trickle of men coming and going, and the things that happened to them provided a minor amount of spiritual sustenance for the others. Leave lasts eighteen days and starts when your feet touch American soil. It seems to consist mostly of getting drunk with friends and trying to meet, impress, and seduce women who won't care that the association will be measured in days, if not hours. When Pemble went home on leave he had to change planes in Texas, and as he was walking through the first-class section on his flight to Oregon a man jumped up, grabbed Pemble's boarding pass, and told him they were trading seats. Pemble's uniform was ripped and filthy, and he sat in first class for the first time in his life reeking of combat and drinking champagne. He took a commuter train from the airport to Beaverton and walked into a Hooters restaurant and ordered a beer. The waitress saw him in his uniform and sat down next to him and started asking questions. At one point she wanted to know what he'd done to get his combat infantry badge.

'I just had to get shot at,' Pemble answered.

Her next question was whether or not he had a girlfriend.

Pemble's parents didn't know he was coming home on leave—he wanted to surprise them—so he walked several miles from the train station with an assault pack over his shoulder and people staring at him as they drove by. His parents were both at work and the house was locked so he got a ladder out of the garage, put it to a second-story window, and climbed in. After a while he got bored sitting home alone so he went out and knocked at the house of a Vietnam vet who lived next door. The vet understood without having to ask and pulled some whiskey out of the cabinet and they spent the rest of the afternoon drinking. When Pemble's parents finally came home he was asleep on their couch, filthy and exhausted and drunk.

Everyone reacts differently to going home. The first time Hijar sat down to a hot meal he burst into tears. Cortez didn't know whether he should act like a man or a boy when he saw his mom at the airport, but it didn't matter because it was his brother-in-law who picked him up and they just went out and got drunk. Jones thought the rattling of the pipes when he ran the water sounded just like the .50 and stood there listening to it for so long that his wife finally asked what was wrong. Everyone jerked at loud noises and dreamed about combat, and everyone worried about their brothers back in the Korengal. It was the kind of combat where one man could make all the difference, but you couldn't be that man if you were home partying with your friends.

And then there were the questions. Moreno went home to Beeville, Texas, and got into a conversation with a stranger who finally asked what he'd wanted to ask all along, which was whether Moreno had killed anyone. Moreno just looked at him. "Keep in mind I've never met this guy," Moreno said. "I'm like, 'Yo, we don't like talking about that.' And he was like, 'If I killed someone I'd let you know.' His eyes were rolling toward the back of his head and this and that and I was like, 'Dude, it's different when you see your best friend laying there dead. You think you're a badass until you've seen a fallen soldier laying there not breathing anymore and then it's a different fucking story.'"

Moreno thought of leave primarily as eighteen days when he didn't have to worry about getting shot. He was one of those rare things, a good soldier who didn't like combat, and as far as he was concerned if they never got into another firefight it was fine with him. Once we got hit pretty hard and an RPG came in and exploded against the sandbags right next to where Moreno was standing. There were only a few weeks to go in the deployment and Moreno dropped into a hole and came back up shaking his head in disgust. Meanwhile Steiner was running around with a big grin on his face. "It's like crack," he yelled, "you can't get a better high." I asked him how he was ever going to go back to civilian life.

He shook his head. "I have no idea."

8
—

THE MISSION EVERYONE'S BEEN GETTING nervous about is Karingal. They've never gone there without getting shot at and the fact that there hasn't been a TIC in weeks only means the enemy has saved up plenty of ammo. Karingal is only a few clicks south of Loy Kalay but the approach is wide open to enemy positions on 1705 and the inhabitants are hard-core Taliban — the guys say they can tell by the looks in their eyes. The town's only saving grace is that there's supposed to be one very beautiful girl there, Moreno caught a glimpse of her once (right before they got lit up from the south). Otherwise all the hot girls are in Upper Obenau.

Patrols never leave at the same time or follow the

same routes, and the mission to Karingal is set for midafternoon with the sun just starting to throw cold blue shadows across the valley. We leave the wire through the southern gate and contour across the draw, moving quickly through the open spots and only stopping behind trees so the patrol is harder to spot. You never walk up on the man in front of you because clusters get targeted, and you never speak over a whisper. If you step carelessly and knock stones down the slope, heads turn and men stare. We cross over the high road and continue southward into a pretty little valley above a creek slotted deeply into a draw. The creek comes down from the high peaks muttering between boulders and over rock shelves and we have to walk way up the valley before we can cross over and double back on the other side. Snow is lying deep in the northern exposures and melting busily on the south-facing slopes as if winter weren't happening there, and if you stopped to feel the sun on your face, you could imagine the war wasn't either.

We exit the draw somewhere north of Karingal and move quickly down the road, boots crunching double-time in the snow and the men silent and tense. The sounds of village life rise to meet us, children shouting and the cry of a baby and once in a while a rooster or the patient agonies of livestock.

KILLING

We're moving on the village single file as fast as we can and sweating heavily in our body armor, trying to get close before the local men can get up to their fighting positions. Gillespie pauses briefly before turning the ridgeline outside town and we start down the last stretch with 1705 looming above us like the hull of a huge gray battleship. No cover except six inches of frozen mud if you squeezed yourself down into the tire ruts in the road.

The village has gone silent now except for one dog, then another furiously baying our arrival. We clamber down the final slope into town to find every door closed and every window shuttered tight. I follow O'Byrne to the edge of the village and he takes up a position behind some trees and watches the ridgeline to our south. That's where it will come from if it comes at all. A family is clustered on the back porch of a house, children crying and a woman trying to pull everyone indoors. A chicken wanders through it all pecking the ground. A mortar booms in the distance, something must be going on up-valley. O'Byrne spots an old man moving fast through the lower village hoping we won't see him and O'Byrne shouts and the old man looks up and nods and starts making his way toward us. He's using an ax as a walking stick and moves impossibly fast up the steep slopes. He must be at least sixty, and moments after O'Byrne calls to him he's standing before us not even breathing hard. An Afghan soldier relieves him of his ax. Through an interpreter the man says he's visiting from Yaka Chine because his son has a wounded leg. Gillespie tells him to take us there and we start off through the village doing our best to keep up with him.

The son is about ten and faces us bravely while Doc Old peels the bandage off his leg. Old has written "I'll fuck your face" in Magic Marker on the front of his ammo rack, but whatever that means, it doesn't seem to impede his concern for the boy. He's been shot in the shin but the wound is months old and has turned gelatinous and brown. I can see the white of his shinbone and a small hole in front where a bullet went in. "Looks like one of ours," Old says, meaning the hole is so small it's probably from an American M4. AK rounds are a lot bigger and do considerably more damage. The father claims the boy got his wound by falling down, but that's clearly absurd and the boy looks like he'd rather lose his leg than stand here any longer with these soldiers gathered around him. Doc Old kneels in front of him to put on a new bandage and when he's done he looks up and says he should get it checked out at the KOP. To me it looks like he's going to lose his leg at the knee. The old man glances around apologetically and shakes his head.

"All we're going to do is help his son," Gillespie tells the translator. "He needs to tell me a good reason why he shouldn't go back to the KOP."

The translator asks the man a long question and gets a long answer back. "He is tired right now and this is the praying time."

"How long does it take to pray?" Gillespie says. "Because if he needs to pray he can pray right now. It's just the right thing for us to do. I mean just 'cause you're tired...it's your *son*."

In retrospect the old man's reluctance made perfect sense—he knew what was going to happen and didn't want to be around us when it did—but eventually Gillespie convinces him to come with us. The old man ducks into his house and comes out with a blanket and knots it over his shoulders and puts his son inside it. He falls in line and we leave the village like we came in, fast and single file, and the first burst of AK comes before the men have even gotten to the road. I'm walking behind Gillespie in the gray-dark and I hear him say, "Fuck," and we flatten ourselves against a stone wall. There are three or four detonations and I can feel the bottom drop out of my stomach, this is my first contact since getting blown up and somehow all the fight's gone out of me, I have no interest in any of this. I crouch against the wall and watch the men I'm with try to figure out what to do.

"Anyone got contact with Two-One, over?" Gillespie says into his radio. "Two-One" means First Squad — Sergeant Mac's men. They're at the top of the village covering our movement.

"Two-One, Two-One, just call," someone repeats.

"Fuck," Gillespie says for the second time and starts moving toward the top of the town. Stichter starts calling mortars down on Kilo Echo 2205, one of the preset targets on a ridgeline to our south, and we churn through town at a dead run, the SAW gunners gasping under their loads. Halfway up the hill Pemble reports he's established communication with Two-One and that the detonations were outgoing 203 rounds: everything's fine. Later we find out that a bullet splintered some wood just above O'Byrne's head, but that's nothing new, and we form up outside the village and move out along the road we came in on.

The old man walks bent forward with his arms clasped behind his back to support the injured boy and I have the impression he could outwalk all of us straight up a mountain if he had to. The plan is to move back to Loy Kalay along the road and deliver the old man and the boy to a Destined Company patrol that has rolled down there in Humvees. It takes the gun team a while to climb down to the road, though, so by the time we start north it's been a good hour since the shooting. First Platoon walked straight into a night ambush on Rock Avalanche, and it seems like it would be an incredibly easy thing to do to us as well — just get a little bit ahead on the road and take out the whole lead squad with machine guns and RPGs.

While we're waiting for the gun team to join us I have time to decide where I want to be in the line. O'Byrne is up front with the rest of his fire team — Money and Steiner and Vaughn. If we walk into an ambush they're going to take the brunt of it, but they're the guys I've been bunking with and know best. When you're entirely dependent on other men for your safety you find yourself making strange unconscious choices about otherwise very mundane things: where to walk, where to sit, who to talk to. You don't want to be anywhere near the ANA on patrol because they're almost as likely to kill you by accident as they are to kill the enemy on purpose. You don't want to be near the new guys in case they freeze or shoot so much they draw fire or jam their guns. You don't want to be near the cowboys, either, or the guys who have to glance over at their team leader before they dare do anything. It's subtle, what you want—I'm not sure there are even words for it—but at night on a frozen road outside an enemy village the choices you make reflect something real. I pick up my pack and move forward.

Thirty feet between Steiner and me, thirty feet between me and Vaughn. O'Byrne walking point, as usual. No sound but the scrape of boots on frozen dirt and occasionally a dog barking in the villages below. God knows how, but they sense strange men are moving through their valley and they don't like it. There's no moon but the stars are fierce and leak just enough light to see a bit of the road and the shapes of the men ahead. I try to avoid walking through puddles because the skim ice shatters with a disastrous clarity in the frozen air. The wind shifts heavily through the holly trees around us. I run scenarios in my mind about where I'll go if we suddenly get lit up, but most stretches of road have no cover so my best option is to just lie down so I don't get hit by gunfire from the men behind me.

We pass quietly below the dark masses of the mountains and occasionally we see a porch light burning down in the valley like a lone planet in an inverted sky. A long time later we're still on the road when a sick, hollow little whistle passes overhead. A few minutes later it happens again. No one knows what it is but later I find out they were sniper rounds fired from way down-valley—off-target but still boring fiercely through the darkness bearing their tiny loads of death.

Those rounds hit pretty close to you in Karingal?" I overhear someone ask O'Byrne after the patrol.

"Yeah, they were pretty fucking close."

"When you didn't radio back we thought you might have been hit. But we didn't hear any screaming, so we figured you were okay."

"Yeah—"

"—or he was hit in the mouth," someone else offers.

Even O'Byrne has to laugh.

BOOK THREE

LOVE

The coward's fear of death stems in large part from his incapacity to love anything but his own body. The inability to participate in others' lives stands in the way of his developing any inner resources sufficient to overcome the terror of death.

—J. Glenn Gary, *The Warriors*

1
—

THAT SPRING STEINER GOT SHOT IN THE HEAD while pinned down at the Aliabad cemetery. Third Platoon was putting in a new outpost on the spot where Murphree lost his legs and Second Platoon's job was to set up on the crest of Hill 1705 and overwatch them while they worked. They were going to go in at dusk and work all night and hope to be done by dawn. Since the site was accessible by road they used prepoured concrete barriers trucked down on flatbeds and unloaded by bulldozer, and the next morning Gillespie decided to move his men off the mountain because the job was done. There was airpower in the next valley over and it was as good a time as any, but some of the team leaders wanted to wait until dark. "That's why we have night vision gear," O'Byrne said, "so that we can walk at night when the enemy can't see us."

O'Byrne tried to raise the point with the lieutenant, but Sergeant Mac finally told him to stop being a bitch. 'If I was a bitch I wouldn't have joined the Army in the first place,' O'Byrne answered. The other side of the coin was that they were deep in enemy territory without much cover, and if they stayed where they were all day, they'd probably get attacked as well. It was a shitty deal all the way around. The men started down the steep slopes of 1705 and as soon as they moved out of position, a single gunshot cracked through the valley. "Right then we should have fucking held back and stopped moving," O'Byrne told me later. "It wasn't our first day. We all knew what the fuck that shot meant."

The road north of 1705 has no cover at all and is exposed to almost every enemy position in the southern half of the valley; it's the kind of place soldiers literally have bad dreams about. When everyone got down to the road, O'Byrne told the men behind him that he was simply going to run, and then he turned and headed for the next bit of cover three hundred yards away. O'Byrne made it to a low rock wall south of Aliabad without taking fire and took a knee to cover everyone else.

The rest of his team came tumbling in after him and then Gillespie and Patterson gasped past and finally Weapons Squad came into view. They were staggering under their loads and still strung along the road when the first burst came in. That was followed by a massive barrage from virtually every enemy position in the southern valley, and O'Byrne watched the rock wall he was hiding behind start to disintegrate from the impacts. He was still furious they hadn't waited until dark. 'This is the day I'm going to die,' he thought.

The rest of O'Byrne's team was pinned down just as badly. Steiner was lying flat on the ground next to Stichter, and when he tried to get up a burst from a PKM rattled into the wall in front of him and lacerated his face with stone shards. He dropped down to regain his composure and then sat up again just in time to catch the next burst. A round drilled straight into his helmet and snapped his head back so hard that he hit Stichter in the face and almost broke his nose. Stichter screamed for a medic and someone else yelled that Steiner had taken a round in the head, and Steiner slumped to the ground with a hole in his helmet and blood running down his face.

Steiner lay there unable to see or move, wondering whether the things he was hearing were true.

Had he been hit in the head? Was he dead? How would he know? The fact that he could hear the men around him should count for something. After a while he could see a little bit and he sat up and looked around. The bullet had penetrated his helmet to the innermost layer and then gone tumbling off in another direction, looking for someone else to kill. (The blood on his face turned out to be lacerations from stone fragments that had hit him.) The other men glanced at Steiner in shock—most of them thought he was dead—but kept shooting because they were still getting hammered and firepower was the only way out of there. Steiner was in a daze and he just sat there with a bullet hole in his helmet, grinning. After a while he got up and started laughing. He should be dead but he wasn't and it was the funniest thing in the world. "Get the fuck down and start returning fire!" someone yelled at him. Steiner laughed on. Others started laughing as well. Soon every man in the platoon was howling behind their rock wall, pouring unholy amounts of firepower into the mountainsides around them.

"It was to cover up how everyone was really feeling," Mac admitted to me later.

Three Humvees drove down from the KOP to pick up Steiner, but he refused to go with them—he wanted to stay with his squad. When the platoon finally started running up the road toward Phoenix, Steiner found himself floating effortlessly ahead of the group despite carrying sixty pounds of ammo and a twenty-pound SAW. It was one of the best highs he'd ever had. It lasted a day or two and then he sank like a stone.

"You start getting these flashes of what could've been," Steiner said. "I was lying in bed like, 'Fuck, I almost died.' What would my funeral have been like? What would the guys have said? Who'd have dragged me out from behind that wall?" Steiner was doing something known to military psychologists as "anxious rumination." Some people are ruminators and some aren't, and the ones who are can turn one bad incident into a lifetime of trauma. "You can't let yourself think about how close this shit is," O'Byrne explained to me later. "Inches. Everything is *that* close. There's just places I don't allow my mind to go. Steiner was saying to me, 'What if the bullet—' and I just stopped him right there, I didn't even let him finish. I said, 'But it didn't. It *didn't*.'"

In some ways the incident took more of a toll on O'Byrne than on Steiner himself. O'Byrne thought he could protect his men, but behind that rock wall in Aliabad he realized it was all beyond his control. "I had promised my guys none of them would die," he said. "That they would all go home, that

I would die before they would. No worries: you're going to get home to your girl, to your mom or dad. So when Steiner got shot I realized I might not be able to stop them from getting hurt, and I remember just sitting there, trembling. That's the worst thing ever: to be in charge of someone's life. And then if you lose them? I could not imagine that. I could not imagine that day."

It wasn't even fighting season, and the men at Restrepo were having one close call after another. Olson was on overwatch with the 240 when a round hit a branch above his head and the next one smacked into the dirt next to his cheek. He thought it was from the sniper rifle that the enemy took off Rougle on Rock Avalanche. A round splintered wood next to Jones's head in the south-facing SAW position. O'Byrne was leaning over to help an Afghan soldier who'd just taken a sniper round through the stomach — he died — when a second one came in and missed him by inches. Buno was doing pull-ups when a Dishka round went straight through the hooch he was in. On and on it went, lives measured in inches and seconds and deaths avoided by complete accident. Platoons with a 10 percent casualty rate could just as easily have a 50 percent casualty rate; it was all luck, all God.

There was nothing to do about it except skate through on prayers and good timing until the birds came in and took them all home.

The men had been out there talking on the radios for almost a year and found themselves saying "break" and "over" while on the KOP phones to their girlfriends and wives. Relationships frayed and ground to an end and old pickup lines were dusted off and evaluated for future use. The men would never say they were in the Army when they met women; far better to go with "dolphin trainer" or "children's book writer." One guy had a lot of success claiming he was Alec Baldwin's son. Every time Cantu rotated down to the KOP, men would come in to get inked up in ever more outlandish ways. Vengeful dragons started to curl around men's torsos and bombs and guns sprouted from their biceps. "Living to die/Dying to live"; "Soldier for God"; "Soldier of Fortune." A new private nicknamed Spanky overreached a bit and tattooed his left arm with a face that was half angel, half devil. When Sergeant Mac saw it he demanded to know what the fuck it meant.

"It represents the angels and devils I have to wake up to every morning, Sar'n," Spanky said.

After the laughter died down Mac told him he

was better off saying he got really fucked up one night and doesn't remember getting it. "Now repeat that a few times so it sounds believable," Mac said.

The rains come in late March and the Pech quickly gets so big and violent that enemy fighters can't cross it on foot. Nothing but combat aircraft can fly out of Bagram and logistics backs up days and then weeks. I pass through Bagram in early April and spend a few days waiting for the clouds to lift enough to see the mountains. No mountain, no flight, but I'd usually hang out at the rotary terminal just in case. No matter how many times you've heard it, you always turn toward the flight line when the 15s and 16s take off, a sound so thunderous and wrong that it would seem to be explainable only by some kind of apocalypse. Then the deltoid shape rising with obscene speed into the Afghan sky, its cold-blue afterburners cutting through the twilight like a welder's torch.

One day I meet a man in civilian clothes who never moves a foot or two from a long black carrying case. We're in a plywood building filled with bored soldiers watching women's college basketball, and when I ask him what he does, he just nods toward the case and says, "We identify guys in the mafia and take them off the battlefield one at a time." A day later at Jalalabad I catch a Black Hawk headed to Camp Blessing that has just dropped off an Afghan soldier in handcuffs and another one in a body bag. Blessing's 155s are going full bore supporting a valley-wide firefight in the Korengal—every position engaged, mortars ranged in on Restrepo and the KOP—and I walk down to the batteries to watch. The great dark barrels are jacked high in the air and snort smoke sideways out their muzzle brakes every time they shoot. They pound the Korengal for an hour and then fall silent with a kind of reluctance and I walk back up the hill to lie back down on my bunk and wait for the weather to clear. Rear-base limbo: an ill blend of apprehension and boredom that is only relieved by going forward where things are even worse.

I killed my first bear with a bow and arrow in Alaska," Lambert says.

After days of waiting around air bases I've finally made it out to Restrepo. It's a slow, hot day—the storm systems have been pushed out to the west—and the talk has turned to hunting.

"Do you have a sidearm with you when you hunt like that?" Patterson asks.

"Fuck yeah."

Lambert says that when he was a kid he'd get

up early to go duck hunting and would show up at school covered in duck blood.

"You ever go frog gigging?" Patterson asks.

"Fuck yeah," says Lambert.

"You ever go squirrel hunting?"

"Fuck yeah. With a little four-ten?"

"You ever go cow hunting?"

"Come on..."

Patterson tells a story about a cow that got caught in the crotch of a tree and no one could get it out. "We tried shooting it out but that didn't work either," he says.

The topic of cow hangs heavily in the air. A few weeks earlier the men spotted a lone cow wandering along the ridge and chased it into the concertina wire that's strung around the base. Once the cow was tangled up they didn't have much choice but to gaffer-tape a combat knife to some tentpoles and kill it caveman-style. By coincidence—or not—a black kid named Lackley, who works full-time as a cook down at the KOP, had just made the trek up to Restrepo to get into a firefight and claim his combat action badge. (It worked.) Once the cow was dead Lackley and Murphy gutted it and cut the head off with a Christmas tree saw and then Lackley prepared a recipe that became known as "same-day cow." He cut strips of meat off the haunches and wrapped them around onions that he got from the Afghan soldiers and then grilled them up on a bonfire outside the Weapons Squad hooch. He used Hesco siding stripped of its liner as a grill. Aside from a couple of frozen steaks they carried up from the KOP it was the first red meat the men had had at Restrepo in almost a year.

The meal was some kind of *Lord of the Flies* turning point—there were only four months to go and standards were starting to slip—but there were consequences. One afternoon soon after I arrive, three old men come walking in from Obenau and stop at the front gate. At first Patterson is pleased—this is the first time elders have made the trip to Restrepo, which can only mean good things about the hearts-and-minds campaign—but not everyone is convinced. "I think this is about the cow," O'Byrne tells me in a low voice as we walk over to where the meeting is going to happen. The elders sit on a row of sandbags by the ANA hooch and Patterson and Abdul, the interpreter, sit facing them. The elders don't take long to get to the point.

"The cow?" says Patterson. "The reason why we killed it was because it ran into our concertina wire and, uh, it was mangled inside the concertina wire, so we had to kill it to put it out of its misery. That's why we killed it."

"They are asking because it's illegal," says Abdul.

"Illegal?"

"Yeah, illegal."

"Like, it was caught in the wire and it was already dead in the wire, so that's, I mean, there was nothing else that we could really do."

"The owner of the cow is a poor person, he is a poor guy," says Abdul, "so what is your opinion about the cow? What do you want to do? Just tell them."

"Like how much does a cow cost?" says Patterson.

"Like five hundred bucks."

"Five hundred bucks? Is that Afghani or American?"

"Of course, American."

Patterson says he has to check with his commander and he gets up and walks into the radio hooch. He gets Kearney on the line and the first thing Kearney wants to know is whether or not his men killed the cow.

"It was tangled up in our wire pretty much dead," Patterson answers. "Two-four ended up cuttin' it up, over."

Kearney says that as long as his soldiers didn't actually kill the cow he doesn't owe any money, but the owners can claim as much HA—"humanitarian aid"—as they want: rice, beans, flour, cooking oil, blankets. Patterson goes back to the elders and delivers the verdict. All they want is money. Patterson says it's HA or nothing, and they ask how much of it they could get.

"Whatever the weight of the cow was, will be the weight of HA," says Patterson.

It's an inspired bit of Old Testament justice, and one of the Afghan soldiers laughs when he hears it. Even the elders smile. After a while they stand up and shake hands and make their way up the steep slopes of the outpost to the southern gate. It's not clear what they're going to do but I'm pretty sure we haven't heard the last of the cow. Later I point out to O'Byrne that they actually *did* kill the cow.

"Well, it was pretty badly tangled up in the wire," he says.

"It was tangled up in the wire because you guys chased it in there."

"Okay," he says, "it's a gray area."

A few days later we leave the hilltop after midnight and go creeping into Karingal with so little illume that even the soldiers have trouble seeing with their night vision gear. There are puddles in the road and stars are reflected in them as if we're walking through fragments of sky. A valley dog barks and another picks it up and by the time we arrive in Karingal the town is deserted except for one teenage boy who produces a sullen evasiveness that is unmistakable even without a common language. We get hit on the way out just as everyone expected — "Another well-timed patrol so we can get lit the fuck up," as Moreno once said — and we come back at a run up a pretty creekbed with mortars shrieking over our heads and Restrepo's .50 hammering away protectively. At one point someone fires two or three bursts from behind a rock wall and Alcantara wants to know what the man is shooting at.

"I don't know, I just figure *one* of us should fucking return fire," comes the answer.

We make it back to the base an hour later, sprinting the last stretch where Kim got pinned down weeks earlier and staggering in the south gate drenched like we'd all just jumped in a pond. The shooting has died down but starts up again half an hour later and then gets firmly settled by a pair of Apaches that come buzzing into the Korengal like angry insects. The men sit around shirtless, smoking cigarettes and watching the Apaches do their work against the flanks of 1705. "You thought that shit was funny this morning, huh?" someone yells after a long groan of 30 mike-mike into the mountainside. "Shoot at us again, bitch."

Prophet has been picking up a lot of chatter about moving weapons and ammo around the valley and the enemy keeps talking about "the thing" and "the big machine." The men assume it's a Dishka. Kearney has a plan to air-assault Third Platoon onto the Sawtalo Sar ridge to try to find it, and Second Platoon's job will be to man Phoenix and some of Third's other positions while they're on the mountain. That's planned for the end of April, which leaves Restrepo a couple of weeks to conduct their own patrols before they get sucked into the larger mechanics of a company-level operation. The villagers in Loy Kalay have been complaining about Taliban fighters that move into their village after dark and harass them, and Patterson comes up with a plan to set up an ambush outside Karingal and surprise them on their way back. It will mean walking down-valley at night, hiding outside the village, and not moving a muscle until it gets dark again. The site for the ambush will be a low rock wall across a small valley outside Karingal. The stakes are high: if we're spotted there, fighters in town can keep us pinned down behind the wall while their brothers in Darbart come down on us through the holly forests of 1705.

The mission is scheduled to go out shortly before midnight, and after dinner I start assembling my gear: a CamelBak full of water, one MRE, a rain poncho, a fleece jacket, and a handful of coffee crystals to pour into my drinking water to get me through the wake-up. Anderson wanders over and watches me for a while without saying anything and finally asks if I want to borrow an old uniform he has. I ask him why.

"It would be a lot better if we didn't get spotted," he says.

When soldiers use understatement it's generally worth paying attention, but I turn him down because wearing military clothing seems like such a blatant erosion of journalistic independence. I doubt I'm more visible than the soldiers anyway— I'm dressed in muted colors that long ago turned Korengal-gray—but as I continue packing I realize that that's not really the point. If we get compromised I'll be the only guy in civilian clothes, and suppose someone gets hit? Suppose someone gets killed? Like every other reporter out there I'm eating Army food, flying on Army helicopters, sleeping in Army hooches, and if I were in the Korengal on my own, I'd probably be dead in twenty-four hours.

Whatever boundaries may have blurred between me and the Army, the blurring didn't start with a shirt.

I finish packing and find Anderson in his bunk and tell him I'll take the clothes after all. He tosses them to me without a glance.

2

—

I'M ON MY BACK BEHIND A LOW ROCK WALL
with a man ten feet to the left of me and another
ten feet to the right. It's so dark in the shadows I
have no idea who they are. Holly oaks are bent over
us like malevolent old people and moonlight turns
the hillsides to pewter. It's very cold and I wrap
myself in an Army poncho and try to think myself
off the mountain to someplace nice. I delay putting on my jacket because the cold is more bearable
knowing that I've still got something in reserve.
After a few hours a thin gray light finally infiltrates
the world and begins reassembling the rocks and
the trees around me. We're on a steep hill facing
Karingal with every man propped against his ruck

and more men above and behind and below. The Claymores are out and no one speaks. Everyone is watching the valley emerge from the safety of night toward whatever's going to happen next.

Karingal is a few hundred yards away. There is a stream at the base of our hill and then a series of wheat terraces and finally the first houses of town. People stir as soon as it's light enough to see: voices, the cries of children, an ax smacking into wood. Teenage boys chase their family's goats up the steep dry slopes west of town to graze the higher elevations. Two girls, little dabs of color against the green terraces, make their way to the stream below us and crouch to wash themselves. They can't be fifty yards away. One old woman walks into the fields to relieve herself and others shuffle along a trail with bundles of firewood on their heads. No one has any idea we're here. Finally there's a man in olive drab moving fast along the high road toward Loy Kalay. He looks around continually and is soon joined by two other men on the same road. One has a shaved head. Next to me, Pemble studies them through binoculars and writes things down in a notebook. If he sees a gun or a radio they'll be killed.

"We've seen about ten pax—fighting-age males— moving from Karingal to Loy Kalay and back," Pemble tells me in a whisper. I can barely hear him over the rushing of the stream below us. "Two of them were wearing BDU jackets and they seem to be pulling security—one guy will come out, scan around, there's another guy just chillin' on a rooftop."

BDUs are what the Army calls foliage-based camouflage. O'Byrne is whispering into his radio that wearing them is a killable offense, just like carrying a radio or a gun, but Patterson isn't sure. (Patterson is the platoon sergeant, but he's leading the patrol because Gillespie is away on leave.) After a few minutes the fighters disappear from sight and I watch the expression on O'Byrne's face go foul. He's lost his chance to kill those guys and—I know exactly what he's thinking—they might be the very guys who kill an American next week or next month. There are other considerations, though. The enemy has observation posts as well, and they know exactly where the Americans go in the valley. This is one of the first times that a patrol has set up in their backyard and not been spotted. Enemy fighters are walking back and forth on an otherwise hidden road without any idea that infidels are watching them from two hundred yards away. Patterson could kill two guys now, or he could come back with a better plan and kill ten later.

By midmorning young boys start to play along

the banks of the stream, and when I close my eyes, all I can hear are their shouts and the steady wash of the rapids. The only way to know I'm at war is to open my eyes and look around at all the men with their guns. The sun finally reaches our hillside and spreads over us like warm oil and I close my eyes again and listen to the children, and a while later I wake up to silence and cumulus clouds sliding across a pale blue sky. Hoyt has a pinch of dip in his mouth and dribbles methodically into the dirt beside him. Pemble stares placidly at the mountain-side. Patterson studies the village through binos and checks what he sees against the entries in Pemble's notebook.

Once in a while a man in the village looks in our direction and then looks away. It's inconceiv-able that he could see us — dirty, unmoving faces in a chaos of rocks and foliage — but still, I have to fight the urge to duck behind the rock wall. No motion at all: roll to the side to piss and if you need to stretch, do it one limb at a time and very slowly. Cumulus clouds drag their shadows across the flat geometry of the terraces and then up into the hills and OP Dallas test-fires their .50 and the sun seems to stall around the noon point and then start its slide toward the western ridges. The valley colors deepen and by midafternoon Karingal contracts back in on itself: goatherds coming down off the hillsides and old men making their way across the terraces and women and children collecting on the rooftops. We leave our wall at the last blue tones of dusk and creep north off the hill and toward safety. We're undetected except for the valley dogs that almost choke with outrage as we pass them in the dark.

Midafternoon and we're sitting in the shade of concealment netting that's been draped over the courtyard. There hasn't been a firefight in weeks and the men are getting a little weird: disputes with a strange new edge to them and a sullen tension that doesn't bode well for the coming months. April is supposed to be the start of fighting season, and the fact that nothing has happened yet produces a cruel mix of boredom and anxiety. If the men were getting hammered they'd at least have something to do, but this is the worst of both worlds: all the dread and none of the adrenaline. A visiting combat medic named Doc Shelke is talking about the Hindu religion and Abdul, the Afghan interpreter, happens to overhear him.

"Hindu is bullshit," he says.

Shelke looks like he might be from India. He

maintains his calm. "The last time a terp said something like that, I talked shit about Islam until he cried," he says.

It was a stupid thing for Abdul to say and he doesn't speak English well enough to make this a fair fight, or even interesting. In an attempt to head off another hour of boredom O'Byrne weighs in with his own religious views. "I don't believe in heaven or hell and I don't want an afterlife," he says. "I believe in doing good in your life, and then you die. I don't believe in God and I've never read the Bible. I don't believe in that shit because I don't *want* to."

An awkward silence. Another sergeant says something irrelevant about an upcoming patrol.

"What—the conversation gets serious and you change the subject?" O'Byrne says. "We're talking about *religion*. You can't have a half-assed conversation about religion."

More silence. No one knows what to say. "Mommy hit Daddy and then Daddy hit Mommy," a private finally tries.

The mood eases when Airborne, a puppy that Second Platoon took from the Afghan soldiers, wanders into the courtyard. They named him Airborne because the soldiers who are going to take over in July—Viper Company of the First Infantry

Division—are just regular infantry, and the idea was to remind them of their inferiority every time they called for the dog. (It backfired: I was told someone from Viper just took Airborne out to the burn pit and shot him.) Airborne usually hangs around the base barking whenever anything moves outside the wire, but a few days ago he went missing and eventually turned up at the KOP. Someone tied him up with 550 cord, but he quickly chewed through that and followed the next switch-out up to Restrepo.

Now Airborne wanders from man to man, chewing on their boots and getting rolled in the dust by rough hands. "So you think you're tough, huh?" Moreno says, cuffing him in with quick boxer jabs. "Take that, you little bastard." Company net suddenly intrudes from the radio room: "Be advised that they dropped a thirty-one and a thirty-eight in Pakistan," a voice says. Everyone stops watching Airborne and looks up: thirty-ones and thirty-eights are bombs. They're not supposed to land in other countries.

The only men I ever saw pray at Restrepo were Afghans, and the topic of religion came up only once the entire time I was out there. It was a beautiful evening in the spring and we were sitting on the ammo hooch smoking cigarettes and talking about a recent TIC. One by one the men left until I was alone with Sergeant Alcantara, who decided to tell me about a recent conversation he'd had with the battalion chaplain. Heat lightning was flashing silently over the valley and we could hear Apaches working something farther north along the Pech.

'Father, basically God came down to earth and in the form of Christ and died for our sins — right?' Al asked.

The chaplain nodded.

'And he died a painful death, but he knew he was going to heaven — right?'

Again the chaplain nodded.

'So how is that sacrifice greater than a soldier in this valley who has *no idea* whether he's going to heaven?'

According to Al, the chaplain had no useful response.

Religion gives a man enough courage to face the overwhelming, and there may have been so little religion at Restrepo because the men didn't feel particularly overwhelmed. (Why appeal to God when you can call in Apaches?) You don't haul your cook up there just so that he can be in his first firefight unless you're pretty confident it's going to end well. But even in the early days, when things were definitely *not* ending well, the nearly narcotic effect of

a tightly knit group might have made faith super-
fluous. The platoon *was* the faith, a greater cause
that, if you focused on it entirely, made your fears
go away. It was an anesthetic that left you aware
of what was happening but strangely fatalistic
about the outcome. As a soldier, the thing you were
most scared of was failing your brothers when they
needed you, and compared to that, dying was easy.
Dying was over with. Cowardice lingered forever.

Heroism is hard to study in soldiers because they
invariably claim that they acted like any good soldier would have. Among other things, heroism is a
negation of the self—you're prepared to lose your
own life for the sake of others—so in that sense,
talking about how brave you were may be psychologically contradictory. (Try telling a mother she
was brave to run into traffic to save her kid.) Civilians understand soldiers to have a kind of baseline
duty, and that everything above that is considered
"bravery." Soldiers see it the other way around:
either you're doing your duty or you're a coward.
There's no other place to go. In 1908, five firemen
died in a blaze in New York City. Speaking at the
funeral, Chief Ed Croker had this to say about their
bravery: "Firemen are going to get killed. When
they join the department they face that fact. When
a man becomes a fireman his greatest act of bravery

has been accomplished. What he does after that is all in the line of work."

You don't have to be a soldier to experience the weird comfort of that approach. Courage seems daunting and hard to attain, but "work" is mundane and eminently doable, a collective process where everyone takes their chances. My work was journalism, not war, but the same principles applied. I was constantly monitoring my fear levels because I didn't want to freeze up at the wrong moment and create a problem, but it never happened, and after a couple of trips I felt my fear just kind of go away. It wasn't that I was less afraid of dying; it was that dying made slightly more sense in the context of a group endeavor that I was slowly becoming part of. As a rule I was way more scared in my bunk at night, when I had the luxury of worrying about myself, than on some hillside where I'd worry about us all.

Because I didn't carry a gun I would always be relegated to a place outside the platoon, but that didn't mean I was unaffected by its gravitational pull. There was a power and logic to the group that overrode everyone's personal concerns, even mine, and somewhere in that loss of self could be found relief from the terrible worries about what might befall you. And it was pretty obvious that if things got bad enough — and there was no reason to think they couldn't — the distinction between journalist and soldier would become irrelevant. A scenario where I found myself stuffing Kerlix into a wound or helping pull someone to safety was entirely plausible, and that forced me to think in ways that only soldiers usually have to. When Chosen got hit at Aranas they suffered a 100 percent casualty rate in a matter of minutes, and the firefight went on for another three hours. The idea that I wouldn't start helping — or fighting — in that situation was absurd.

The offers of weapons started on my first trip and continued throughout the entire year. Sometimes it was a hand grenade "just in case." Other times it was an offer to jump on the 240 during the next contact. ("We'll just show you where to shoot.") Once I told Moreno that if I weren't married I'd have been out there the full fifteen months, and he laughed and said that in that case, they'd definitely have me carrying a weapon. The idea of spending long stretches in the Korengal without shooting anything made as little sense to the soldiers as, say, going to a Vicenza whorehouse and just hanging out in the lobby. Guns were the *point*, the one entirely good thing of the whole shitty year, and the fact that reporters don't carry them, shoot them, or accept the very generous offers to "go ahead and get some" on the .50 just made soldiers shake their heads. It was a hard thing to explain to them that maybe you could pass someone a box of ammo during a firefight or sneak 100 rounds on a SAW down at the firing range, but as a journalist the one thing you absolutely *could not* do was carry a weapon. It would make you a combatant rather than an observer, and you'd lose the right to comment on the war later with any kind of objectivity.

To refuse a weapon was one thing, but that didn't mean you couldn't know anything about them. One hot, boring afternoon in the middle of the spring fighting season, Sergeant Al decided that Tim and I should be able to load and shoot every weapon at the outpost, and clear them if they jammed. We went over to the Afghan hooch and started with an AK. It was light and cheap-feeling, as if it were made out of tin, and Al said it has no internal recoil, so the entire force of the discharge goes straight into your shoulder. That makes it highly inaccurate after the first shot in a burst but mechanically so simple that it requires virtually no maintenance. You could hide it under a rock and come back six months later and it would still shoot.

The M4 fires a much smaller bullet, which means you can carry more ammunition for the same weight, but it's not accurate over distance and tends to jam. Several times I've been in firefights where the man next to me was swearing and desperately trying to clear his weapon. The SAW was the smallest belt-fed weapon at Restrepo and had such a simple design that a monkey could have operated it. You pop open the feed-tray cover, lay the ammo belt into the receiver, slap the cover closed, and pull back the charging bolt; now you're ready to fire 900 rounds a minute. The 240 is almost identical but larger and slower and the .50 is larger still, a barrel you could stick your thumb down and rounds the size of railroad spikes. With the .50 you could hit virtually anything in the valley you could see. During the Vietnam War, an American gunner supposedly attached a telescopic sight to his .50 and, with a single shot, knocked a messenger off a bicycle at two miles. It's such a perfect weapon that the design has not changed in any meaningful way since World War I.

As a reporter it was hard to come to any kind of psychological accommodation with the weapons because they were everywhere—you couldn't sit on someone's bunk without moving an M4 or some grenades—and they only got more compelling as time went on. They had a kind of heavy perfection that made them impossible to ignore. What you *really* wanted to do was use them somehow, but that was so wildly forbidden that it took you a while to even admit you'd had the thought. After that you'd find yourself trying to imagine situations where it might be permissible without the obvious ethical problems. The only one I could come up with was a scenario that was so desperate and out of control—a hundred Taliban fighters coming up the draw and through the wire—that picking up a gun would be simply a matter of survival. That was too horrific to actually hope for, so I didn't, but I'd find myself thinking that if it *were* to happen, I hoped I'd be there for it.

It's a foolish and embarrassing thought but worth owning up to. Perfectly sane, good men have been drawn back to combat over and over again, and anyone interested in the idea of world peace would do well to know what they're looking for. Not killing, necessarily—that couldn't have been clearer in my mind—but the other side of the equation: protecting. The defense of the tribe is an insanely compelling idea, and once you've been exposed to it, there's almost nothing else you'd rather do. The only reason anyone was alive at Restrepo—or at Aranas or at Ranch House or, later, at Wanat—was because every man up there was willing to die defending it. In Second Platoon Tim and I were the only ones who benefited from that arrangement for "free," as it were, and it's hard to overstate the psychological significance of that. (Once Tim found himself throwing ammo to a couple of guys who were stuck behind a Hesco during a fight, but that was as close as we ever got to actually *doing* anything.) There was a debt that no one registered except the men who owed it.

Collective defense can be so compelling—so addictive, in fact—that eventually it becomes the rationale for why the group exists in the first place. I think almost every man at Restrepo secretly hoped the enemy would make a serious try at overrunning the place before the deployment came to an end. It was everyone's worst nightmare but also the thing they hoped for most, some ultimate demonstration of the bond and fighting ability of the men. For sure there were guys who re-upped because something like that hadn't happened yet. After the men got back to Vicenza, I asked Bobby Wilson if he missed Restrepo at all.

"I'd take a helicopter there tomorrow," he said. Then, leaning in, a little softer: "Most of us would."

3
—

NOTHING FOR WEEKS BUT THE OMINOUS buildup of ammo in the valley and enemy commanders saying strange, enigmatic things into their radios. "I'll bring the Dishka and the milk," a commander radioed once, though no one knew whether that was code for something or he was actually bringing real milk somewhere. According to the radio chatter there are a dozen mortar rounds in the valley, ammo for an 88 mm recoilless, and even some Katyusha rockets. In 2000 I'd gone through a Taliban rocket attack with a group of Tajik fighters in the north, and it was nothing I ever wanted to repeat. The rockets came in with a shrieking whistle that made me weird about teakettles and subway brakes for years.

One morning Patterson leads a patrol along the high road and then up the western spur through sweet-smelling sage and past an enemy fighting position littered with old brass. From there we could see over the tops of the Hescos straight into Restrepo. Patterson calls in the grid numbers to the KOP so the mortars hit it next time they take fire from that direction, and we continue climbing. We come out on a summit known as Peak One that the Americans and the Taliban more or less share. "When we're up here it's ours and as soon as we leave it's theirs," Mac says. There are American fighting positions facing south toward Yaka Chine and Taliban positions facing north toward the KOP. All of them are filled with garbage.

A monkey watches us at a safe distance from a rock, and someone says that if it's holding a radio we can shoot it. We sit for a while looking south toward Yaka Chine and eventually we descend to a little plateau where the enemy has set up more fighting positions. Nothing moves in the valley and we continue off the plateau and down the spur back to Restrepo. It's not even noon when we walk in the south gate and drop our gear and strip off our shirts. We sit on the ammo hooch drinking Gatorade and playing with Airborne, and after a while a single boom rolls through the valley.

"Road construction," Patterson says.

I'm already lunging for my vest and helmet and I sit back down a little sheepishly. Another boom rolls past and everyone looks at each other. A third boom.

"That's not road construction," someone says.

Vegas is getting shelled and Dallas is getting hit and the KOP starts taking fire from the north. I crawl up to the LRAS position to watch mortars drop into the northern Abas Ghar and I'm up there for a few minutes with Cantu when rounds start snapping above our heads. Soon Mac scrambles up alongside us with a 240 and starts lighting up the Donga and Marastanau spurs and then Olson brings up another one to hit the ridges to the south and finally Bone arrives to start dropping bombs. Bone is the radio call sign for the B-1 bombers; they fly so high you can't see or hear them, but the forward observer will say something like "bombs incoming," and then you become aware of a strange, airy, rushing sound. Then a flash, a boil of smoke unfolding like a dirty flower across the valley, and finally a shuddering compression of air that reaches you seconds later.

Bone drops bombs to the south and east and

the shooting stops and the men sit around smoking cigarettes and waiting to see what will happen. Most of them went through the firefight shirtless and a few didn't even bother putting on their helmet or armor. After a while Lambert pokes his head up through the cutout to the .50 cal pit and says, "They just got radio chatter saying, 'Go back to your positions and fire again.'"

Mac's made himself comfortable against the sandbags and doesn't even bother getting up. "Apparently we didn't do enough damage to them and they want some more," he says. "They want their seventy-two virgins."

Prophet says a group of foreign fighters has just come into the valley, and local commanders wanted to provide them with a good fight. And once the foreigners use up their ammo they'll have to pay locals to carry more from Pakistan, so there's even a financial incentive to keep shooting. Sometimes the fight in the valley could seem like a strange, slow game that everyone—including the Americans—were enjoying too much to possibly bring to an end.

Half an hour later another convulsion of firepower sweeps through the American positions. Olson pins someone down with his 240 on Spartan Spur and I can stand directly behind him, his shoulder vibrating with the recoil, and watch tracers arc and wobble across the draw and finger their way around the ridge. Now it's dusk and the men sit in the courtyard, faces still dirt-streaked from the patrol, talking about the TIC. It's the best thing that's happened in weeks, and there probably won't be another like it for at least that long. Murphy starts wondering aloud which side the sherbet spoon goes on at a formal table setting. He is a forward observer and is still amped from having spent the afternoon calling in corrections to 2,000-pound bomb strikes. He's from a well-off family and had already made the mistake of telling the others that he'd gone to etiquette school.

"Sherbet spoons? Are you fucking kidding me?" Moreno says. Moreno grew up in Beeville, Texas, and worked as a corrections officer at a state prison.

"Like when you go to a country club or something," Murphy says.

"Well that explains it."

Murphy ignores him and tells a story about how his grandfather built him a train set when he was young. It's hard to know if this is a misguided attempt to impress or some strange eruption of post-TIC openness.

"Well, my grandfather was shot in a bar fight," Moreno says. "Different fuckin' lives."

WAR

• • •

Mefloquine dreams, the unwelcome glimpses into your psyche that are produced by the malaria medication everyone takes. The medic distributes the pills every Monday, and that night is always the worst: I'm sawing someone in half with a carpentry saw for no reason that I can explain; I'm choking with sorrow and remorse over something that ended twenty-five years ago; I'm preparing for combat and the men around me are glancing at each other, like, "This is it, brother, see you on the other side." I always wake up without moving, my eyes suddenly wide open in the darkness. Men snoring softly around me and the generator thumping in some kind of frantic heartbeat. The side effects of mefloquine include severe depression, paranoia, aggression, nightmares, and insomnia. Those happen to be the side effects of combat as well. I go back to sleep and wake up the next morning edgy and weird.

There are two months left to the deployment and the men devise all kinds of ways to quantify that: number of patrols, number of KOP rotations, number of mefloquine Mondays. It's starting to dawn on them that they'll probably never walk to the top of Honcho Hill again or get dropped onto the Abas Ghar. When they're down at the KOP they use the communal laptops to try to arrange girlfriends for themselves when they get back. The men who already have girlfriends arrange to have them stock up on beer, steak, whatever they've been craving for the past year. The men will fly into Aviano Air Base, take a two-hour bus ride to Vicenza, turn in their weapons, and then form up on a parade ground called Hoekstra Field. As soon as they're discharged they can do whatever they want. The drinking starts immediately and continues until unconsciousness and then resumes whenever and wherever the men wake up. They find themselves at train stations and on sidewalks and in police stations and occasionally at the medical facilities. In past years one drunken paratrooper was struck by a train and killed and another died of an overdose. They'd made it through the dangers of combat and died within sight of their barracks in Vicenza.

"Y'all will only be remembered for the last thing you ever did," Caldwell warned them one warm spring night. He'd hiked up to Restrepo to make sure the men were all squared away for the return home, and he left them with his own story about why he quit drinking. ("My kids were upset, my wife wasn't talking to me . . . I just told her, 'Don't worry, it's taken care of,' and I never drank again.")

With summer come the twin afflictions of heat and boredom. A poor wheat harvest creates a temporary food shortage in the valley, which means the enemy has no surplus cash with which to buy ammo. Attacks drop to every week or two—not nearly enough to make up for the general shittiness of the place. The men sleep as late as they can and come shuffling out of their fly-infested hooches scratching and farting. By midmorning it's over a hundred degrees and the heat has a kind of buzzing slowness to it that alone almost feels capable of overrunning Restrepo. It's a miraculous kind of antiparadise up here: heat and dust and tarantulas and flies and no women and no running water and no cooked food and nothing to do but kill and wait. It's so hot that the men wander around in flip-flops and underwear, unshaved and foul. Airborne panting in the shade, someone burning shit out back, a feeble breeze making the concealment netting billow and subside like a huge lung.

The men ran out of things to say about three months ago, so they just sit around in a mute daze. One day I watch Money come out of the hooch, look around, grunt, and go back inside for another three hours' sleep. A summer shower comes through, briefly turning the air sweet and pungent, but the raindrops are small and sharp as needles and do almost nothing for the heat. "I used to live a thousand feet above sea level, and we'd find seashells in the rocks along the side of the road," O'Byrne finally says. No one answers for about five minutes.

"You ever go to military school?" Murphy finally asks.

"Fuck no, my parents couldn't afford that shit," O'Byrne says. "Getting locked up was my military school."

Boredom so relentless that the men openly hope for an attack. One crazy-hot morning Lieutenant Gillespie wanders by muttering, "Please, God, let's get into a firefight." I think it was Bobby who finally came up with the idea of sending Tim and me down to Darbart wearing burkas made out of American flags. (Surely *that* would kick something off.) Every American sniper in the valley would cover us from the hilltops.

"That's a weird image," Tim finally says, shaking his head.

Bobby is a 240 gunner from Georgia and Jones's best friend: one black guy and one unreconstructed Georgia redneck wandering around Restrepo looking for trouble like a pair of bad guys in a spaghetti western. Bobby has a tattoo of a sunburst around one nipple and a massive branding scar in the shape of a heart above the other. The heart has an arrow through it. He says he joined the Army because his girl left him while he was on a bender, which sent him on another bender, which eventually put him unconscious on his father's front lawn. When he woke up he and his father got drunk, and then Bobby went down to the recruiter's office and tried to join the Marines. The Marines wouldn't take him so he walked down the hall and joined the Army instead.

Bobby's scene was so far out there that even his fellow soldiers had trouble wrapping their minds around it. "Just a pile of fuck, a big stupid redneck," as Jones described him, except that he wasn't: his aunt had adopted a black child and Bobby — slow-speaking, foul-mouthed, and outrageous — was one of the smartest and most capable guys in the entire company. One day the generator wouldn't start and Bobby told O'Byrne to kick it halfway up the side, just above the fuel filter. The machine started immediately. "He had what I call 'man knowledge,'" O'Byrne told me. "He wasn't very polished but he had all the knowledge a man needs to get by in the world."

The trick to understanding Bobby was to understand that he was so clear about who he was that he could, for example, spout the most egregious racist bullshit and not come across as a true bigot.

(It was, quite possibly, his way of making fun of people who really *did* talk that way.) Before the deployment, Bobby said some unforgivable things to a black MP who was trying to arrest him for drunk and disorderly, but you had to reconcile that with the fact that the only black guy in the platoon was his best friend. It was about authority, not race, but you'd have to know Bobby pretty well to even bother understanding that. "There ain't a racist bone in his body," Jones said. "You call me nigger and Bobby's standing around, and I'd be surprised if I could hit you first."

There were plenty of guys in the platoon who were as brave as Bobby, but none exuded quite the same sense of just *not caring*. He'd sit cross-legged behind the 240, stubby fingers barely able to fit inside the trigger guard, grinning like a fiend just waiting to get into it. That bought him a lot of slack in other, more confusing aspects of his character. Bobby claimed a kind of broad-spectrum sexuality that made virtually no distinction between anything, and as the months went by that expressed itself in increasingly weird ways. He would take someone down with a quick headlock and create a kind of prison-yard sense of violation without actually crossing some ultimate line. He had thick limbs and crazy farmhand strength and when he teamed up with Jones—which was most of the time—you'd need half a squad to defend yourself. Ultimately, it made me think that if you deprive men of the company of women for too long, and then turn off the steady adrenaline drip of heavy combat, it may not turn sexual, but it's certainly going to turn weird.

And weird it was: strange pantomimed man-rapes and struggles for dominance and grotesque, smoochy come-ons that could only make sense in a place where every other form of amusement had long since been used up. Bobby wasn't gay any more than he was racist, but a year on a hilltop somehow made pretending otherwise psychologically necessary. And it wasn't gay anyhow: it was just so hypersexual that gender ceased to matter. Someone once asked Bobby whether, all joking aside, he would actually have sex with a man up here. "Of course," Bobby said. "It would be gay not to."

"Gay *not* to?" O'Byrne demanded. "What the fuck does that mean?"

Bobby launched into a theory that "real" men need sex no matter what, so choosing abstinence can only mean you're not a real man. Who you have sex *with* is of far lesser importance. The men knew it made no sense—Bobby's weird brilliance—but no one could quite formulate a rebuttal. The less

308

fighting there was, the weirder things got until men literally moved around in pairs in case they ran into Bobby and Jones. "One day that shit's gonna go too far and someone's actually going to get raped," O'Byrne said to me one night. "Like literally, *raped*. They won't know when to stop and then it's gonna be too late."

Bobby told me that after the deployment he was planning on visiting his wife, buying a motorcycle, and then driving south into Mexico. He was going to live out some south-of-the-border fantasy for a while and then decide whether to go AWOL or return home. The last I heard he was at Fort Bragg, challenging assumptions in the 82nd Airborne.

I pass through Bagram in late May when the first replacement units are starting to come in. I get space-blocked on a flight that requires showing up at the terminal at four in the morning, just as the sky is getting light. A dozen soldiers are watching NASCAR on a big flat-screen and the room slowly fills with more men in clean uniforms carrying new guns. They're headed to the firebases to the east and south and they look ten years younger than the men they'll be replacing. They're combat infantry, the ultimate point of all this, the most replaceable

part of the whole deadly show. (Two years earlier a story made the rounds about a MEDEVAC
pilot who disobeyed direct orders, turned off his
radio, and landed in heavy ground fire to pick up a
wounded Battle Company soldier. The man lived,
but the incident gave some soldiers the feeling that
if the military had to choose between a grunt and
a Black Hawk, they'd probably go with the Black
Hawk.) The men take a perverse pride in this, cul-
tivate a certain disdain for anyone who has it better, which is basically everyone. Combat infantry
carry the most, eat the worst, die the fastest, sleep
the least, and have the most to fear. But they're the
real soldiers, the only ones conducting what can
be considered "war" in the most classic sense, and
everyone knows it. I once asked someone in Second
Platoon why frontline grunts aren't more admired.

"Because everyone just thinks we're stupid," the
man said.

"But you do all the fighting."

"Yeah," he said, "exactly."

Out east, I'm told, the war is tipping very slightly
toward improvement. Kunar is now such a deadly
place for insurgents that the cash payment for
fighting there has gone from five dollars a day per
man to ten. The "PID and engage" rate—where
the enemy is spotted and destroyed before he can

attack—has gone from 4 percent of all engagements to almost half. Battle Company trucks hit an IED in the northern Korengal but no one was hurt, and the Taliban have been painting Pakistani cell phone numbers on rocks, trying to enlist fighters. They took out the LRAS with a sniper round and grabbed an old man and a fifteen-year-old boy who worked at the KOP and cut their throats a few hundred yards outside the wire. Men on base could hear them screaming as they died. Public affairs will tell you that the Taliban are getting more brutal because they're losing the war, but pretty much everyone else will tell you they started out brutal and aren't losing shit.

I catch a flight to Blessing and fly into the Korengal on a Chinook filled with Chosen Company soldiers. They'll be in the valley for a few days to cover for elements of Battle who are going for a "rest-and-refit." Third Platoon is planning an early morning operation to clear the town of Marastanau, across the valley, and the lieutenant invites me along, but in the interest of getting a real night's sleep I turn him down. We're woken up by gunfire anyway: Third Platoon hit from three directions and pinned down behind a rock wall with plunging fire coming in from the ridges and U.S. .50 cal shrieking over their heads in the other direction. The battle goes on for an hour, white phosphorus rounds flashing and arcing out over the mountainsides like enormous white spiders. The Apaches and A-10s show up and do some work and finally it's over and everyone shuffles back to the fly-crazed darkness of their hooches to get a few more hours of sleep.

A few days after I arrive, Kearney puts together a shura of valley elders, and the provincial governor flies in for it. The meeting starts in what must have been a rather incredible way for the locals: a young American woman from USAID speaking in Pashto about plans for the valley. After that, the governor gives a passionate speech about what this area could be if the locals stopped fighting and accepted government authority. He's dressed in a suit and vest, and it's quite possibly the first suit and vest the locals have ever seen. When he's done a young man stands up, eyes bright with hate, and says that the Americans dropped a bomb on his brother's house in Kalaygal and killed thirteen people. "If the Americans can't bring security with their guns and bombs, then they should just leave the valley," he shouts. "Otherwise there will be jihad!"

The governor is having none of it. "We've all done jihad and lost family members," he says. "But the Taliban are shooting at Afghan soldiers. Why? They are Muslims too. If you're not man enough to keep the Taliban out of the valley, then I'm sorry, you're going to get bombed."

For a minute the young man is too stunned to respond. Then there's a sudden knocking of gunfire from down-valley and Kearney rushes out of the room to direct the mortars. Second Platoon has gotten hit on their way back from Loy Kalay, pinned down in the open stretch just outside the base. They make it into the wire behind a curtain of high explosives and the shura lurches on to the rumble of explosions and A-10 gun runs. After an hour or so the elders gather themselves up and walk back out the front gate, and Tim and I catch a switch-out that's headed up to Restrepo.

We come walking in the south gate late that afternoon and drop our packs in front of First Squad hooch. Nothing has changed except that Airborne is now big enough to go out on patrols. I've been coming to this hilltop for almost a year, and to my amazement the place has started to carry the slight tang of home.

4
—

COFFEE AT RESTREPO WAS A PROBLEM BECAUSE no one drank it so you were more or less on your own in that regard. Certain MREs include packets of coffee, powdered milk, and sugar, but I always found it hard to remember which ones they were—as opposed to, say, the breakfast tea or cider mix—and that meant pawing through the garbage to find enough ingredients for a good cup. Once the precious powders were in hand I'd go to the command center and empty a bottle of water into the electric kettle and plug it in. The command center was a dark, secure bunker next to Gillespie's bunk where the radios were stacked, and there was usually so little light that finding the kettle required some feeling around.

While the water was heating I'd scout a place to sit. Pretty much everything was uncomfortable at Restrepo — there was one chair but it was almost always taken, the sandbags were hard as rocks, and the round plastic Javelin case next to First Squad hooch made your ass numb in minutes — but finding a good seat was important. You'd only get one cup of coffee a day, and considering what's *not* available at Restrepo, that cup was pretty much the most pleasurable thing that was going to happen to you until you got home. I liked to drink my coffee sitting with my back against a Hesco beneath the south-facing SAW position. Nothing random could hit you there, and you were inside the courtyard looking north up the valley. In front of me was a pile of sandbags holding up a fiberglass pole for the concealment netting, and I could brace my legs on the sandbags and use my knees to write against. The netting broke up the direct sunlight and gave things a mottled, wobbly feel that could make you dizzy if you stared at the shadows for too long.

I usually put together my coffee around midmorning and then settled into my spot to work on my notes, but one morning Gillespie sends out a patrol to Obenau and we don't come back until midday. We come walking into the wire to word from Prophet that we're about to get hit. For weeks there's been intel about ammo coming into the valley—mortars, rockets, crates of Dishka rounds—the kinds of things you'd use against a fortified position rather than men on foot. The attack is supposed to come around 12:30 that afternoon, but the hour comes and goes without a shot, and the men sink back into their slow-motion heat trance. It's one of those dead afternoons in the Korengal where nothing moves and you barely have the energy to wave the flies off your face. I mix up my coffee and settle into my spot to talk to Gillespie. Richardson is brushing his teeth. A few Afghan soldiers are standing around the ammo hooch. Most of the Americans are in their bunks. Airborne is asleep in the shade near the muddy spot created by the water bladder.

I'm just raising the mug to my lips for a first sip when the air around us compresses with a *WHUMP*. Gillespie and I just look at each other—could it be? Then comes a flurry of sick little snaps and the inevitable staccato sound in the distance. That first burst, I find out later, hit the guard tower and splintered plywood a few inches from Pemble's head. Richardson is on the SAW so fast that he has to spit out his last mouthful of toothpaste between bursts.

Gillespie jumps up and runs into the radio room, and everywhere men are grabbing their vests and sprinting for their positions. My cup of coffee gets knocked over almost immediately. On the radio I can hear Kearney yelling, "ALL BATTLE ELEMENTS THIS IS BATTLE-SIX THIS IS THE TIC WE WERE TALKIN' ABOUT THE KOP IS TAKING INDIRECT, OVER."

"Indirect" means mortars. They're shot upward out of a tube and come down from above, which makes them harder to take cover from. (They're also harder to suppress because, unlike guns, mortars can be completely out of sight behind a ridge. All the mortarman needs is a spotter calling in corrections to walk the rounds onto the target.) The KOP is essentially the Mothership, and without her, every outpost in the valley would be indefensible. The job of the outposts is to keep the KOP from getting attacked so that the KOP, in return, can support the outposts. Grenades and mortars start coming in and detonating against our own fortifications and we're taking gunfire from three different directions to the south. Gillespie is out on the ammo hooch trying to see where the grenades are coming from and shouting into his radio and the Afghans are standing around reluctant and confused and the Americans are running shirtless and whooping to their guns. During the lulls they put wads of chew under their lips or light cigarettes. Olson's on the .50 alternating bursts with Jones, who's above him on the 240, and Pemble is so upset about almost getting killed that he empties a whole can of linked grenades into the ridges to the south.

The fight lasts ten or fifteen minutes and then the A-10s show up and tilt into their dives. Ninety rounds a second the size of beer cans unzipping the mountainsides with a sound like the sky ripping. The men look up and whoop when they hear it, a punishment so unnegotiable it might as well have come from God.

One night a few weeks later I'm sitting on the ammo hooch listening to the monkeys in the peaks. A temperature inversion has filled the valley with mist and the mist is silver in the moonlight and almost liquid. Airborne is asleep but keeps popping his head up to growl at some threat impossibly far below us in the valley. There's been a big fight over by the Pakistan border and F-15s and -16s have been powering overhead all evening looking for people to kill. O'Byrne wanders out and we start talking. His head is shaved but dirt sticks to the stubble so you can see where his hair ought to be. He says he signed a contract with the Army that's almost up, and he has to figure out whether to reenlist.

"Combat is such an adrenaline rush," he says. "I'm worried I'll be looking for that when I get home and if I can't find it, I'll just start drinking and getting in trouble. People back home think we drink because of the bad stuff, but that's not true... we drink because we miss the good stuff."

O'Byrne is also worried about being alone. He hasn't been out of earshot of his platoonmates for two years and has no idea how he'll react to solitude. He's never had to get a job, find an apartment, or arrange a doctor's appointment because the Army has always done those things for him. All he's had to do is fight. And he's good at it, so leading a patrol up 1705 causes him less anxiety than, say, moving to Boston and finding an apartment and a job. He has little capacity for what civilians refer to as "life skills"; for him, life skills literally keep you alive. Those are far simpler and more compelling than the skills required at home. "In the Korengal, almost every problem could get settled by getting violent faster than the other guy," O'Byrne told me. "Do that at home and it's not going to go so well."

It's a stressful way to live but once it's blown out your levels almost everything else looks boring. O'Byrne knows himself: when he gets bored he starts drinking and getting into fights, and then it's only a matter of time until he's back in the system. If that's the case, he might as well *stay* in the system — a better one — and actually move upward. I suggest a few civilian jobs that offer a little adrenaline — wilderness trip guide, firefighter — but we both know it's just not the same. We are at one of the most exposed outposts in the entire U.S. military, and he's crawling out of his skin because there hasn't been a good firefight in a week. How do you bring a guy like that back into the world?

Civilians balk at recognizing that one of the most traumatic things about combat is having to give it up. War is so obviously evil and wrong that the idea there could be anything good to it almost feels like a profanity. And yet throughout history, men like Mac and Rice and O'Byrne have come home to find themselves desperately missing what should have been the worst experience of their lives. To a combat vet, the civilian world can seem frivolous and dull, with very little at stake and all the wrong people in power. These men come home and quickly find themselves getting berated by a rear-base major who's never seen combat or arguing with their girlfriend about some domestic issue they don't even understand. When men say they miss combat, it's not that they actually miss getting shot at — you'd have to be deranged — it's that they miss being in a world where everything is important and nothing is taken for granted. They miss being in a world where human relations are entirely governed by whether you can trust the other person with your life.

It's such a pure, clean standard that men can completely remake themselves in war. You could be anything back home — shy, ugly, rich, poor, unpopular — and it won't matter because it's of no consequence in a firefight, and therefore of no consequence, period. The only thing that matters is your level of dedication to the rest of the group, and that is almost impossible to fake. That is why the men say such impossibly vulgar things about each other's sisters and mothers. It's one more way to prove nothing can break the bond between them; it's one more way to prove they're not alone out there.

War is a big and sprawling word that brings a lot of human suffering into the conversation, but combat is a different matter. Combat is the smaller game that young men fall in love with, and any solution to the human problem of war will have to take into account the psyches of these young men. For some reason there is a profound and mysterious gratification to the reciprocal agreement to protect another person with your life, and combat is virtually the only situation in which that happens regularly. These hillsides of loose shale and holly trees are where the men feel not most *alive*—that you can get skydiving—but the most utilized. The most necessary. The most clear and certain and purposeful. If young men could get that feeling at home, no one would ever want to go to war again, but they can't. So here sits Sergeant Brendan O'Byrne, one month before the end of deployment, seriously contemplating signing back up.

"I prayed only once in Afghanistan," O'Byrne wrote me after it was all over. "It was when Restrepo got shot, and I prayed to god to let him live. But God, Allah, Jehovah, Zeus or whatever a person may call God wasn't in that valley. Combat is the devil's game. God wanted no part. That's why our prayers weren't answered: the only one listening was Satan."

In November 1943, ten rifle companies from the First Infantry Division arrived in England to prepare for the invasion of Nazi-occupied France. The men had fought their way across North Africa and Italy and were now poised to spearhead the biggest and most decisive action of World War II. (The men had seen so much combat that a sour refrain had begun to make the rounds: "The Army consists of the First Infantry Division and eight million replacements.") As these men prepared for the invasion, they were asked to fill out questionnaires prepared by a new entity known as the Army Research Branch. The goal of the study was to determine whether mental attitude among soldiers was any predictor of combat performance. Similar questionnaires were also given to new units who had just arrived from the United States — "cherries," as they were already known back then.

Several months later these men sprinted into the artillery and machine-gun fire that was plowing up the beaches of Normandy, overran the German positions, and eventually went on to liberate Paris. Combat losses over the course of those two months were around 60 percent, and even higher for officers. What interested sociologists at the Research Branch, however, were *non*-combat losses — men who went mad from trauma and fear. For every four men felled by bullets there was, on average, one removed from the battlefield for psychological reasons. Such losses varied from unit to unit and were thought to closely reflect the fighting ability of those groups. The Army wanted to know whether that ability could be determined *beforehand*, simply by asking questions.

LOVE

It could, as it turned out. The Research Branch—which went on to publish its findings in a classic volume called *The American Soldier: Combat and Its Aftermath*, edited by sociologist Samuel Stouffer—found that in ten out of twelve regiments, companies with poor attitudes were far more likely than others to suffer noncombat casualties. Stouffer calculated that the chance of that happening randomly, with no statistical connection between the two, was less than 2 percent. The study went on, questionnaire after questionnaire, to attempt to pry from the minds of thousands of soldiers what exactly enabled them to function in an environment as hellish and confusing as modern combat. All things being equal, some men make better soldiers than others, and some units perform better than others. The traits that distinguish those men, and those units, could be called the Holy Grail of combat psychology. They could be called the basis for what people loosely refer to as "courage."

An Israeli study during the 1973 Yom Kippur War found that high-performing soldiers were more intelligent, more "masculine," more socially mature, and more emotionally stable than average men. Moreover, attack divers who exhibited behavioral problems in tightly run kibbutz communities turned out to be far better fighters than "conform-ist" divers who never got in trouble. At the other end of the spectrum, eight out of ten men who suffered psychological collapse in combat had a problem at home: a pregnant wife, a financial crisis, a recent death in the family. Those collapses were most likely to be caused not by a near-death experience, as one might expect, but by the combat death of a close friend. That was certainly true at Restrepo as well. Nearly every man had missed death by a margin of inches, but those traumas were almost never discussed. Rather, it was the losses in the unit that lingered in men's minds. The only time I saw a man cry up there was when I asked Pemble whether he was glad the outpost had been named after Doc Restrepo. Pemble nodded, tried to answer, and then his face just went into his hands.

Cortez was another man who struggled with the loss of Restrepo. "His death was a bit hard on us," he told me, months later, with typical understatement. "We loved him like a brother. I actually saw him as an older brother, and after he went down, there was a time I didn't care about anything. I didn't care about getting shot or if I died over there. I'd run into the open and not care and I'd be getting chewed out by a team leader and not care. I wasn't scared, honestly, but I just didn't care. I didn't care if I died or not."

Someone finally pointed out to Cortez that if he got hit, someone else was going to have to run through gunfire to save him, and the idea that he might get one of his brothers killed was enough to get him to knock it off. His reaction points to an irony of combat psychology, however—the logical downside of heroism. If you're willing to lay down your life for another person, then their death is going to be more upsetting than the prospect of your own, and intense combat might incapacitate an entire unit through grief alone. Combat is such an urgent business, however, that most men simply defer the psychological issues until later. "A tired, cold, muddy rifleman goes forward with the bitter dryness of fear in his mouth into the mortar bursts and machine-gun fire of a determined enemy," Stouffer wrote in *The American Soldier*. "A tremendous psychological mobilization is necessary to make an individual do this, not just once but many times. In combat, surely, if anywhere, we should be able to observe behavioral determinants of great significance."

Some of those behavioral determinants—like a willingness to take risks—seem to figure disproportionately in the characters of young men. They are killed in accidents and homicides at a rate of 106 per 100,000 per year, roughly five times the rate of young women. Statistically, it's six times as dangerous to spend a year as a young man in America than as a cop or a fireman, and vastly more dangerous than a one-year deployment at a big military base in Afghanistan. You'd have to go to a remote firebase like the KOP or Camp Blessing to find a level of risk that surpasses that of simply being an adolescent male back home.

Combat isn't simply a matter of risk, though; it's also a matter of mastery. The basic neurological mechanism that induces mammals to do things is called the dopamine reward system. Dopamine is a neurotransmitter that mimics the effect of cocaine in the brain, and it gets released when a person wins a game or solves a problem or succeeds at a difficult task. The dopamine reward system exists in both sexes but is stronger in men, and as a result, men are more likely to become obsessively involved in such things as hunting, gambling, computer games, and war. When the men of Second Platoon were moping around the outpost hoping for a firefight it was because, among other things, they weren't getting their accustomed dose of endorphins and dopamine. They played video games instead. Women can master those skills without having pleasure centers in their brains—primarily the mesocorticolimbic center—light up as if they'd just done a line of coke.

One of the beguiling things about combat and other deep games is that they're so complex, there's no way to predict the outcome. That means that any ragtag militia, no matter how small and poorly equipped, might conceivably defeat a superior force if it fights well enough. Combat starts out as a fairly organized math problem involving trajectories and angles but quickly decays into a kind of violent farce, and the randomness of that farce can produce strange outcomes. "Every action produces a counteraction on the enemy's part," an American correspondent named Jack Belden wrote about combat during World War II. (Belden's observations were so keen that he was quoted in *The American Soldier*.) "The thousands of interlocking actions throw up millions of little frictions, accidents and chances, from which there emanates an all-embracing fog of uncertainty."

Combat fog obscures your fate—obscures when and where you might die—and from that unknown is born a desperate bond between the men. That bond is the core experience of combat and the only thing you can absolutely count on.

The Army might screw you and your girlfriend might dump you and the enemy might kill you, but the shared commitment to safeguard one another's lives is unnegotiable and only deepens with time. The willingness to die for another person is a form of love that even religions fail to inspire, and the experience of it changes a person profoundly. What the Army sociologists, with their clipboards and their questions and their endless meta-analyses, slowly came to understand was that courage *was* love. In war, neither could exist without the other, and that in a sense they were just different ways of saying the same thing. According to their questionnaires, the primary motivation in combat (other than "ending the task" — which meant they all could go home) was "solidarity with the group." That far outweighed self-preservation or idealism as a motivator. The Army Research Branch cites cases of wounded men going AWOL after their hospitalization in order to get back to their unit faster than the military could get them there. A civilian might consider this an act of courage, but soldiers knew better. To them it was just an act of brotherhood, and there probably wasn't much to say about it except, "Welcome back."

Loyalty to the group drove men back into combat—and occasionally to their deaths—but the group also provided the only psychological refuge from the horror of what was going on. It was conceivably more reassuring to be under fire with men you trusted than to languish at some rear base with strangers who had no real understanding of war. It's as if there was an intoxicating effect to group inclusion that more than compensated for the dangers the group had to face. A study conducted in the mid-1950s found that jumping out of a plane generated extreme anxiety in *loosely* bonded groups of paratroopers, but tightly bonded men mainly worried about living up to the standards of the group. Men were also found to be able to withstand more pain — in this case, electric shocks — when they were part of a close group than when they were alone.

In the early 1990s, an English anthropologist named Robin Dunbar theorized that the maximum size for any group of primates was determined by brain size — specifically, the size of the neocortex. The larger the neocortex, he reasoned, the more individuals with whom you could maintain personal relationships. Dunbar then compared primate brains to human brains and used the differential to predict the ideal size for a group of humans. The number he came up with was 147.8 people. Rounded up to 150, it became known as the Dunbar number, and it happened to pop up everywhere. A survey of ethnographic data found that precontact hunter-gatherers around the world lived in shifting communities that ranged from 90 to 221 people, with an average of 148. Neolithic villages in Mesopotamia were thought to have had around 150 people. The Roman army of the classical period used a formation of 130 men—called a maniple, or a double century—in combat. Hutterite communities in South Dakota split after reaching 150 people because, in their opinion, anything larger cannot be controlled by peer pressure alone.

Dunbar also found that the size of human hunter-gatherer communities was not spread evenly along a spectrum but tended to clump around certain numbers. The first group size that kept coming up in ethnographic data was thirty to fifty people— essentially a platoon. (Unlike hunter-gatherer communities, platoons are obviously single-sex, but the group identification may still function the same way.) Those communities were highly mobile but kept in close contact with three or four other communities for social and defensive purposes. The larger these groups were, the better they could defend themselves, up until the point where they got so big that they started to fracture and divide. Many such groups formed a tribe, and tribes either fought each other or formed confederacies against other tribes. The basic dichotomy of "us" versus "them" happened at the tribal level and was reinforced by differences in language and culture.

The parallels with military structure are almost exact. Battle Company had around 150 men, and every man in the company knew every other man by face and by name. The molten core of the group bond was the platoon, however. A platoon—with a headquarters element, a radio operator, a medic, and a forward observer for calling in airstrikes—is the smallest self-contained unit in the regular army. Inserted into enemy territory and resupplied by air, a platoon could function more or less indefinitely. When I asked the men about their allegiance to one another, they said they would unhesitatingly risk their lives for anyone in the platoon or company, but that the sentiment dropped off pretty quickly after that. By the time you got to brigade level—three or four thousand men—any sense of common goals or identity was pretty much theoretical. The 173rd had an unmanned observation blimp tethered over Asadabad, for example, and one night a thunderstorm caused it to crash. When the men at Restrepo heard that, they broke into a cheer.

Self-sacrifice in defense of one's community is virtually universal among humans, extolled in myths and legends all over the world, and undoubtedly ancient. No community can protect itself unless a certain portion of its youth decide they are willing to risk their lives in its defense. That sentiment can be horribly manipulated by leaders and politicians, of course, but the underlying sentiment remains the same. Cheyenne Dog Soldiers wore long sashes that they staked to the ground in battle so that they couldn't retreat from the spot unless released by someone else. American militiamen at the Alamo were outnumbered ten to one and yet fought to the last man rather than surrender to Mexican forces trying to reclaim the territory of Texas. And soldiers in World War I ran headlong into heavy machine-gun fire not because many of them cared about the larger politics of the war but because that's what the man to the left and right of them was doing. The cause doesn't have to be righteous and battle doesn't have to be winnable; but over and over again throughout history, men have chosen to die in battle with their friends rather than to flee on their own and survive.

While Stouffer was trying to figure this phenomenon out among American troops, the Psychological Warfare Division was trying to do the same thing with the Germans. One of the most astounding things about the last phase of the war wasn't that the German army collapsed — by the end that was a matter of simple math — but that it lasted as long as it did. Many German units that were completely cut off from the rest of their army continued resisting the prospect of certain defeat. After the war, a pair of former American intelligence officers named Edward Shils and Morris Janowitz set about interviewing thousands of German prisoners to find out what had motivated them in the face of such odds. Their paper, "Cohesion and Disintegration in the Wehrmacht in World War II," became a classic inquiry into why men fight.

Considering the extreme nationalism of the Nazi era, one might expect that territorial ambition and a sense of racial superiority motivated most of the men on the German line. In fact, those concepts only helped men who were already part of a cohesive unit; for everyone else, such grand principles provided no motivation at all. A soldier needs to have his basic physical needs met and needs to feel valued and loved by others. If those things are provided by the group, a soldier requires virtually no rationale other than the defense of that group to continue fighting. Allied propaganda about the moral wrongfulness of the Nazi government had very little effect on these men because they weren't really fighting for that government anyway. As the

German lines collapsed and the German army, the Wehrmacht, began to break up, the concerns of fighting began to give way to those of pure physical survival. At that point, Allied propaganda campaigns that guaranteed food, shelter, and safety to German deserters began to take a toll.

But even then, Shils and Janowitz found, the men who deserted tended to be disgruntled loners who had never really fit into their unit. They were men who typically had trouble giving or receiving affection and had a history of difficult relations with friends and family back home. A significant number had criminal records. The majority of everyone else either fought and died as a unit or surrendered as a unit. Almost no one acted on their own to avoid a fate that was coming to the whole group. When I asked Hijar what it would mean to get overrun, he said, "By a brave man's definition it would mean to fight until you died." That is essentially what the entire German army tried to do as the Western Front collapsed in the spring of 1945.

The starkest version of this commitment to the group is throwing yourself on a hand grenade to save the men around you. It's courage in its most raw form, an instantaneous decision that is virtually guaranteed to kill the hero but stands a very good chance of saving everyone else. (Most acts of heroism contain at least an outside chance of survival—and a high chance of failure.) When Giunta ran into heavy fire to save Brennan from getting dragged off by the enemy, I doubt he considered his own safety, but somewhere in his mind he may have thought he had a chance of surviving. That would not be true with a hand grenade. Throwing yourself on a hand grenade is a deliberate act of suicide, and as such it occupies a singular place in the taxonomy of courage.

It is a particularly hard act to understand from an evolutionary point of view. The driving mechanism of human evolution is natural selection, meaning that genes of individuals who die before they have a chance to reproduce tend to get weeded out of a population. A young man who throws himself on a grenade is effectively conceding the genetic competition to the men he saves: they will go on to have children whereas he won't. From that, it's hard to imagine how a gene for courage or altruism could get passed forward through the generations. Individuals in most species will defend their young, which makes genetic sense, and a few, like wolves, will even defend their mates. But humans may be the only animal that practices what could be thought of as "suicidal defense": an individual male will rush to the defense of another male despite the fact that both are likely to die. Chimpanzees share around 99 percent of human DNA and are the only primate species yet observed to stage raids into neighboring territory and to kill the lone males they encounter. Raid after raid, kill after kill, they'll wipe out the male population of a rival troop and take over their females and their territory. When these attacks happen, other males in the area flee rather than come to their comrade's defense. Researchers have never once observed a chimpanzee turn around to help another male who is getting beaten to death by outsiders.

By that standard, courage could be thought of as a uniquely human trait. Courage would make even more evolutionary sense if it were also followed by some kind of social reward, like access to resources or to females. The glory heaped upon heroes in almost all societies might explain why young men are so eager to send themselves to war—or, if sent, to fight bravely. That would only work in a species that is capable of language, however; acts of bravery can't follow a chimp home from the battlefield any more than acts of cowardice. Without language, courage just becomes suicidal foolishness. But once our ancestors escaped the eternal present by learning to speak, they could repeat stories that would make individuals accountable for their actions—or rewarded for them. That would create a strong incentive not to turn and flee while others fought off the enemy. Better to fight and die than to face ostracism and contempt back home.

Genetic material gathered from contemporary hunter-gatherers suggests that for much of prehistory, humans lived in groups of thirty to fifty people who were loosely related to one another. They married into other groups that spoke the same language and shared the same territory. If you were a young male in that era, dying in defense of your group would make good genetic sense because even if you didn't have children, your relatives would, and it would be your nieces and nephews who passed your genes on to future generations. Our evolutionary past was *not* peaceful: archaeological evidence indicates that up to 15 percent of early humans died in battles with rival tribes. (By comparison, the carnage of the twentieth century produced a civilian casualty rate of less than 2 percent.) Because of our violent past, evolution may have programmed us to think we're related to everyone in our immediate group — even in a platoon — and that dying in its defense is a good genetic strategy. Groups that weren't organized like that may have had a hard time competing with groups that were, so in that way a propensity for bravery and self-sacrifice could have spread through human culture. I once asked Cortez whether he would risk his life for other men in the platoon.

"I'd actually throw myself on the hand grenade for them," he said. I asked him why.

"Because I actually love my brothers," he said. "I mean, it's a brotherhood. Being able to save their life so they can live, I think is rewarding. Any of them would do it for me."

5
—

EARLY MORNING, THE MEN ASLEEP LIKE
hounds in every conceivable position and dressed
in everything from gym shorts to full camo and
boots. Some seem to lie where they fell and others
are curled up like children with blankets dragged
up to their chins. They're surrounded by guns and
radios and ammo and tube-launched rockets and,
here and there, magazine photos of girls in bikinis.
(If those girls only knew where they'd wound up;
if they only knew they'd been nailed to a six-by-six
between old fly strips and belts of SAW ammo.)
Early one morning we take half a magazine of AK
from the ridge above us and I wake up thinking it's
just another bad dream until everyone figures it out

all at once, men falling over each other grabbing rifles and grenades and piling out the door to stand around half-naked in the gray light.

"That's it?" someone asks. "One burst?"

"Weak," Moreno says, walking away.

It's the first contact in over two weeks, and no one can figure out whether the Americans are actually winning or if the enemy just decided not to fight for a while. Sometimes the war could look utterly futile—empires almost never win these things—and other times you'd remember that the enemy doesn't have it so good either. They rarely get closer than five hundred yards, they rarely hit anyone, and they usually lose five or ten fighters in the ensuing airstrikes. Worse still, the locals seem to be souring on the whole concept of jihad. On one patrol an old man gives Patterson the names of the three insurgent leaders in Yaka Chine because their fighters come into Loy Kalay after dark to harass the inhabitants. He says the fighters wear uniforms and night vision gear and always leave town before dawn. "They took my son from the mosque and almost killed him for using tobacco and not having a beard," the old man says. "It's the old Taliban rules."

Stichter asks him what the chances are of us getting shot at on the way out of town, and the old man just shrugs. "Only God knows," he says.

LOVE

"I'd say it's about seventy-five percent," Stichter tells me as we turn to go.

As it turns out we walk back unmolested. A few days later we're all sitting around the courtyard at Restrepo when word comes over company net that a force of Pakistani Taliban just attacked a border outpost manned by a special unit of Afghan soldiers. The Taliban were shooting across the border from positions held by the Pakistani Frontier Corps, so the Afghans called in airstrikes on the Frontier Corps positions. Colonel Ostlund then ordered four more bombs to be dropped on another group of attackers that had just fled back across the border. They were all killed. "If we go to war with Pakistan, I'll reenlist," O'Byrne says. He's shirtless in the late-afternoon heat and sitting in a folding chair that someone stole from a sergeant first class in Kuwait. The sergeant's name — Elder — is written in Magic Marker on the back of the chair, and now it's sitting up at Restrepo getting shot at. The chair even has a drink holder in the armrest.

The men know Pakistan is the root of the entire war, and that is just about the only topic they get political about. They don't much care what happens in Afghanistan — they barely even care what happens on the Pech — but day after day they hear intel about fresh fighters coming in from Pakistan and wounded ones going out. Supposedly there's a medical clinic in Pakistan entirely devoted to treating insurgents. Somewhere in the valley there's a boulder painted with jihadist graffiti, but it's in Arabic instead of Pashto because locals aren't as enthused about the war as the outsiders. You didn't have to be in the Army to notice that Pakistan was effectively waging war against America, but the administration back home was refusing to even acknowledge it, much less take any action. Now an American colonel is bombing Pakistani troops inside their own country and the feeling at Restrepo is, *Finally...*

Advance personnel for Viper Company will start arriving in weeks, and the men have already started talking. They considered Viper Company to be a mechanized unit, meaning they ride around in Humvees and Bradley Fighting Vehicles, and the word is that their mountain-warfare training back home didn't go so well. The men at Restrepo are convinced that Viper will arrive fat and out of shape, and it will be Second Platoon's job to make sure that they suffer appropriately. When a new unit arrives in theater they undergo a week or so of what is known as "right-seat left-seat" patrols. First the old unit leads the patrols, pointing out all the salient features of the area, and the new unit just follows. Then the new unit leads and the old unit follows. That takes about a week, and then the old unit gets on a helicopter and flies away forever and the new guys are on their own.

Right-seat left-seat is how tactical knowledge—the little details that save men's lives—gets passed from one unit to the next. From a combat vet's point of view, right-seat left-seat is also a chance to walk cherries into the ground and demonstrate their staggering weakness. (It actually worked too well: one Viper Company soldier literally wound up on his hands and knees on the last hill to Restrepo.) Most casualties occur in the first few months of a deployment because the new men don't know where they're getting shot at from and the mortar teams don't know what hilltops to hit. The job of Kearney and his soldiers was to explain all this so that the new unit wouldn't have to learn by trial and error at the cost of men's lives.

A crucial part of the handoff is pushing the enemy back so that there is some "white space" on the battlefield, and Kearney came up with a fairly radical plan for doing that: he was going to sweep Yaka Chine. Third Platoon would get dropped onto the ridges west of town, Second Platoon would clear from the south, and Kearney and his headquarters element would direct everything from Divpat.

Locals had said that there were foreign fighters in Yaka Chine walking around openly in military camouflage with weapons over their shoulders. Apparently they'd conceded the northern half of the valley to the Americans but considered themselves immune to attack in the southern half. It was only three miles from Restrepo, but there were so many draws and caves in the hills above town, and so many fighting positions on the high ground, that it would take a brigade-wide effort to get in and out of there safely.

The entire plan hinged on airpower because there was no way to walk down there fast enough to catch the enemy by surprise. Air was now conducted by the 101st Aviation Wing, which had arrived in country only a couple of months earlier, but they'd already crashed so many helicopters that they were reluctant to fly into any landing zones that hadn't been cleared. Kearney was going to use the same two landing zones that he'd used on Rock Avalanche—code-named Grant and Cubs—but they were just small bare patches on the sides of mountains. If a rotor blade so much as clipped a treetop, the helicopter would crash.

The men of Second Platoon are down at the KOP clustered behind the blast wall packing and repacking their gear for the mission: ammo, radio batteries, water, everything you'd need for a forty-eight-hour Armageddon. Yaka Chine is crawling with insurgents; they've got no farther place to go and it's an almost guaranteed firefight. Almost guaranteed casualties. Mace walks up carrying a crate of Claymore mines, which are set up around any static position and detonate outward rather than upward to blunt any ground attack. The men are discussing how much water to bring and how much sleeping gear they'll need and whether to use small assault packs or full rucks. After a while Gillespie wanders up and announces that there's limited space on the birds, so Solowksi won't be going — though I will. It's not exactly that Solowski's getting pulled *for* me, but that's the result. That means not only will the gun team be down a man but the others will have to carry that much more ammo. Later I catch Gillespie by himself and tell him I'd be happy to carry 500 rounds if that would make things easier.

"Let me talk to the gun team," he says. "You might have to."

The medic gives me extra rehydration salts and an IV bag in case I get hit. I've already got a tourniquet and an Israeli bandage in my vest, and a pack of Kerlix. In my chest my heart is slamming. There are times when all of this — the helicopters and the guns and the Afghans and the steep beautiful mountains — just feels like some awesome and dramatic game. And then there are moments when you suddenly understand how real it all is: no way to control what happens next, no way to rewind things back to a better place if it all goes wrong. There's intel about four SA-18 rockets in the valley, the kind that track heat signatures and blow aircraft out of the sky. We could lift off from the KOP and all be dead in minutes. I don't have to go on this mission, I don't even have to be in this valley. Right now I have everything — my life, my safety, my friends and family back home — and I might be allowed one moment of regret before those things are taken from me. One moment of crazy downward acceleration in a Chinook; one moment of dirt unzipping toward me faster than I can get out of its way. "The quick chaotic bundling of a man into eternity," as Melville called it; the last impossible phase shift from being a person to being nothing at all.

I finish packing my gear. The stress is getting to everyone and things are noticeably strange. The men are creeping around the KOP trying to avoid Bobby and Jones or lying inert on their bunks as if they're in some kind of morgue for the semiconscious. I watch one guy pull out his 9 mil and put it to another man's forehead. Right between the eyes but it isn't cocked. It's tempting to calm myself with the idea that everything is in God's hands, but *I'm* the one deciding whether or not to get on the helicopter—not God—so it's hard to see what He has to do with it. The other men don't have a choice so they're spared that particular torment, though of course they have others. Either way, this will be settled—done with, nothing more to worry about—in forty-eight hours. That's the closest you're going to get to reassurance without grasping at some kind of religious help. God let Restrepo die and Rougle die and forty other guys die in this valley—not to mention dozens of civilians—so as a source of comfort He's not that tempting. Maybe O'Byrne had it right: prayers don't get answered because God isn't even *in* this valley.

Across the battalion units are getting ready for the handoff and trying to create enough white space so the new guys don't get killed as soon as they get there. The biggest effort is happening about ten miles to the north in the Waygal Valley, where Chosen Company will simultaneously abandon Outpost Bella and build a new one in the town of Wanat. Bella was the sister base to Ranch House, which almost got overrun the previous August, and after the Americans abandoned Ranch House it was only a matter of time before Bella went as well.

There was no passable road up to Bella so everything had to come in by air, and the mountains
were so high and steep that the Chinooks had a
hard time even dropping off sling loads. They can't
abandon the Waygal altogether, though, because
it was a major infiltration route for fighters moving from sanctuaries in Pakistan toward Kabul
and the interior. The enemy knew Bella was being
abandoned, and there was intel that a force of two
hundred fighters were going to launch an attack in
order to make it appear as if they'd actually driven
the Americans out.

Within hours of pulling out of Bella, Chosen
Company's Second Platoon was going to convoy
the eight kilometers from Blessing to the town of
Wanat to build a permanent base next to the police
station and the district center. They would be going
home in less than two weeks, and building the outpost would be their last mission in Afghanistan.
They had already sent most of their gear back to
Vicenza. A spot for the base had been picked out in
a field just south of the town, near the intersection
of two rivers that had been bridged the year before
by 10th Mountain. It was a crucial piece of terrain
that The Rock had spent nearly a year negotiating
for; unfortunately, that also gave the enemy plenty
of time to prepare. The base would be named

Combat Outpost Kahler, after a platoon sergeant who had been killed by an Afghan security guard in a highly suspect friendly-fire incident six months earlier.

There was a bad feeling about the mission from the beginning. Days beforehand someone had written "Wanat: the movie" on the mission board, and the men were joking about which actors would play them. An Afghan heavy equipment contractor never showed up on the job, and the Americans' one Bobcat had a bulldozer blade but no bucket. That meant it could only fill Hescos to a height of about four feet; everything else would have to be done by hand. Men were spotted moving along the upper ridges but couldn't be killed because they weren't carrying weapons, and on the third night an estimated two hundred foreign and local fighters managed to move into positions around Outpost Kahler. They set up heavy machine guns on the ridges and put a Dishka in a nearby building, aimed point-blank into the base, and riddled the bazaar with more fighters who were mobile inside the innumerable stalls and alleyways. Finally they positioned cadres of men whose job it was to run forward and breach the wire, or die trying.

The Taliban plan was to suppress the base with massive firepower, breach the wire, and drag off dead and wounded American soldiers. There was a small outpost a hundred yards outside the base, and that was particularly vulnerable to being over-run. The Taliban knew that once they were close in they couldn't be hit by artillery, and that Apaches would take at least an hour to get there. That meant it would be a fair fight until then. With luck they could get inside the wire, kill groups of soldiers as their guns jammed, and possibly take over the entire base. It was exactly the nightmare scenario that the men at Restrepo went to sleep dreading; it was exactly the nightmare scenario that few Americans back home even understood could happen. The fact that it didn't happen at Wanat was nothing short of a miracle.

The signal to attack was two long bursts from a heavy machine gun. That was immediately followed by waves of rocket-propelled grenades that took out or suppressed every heavy weapon at the base. There was so much fire coming in that the mortar tubes were sparkling with bullet strikes and no one could get near them. A grenade hit the missile truck almost immediately and set it on fire. The Americans were instantly outnumbered and outgunned and shooting so much that the barrels of their guns were melting. A sergeant named Hector Chaves, who had already been through Ranch

House, saw a Taliban fighter climbing a tree outside the wire so he shot him. Another fighter started climbing the tree so Chavez shot him too. After Chavez shot his third man they finally abandoned the tree and tried something else.

An RPG hit near the mortar pit and tore up a mortarman named Sergio Abad with shrapnel. Abad had transferred out of Battle Company several months earlier, and the last time I'd seen him, he was relaxing at Camp Blessing, just waiting to go home. Now Abad found himself lying wounded in the mortar pit handing ammo to Chavez, who was busy firing over the tops of the sandbags. The 120 mm mortars, which have a killing radius of seventy yards, caught fire, and Chavez and another man grabbed Abad and started pulling him to safety. Halfway across the base they took a burst of machine-gun fire and Chavez went down, shot in both legs. He continued crawling toward cover, pulling Abad behind him, until several men at the command post ran out and rescued them.

Abad died quickly in the command post lying next to Chavez and several other wounded. Chavez was worried he'd been hit in the balls and so in the middle of the firefight he made Staff Sergeant Erich Phillips pull his pants down and make sure everything was okay. It was. The blazing missile truck finally exploded, engulfing an Afghan soldier in flames and sending antitank missiles tumbling across the base. One landed in the command post, and as it sat there the men could hear the motor spinning up and the weapon arming itself. Chavez just lay there, waiting. "I was in so much pain I couldn't move," he told me. "I just said 'Fuck it, I'm done.' Then Sergeant Phillips came over, picked the motherfucker up, walked it out somewhere, and tossed it."

Meanwhile, a hundred yards outside the wire, the outpost was getting overrun. The first barrage of grenades had slammed into the position and wounded or incapacitated every man there. The grenades kept coming and blowing men out of their positions and the weapons out of their hands and even the helmets off their heads. A specialist named Matthew Phillips stood up to throw a hand grenade and was killed before he could pull the pin. Specialist Jason Bogar was ignoring the rounds that were sparking off the boulder in front of him and going cyclic on his SAW. It finally jammed when the barrel turned white-hot and started to melt.

Enemy fighters were swarming toward the position, and the only way to keep them back was to keep up a constant barrage of fire. The weapons couldn't sustain it, though. If a machine gun could

shoot forever, one man could hold off a whole battalion, but they jam. That's how positions get overrun. After Bogar's SAW went down the 240 ran
out of ammo and the men were reduced to shooting with their rifles and throwing grenades. Almost
every man was wounded by this point, some badly.
There was so much gunfire that, psychologically,
it was very hard for the men to expose their heads
above the tops of the sandbags in order to shoot.
Specialists Chris McKaig and Jonathan Ayers
decided to pop up in unison, shoot a burst, and
then duck down again. They did that several times
until Ayers was hit in the face and fell over, dead.

Sergeant Ryan Pitts, the platoon forward observer, was pinned down and badly wounded in the
northernmost position. He'd gotten a tourniquet
onto his shattered leg and started throwing hand
grenades over the top of the sandbags. Between
explosions he got through to the command post by
radio and told them that they were getting overrun.
A three-man team led by First Lieutenant Jonathan
Brostrom left the base and ran through heavy fire
carrying weapons, ammunition, and medical supplies. One of them got hit almost immediately. Brostrom and Specialist Jason Hovater made it to the
outpost and began fighting with the help of another
specialist named Pruitt Rainey. They grabbed the

240 from Pitts—he was too badly wounded to use it—and moved to an adjacent fighting position. At one point a specialist named Stafford heard one of the men scream, "They're inside the wire!" followed by a long burst of gunfire. Then, "He's right behind the fucking sandbag!" and another burst. After that came silence, and Brostrom, Rainey, and Hovater were dead.

By this time there were almost no functioning weapons at the outpost. Three wounded men, unaware that Pitts was lying wounded in the northern position, crawled through the outpost making sure everyone was dead and then started staggering toward the relative safety of the base. They made it amid a hail of gunfire and Pitts, who by now had run out of ammo, realized he was alone up there. Enemy fighters were so close that when he radioed for help he had to whisper. Another relief team was organized and four men left the wire at a run and headed for the outpost. One of them was a private first class named Jacob Sones: "No one wanted to go up there because the way they were shooting, whatever angle they had, it was perfect," Sones told me. "They were laying that place down, they were blowing the shit out of it. We got up there and they were all dead except for Pitts, but at the time you're just like, 'We have to get this done or *everybody's* going to die.'"

As soon as they got there they took another tremendous barrage of grenades. One hit Sergeant Israel Garcia dead on. He died within seconds, Pitts holding his hand and telling him they were going to get him home. The blast "hot-miked" his radio and jammed the platoon frequency. Within minutes everyone on the relief team was dead or wounded. They fought on, picking up jammed weapons and trying to shoot them and throwing them down and looking for more. Sones remembers seeing Specialist Phillips and another man lying dead, embracing each other. Ayers was slumped over a 240, and they had to pull him off to use the gun, which was jammed anyway. The Taliban were even throwing rocks at them, hoping the Americans would think they were grenades and jump out of their positions, where they could be shot.

Sones made his way to Pitts, who was blacking out from blood loss, and together they started trying to crawl back to the main base. Right around then—about an hour into the fight—the first Apaches arrived. They hunted men in the treeline and did gun runs that plowed up the earth thirty yards outside the sandbags. The Apaches finally managed to tilt the battle back in favor of the defenders. Nine Americans were killed and twenty-seven wounded—over half the American force at the base. It was the single costliest firefight of the war. It was the single costliest firefight since Mogadishu. At some point the enemy supposedly managed to drag two dead Americans down several agricultural terraces before abandoning them. They hadn't overrun an American base, but they'd penetrated a position and put their hands on American soldiers. It wasn't a good sign.

Back at the KOP, Battle Company was following the events over the battalion net as they unfolded, and Third Platoon was mobilized to fly in by helicopter and reinforce the position. After Third Platoon left, Kearney gathered the rest of his men around the command center at the KOP and told them what had happened. He stood in a brown T-shirt, twenty-seven years old, all the youth in his face gone, unshaved and grim and angry.

"Proctor, why did you join the Army?" he said, pointing to one of the men.

"To fight for my country, sir."

"Did you expect there was a chance you might get injured or that you might die?"

"Absolutely, sir."

"Anybody join not knowing that might be an option?"

The men shook their heads.

"Okay, the country's at war and you're the ones stepping up and doing it," Kearney went on. "It's like one percent of the whole damn nation is out there doing it. What do you guys think would have happened if we had just stopped at Vimoto, didn't go out there doing our aggressive patrolling, didn't go out there and build OP Restrepo? You guys want to know what would happen? The same shit that happened today up at Chosen Company."

The men are looking down and avoiding each other's gazes. Many are smoking cigarettes and others look close to tears. Kearney repeats the information he has—nine dead, nine wounded—and then tells them that one of the dead is Abad.

"I guarantee you that if he hadn't been doing his job when he died, there'd probably be more soldiers out there dead right now," Kearney says. "So take honor in the fact that you guys trained up one hell of a fucking soldier."

Kearney holds a moment of silence for the dead and then dismisses the men. "Carry me," Jones says to Stichter quietly as he walks past.

6

—

BATTLE COMPANY'S LAST BIG MISSION GOES off at dusk, lines of men moving down the slope to the landing zone and piling into Black Hawks. The 101st refused to fly into Grant and Cubs so the mission got scaled back to Third Platoon flying onto Divpat along with some Scouts and a unit of Pathfinders. The job of the Pathfinders is to clear the top of Divpat so that the next unit can land Chinooks up there. That way Viper Company could pick up where Battle Company left off. Battle will not be sweeping Yaka Chine; Battle will not go out of the valley with one last monster firefight. Most of the men seem relieved. A few are clearly disappointed.

Someone who was probably going to get shot will now be going home alive and whole.

We're there in minutes, the slopes of Divpat rising up fast and then suddenly becoming hard ground right beneath us. Men tumble out of the bird, hitting heavily with their full rucks and immediately going prone in the heavy brush, rifles aimed outward in case we take contact and uniforms rattling in the rotor wash. Then the bird rises up and pounds off to the west, dropping fast off the ridge and then carving back northward for the KOP. It's almost dark by the time everyone is there, and the men wallow through the chest-high brush to set up fighting positions in the cardinal directions. I stay with Kearney, who finds a central place for himself near the 60 mm mortar. The enemy chatter starts almost immediately:

"It's very important to talk to Mullah Nasrullah for permission to go to work tomorrow," one commander says over the radio. "Let's give them a good welcome on Divpat."

Prophet is picking up information that the enemy has a Dishka and a mortar tube and that there are thirty fighters ready to assault up the slopes in the morning. Kearney kneels in the brush studying a laminated map and talking to Ostlund on the radio. His mission is to clear the landing zone for later use, but he and Ostlund have come up with a plan to lure the fighters onto the hill to kill them. The birds are going to come back for what's known as a "false extraction"—they land and take off again, as if picking up men—but the Americans remain in place. When the fighters come up the slopes to check out what the Americans were up to they'll walk straight into the Claymores and the guns.

The illume is a 100 percent and the fighters will be moving into position all night long. The radio chatter stops after a while and Prophet informs us that they've got their detection equipment on "scan" and will now be listening to the ball game. (The White Sox are playing the Cubs and there's probably a certain amount of money at stake.) The moon comes up over the Abas Ghar and we lie in the brush listening to the wind sweeping over the top of Divpat. A surveillance drone buzzes protectively overhead. Everyone sleeps in their clothes and body armor and some men even keep their helmets on. If it starts it'll start fast.

Dawn comes crawling up out of the east with the moon still hung over the valley like a dinner plate and the men wrapped in their ponchos and curled up shivering. More radio chatter but no contact and as soon as the sun has spilled over the top of the Abas Ghar the men disperse to their fighting positions. Kearney strings up camo netting over the brush to create some shade and we sit there waiting. The false extraction is blown already because the Pathfinders bound up their chainsaws cutting through the brush and had trouble rehanging the chains. The medic grew up on a farm and shows them how to cut brush without ruining the saws, and now in broad daylight they go to work finishing their job and blowing the biggest trees off the position with C-4. Over the battalion net it comes in that Destined is in contact to the east.

"Two ANA killed, we've only lost five so far," Ostlund says over the radio. Five American dead would be a major event, but the Afghan soldiers are different, and undoubtedly they feel the same way about us.

Around midmorning Prophet suddenly picks up radio traffic from all over the southern part of the valley. "We are in position and ready to go to work," one fighter says. Another answers, "I will go alone unless you are coming, in which case I'll stay. I will tell you what I see."

Prophet says the signal on the last one is very strong, which means the man is close. Kearney tells me he's probably a spotter whose job will be to call corrections in to the mortarman and the Dishka gunner. Once those have us pinned down the other men will come up the hill to kill us. Kearney has a decision to make: he can take out the spotter with A-10 gun runs and ruin their plan, or he can let it unfold and hope to kill more of them when they come over the top. It doesn't take him long to decide.

"Maybe it would have been better to let them mass for an attack, but this late in the game it's just not worth it," he tells me. The A-10s have finished their business and we're sitting on the side of the hill looking eastward across the valley. It's almost peaceful. "Mortars and a Dishka? I don't need that shit and neither do the boys. For that matter," he says, looking over at me, "neither do you."

VICENZA, ITALY
Three Months Later

Day after day of rain and early, sullen dusks. Second Platoon is about to disperse and will never exist again, as such, but the men are too busy—or messed up—to get overly sentimental about it. Bobby is running a fever of 103, coughing like a diesel engine and drinking all day long. Money marries a woman he met on leave a few months earlier. A soldier from Chosen Company gets taken to the hospital in an ambulance after collapsing in his room shrieking that people are trying to kill him. The toughest guys in the platoon find themselves crying every day, and the more vulnerable guys skirt the edge of sanity. "It's even bothering me," Bobby confides to me over dinner. "And nothing bothers me. Can you imagine what it's doing to some of the other guys?"

The petty tyrannies of garrison life have returned, and the men do not react well to getting reprimanded by other men who have never been to war. O'Byrne gets yelled at for not sitting in an armchair properly, meaning that he looks too comfortable. Solowski goes home on leave and finds out that his mother is days or weeks away from dying of liver disease. He uses up eight days of emergency leave and then has to go AWOL in order to stay by her side until the end. She is saved by an emergency transplant, thank God, but when Solowski returns to Vicenza, he gets busted down a rank and is made to work extra duty. Cunningham creeps out of bed at dawn and stands outside Battle Company barracks shouting "ALLAHU AKHBAR!" into a bullhorn. Men stagger out of bed thinking they're still in the Korengal.

O'Byrne doesn't fare well. He decides to get out of the Army rather than renew his contract, but he can't begin to tackle the paperwork in his state of mind. His sister flies in for a visit, and when they go walking around town, O'Byrne becomes convinced someone is following them and takes defensive action. He was less scared in the Korengal, where people were actually shooting at him, than in Italy, where it's mostly in his head. Eventually his paranoia starts to fulfill itself. He gets attacked in Venice; a guy breaks a bottle over his head and O'Byrne has to jump into a canal to escape. Soon afterward he falls down a flight of concrete stairs and cracks a front tooth and splits open an eyebrow. His explanation, when asked, is that he was attacked by a wolverine.

When I get to Vicenza, O'Byrne has gone AWOL. That's a problem, because his military ID is about to expire, and when it does he'll be in some weird limbo where he won't be allowed on base but he won't be allowed to go home either. One night Second Platoon is having a barbecue and the guys are standing around talking to some Romanian strippers, and O'Byrne finally calls Hoyt's cell phone. Hoyt talks to him for a minute and then hands the phone to me with a "See what I mean?" kind of look. O'Byrne is so upset he can barely talk. He's drunk at a bar in Florence and his wallet is missing and his cell phone has died. He's talking on a cell he borrowed from some guy in the bar. "The Army's trying to kill me," he says. "I don't dare come back. They're trying to kill me."

He finally shows up the next day and Nevala drives him around the base trying to take care of his paperwork. I tag along to see what happens. O'Byrne refers to the base as "Coward's Land," because it's a place where guys who have never done anything but fill out paperwork can boss around guys who have actually *fought for their country. A whole new set of rules apply that seem almost deliberately punitive of the traits that make for a good combat soldier. We park in front of something called the Transition Office, and O'Byrne says, "Come in and watch, this is gonna be good."*

There's a middle-aged black lady behind the desk who seems perfectly nice. O'Byrne takes a mint out of a jar on her desk and gives her one and explains that his paperwork is late and his ID expires in two days. By then he's supposed to be on a plane home.

"The only acceptable reason for not being on that plane is if you're in jail," the woman says. "And if you're not on that plane you'll be arrested and put in jail."

O'Byrne maintains his composure. "So what should I do?" he asks.

"Call your commanding officer," the woman says, "and ask him to have you arrested. That way you won't be breaking the rules when you don't get on the plane."

If she understands the irony at work here she doesn't betray it. "Let me get this right," O'Byrne says. "You want me to ask to get arrested now so I won't get arrested later?"

"That's right," the woman says and returns to her paperwork.

We get up to go and O'Byrne turns to me as we

walk out the door. "See?" he says. "See why I hate the Army?"

The Army that saved O'Byrne from himself is now destroying the very man it created—or at least that's how it seems to O'Byrne. The new battalion commander finally intervenes and sees to it that O'Byrne gets home safely, but civilian life goes even worse than garrison life. Months later, I get a note from him explaining that he wants to go back into the Army. "It's as if I'm self-destructive, trying to find the hardest thing possible to make me feel accomplished," he writes. "A lot of people tell me I could be anything I want to be. If that's true, why can't I be a fucking civilian and lead a normal fucking life? Probably 'cause I don't want to."

You got me there, O'Byrne; you got me there, brother. Maybe the ultimate wound is the one that makes you miss the war you got it in.

SELECTED SOURCES AND REFERENCES

Book One: FEAR

Ackerl, Kerstin, Michaela Atzmueller, and Karl Grammer. "The Scent of Fear." *Neuroendocrinology Letters*, Vol. 23, No. 2, April 2002.

Arthurs, Cmd. Sgt. Maj. Ted G. *Land with No Sun: A Year in Vietnam with the 173rd Airborne*. Stackpole Books, 2006.

Azar, Beth. "Exposure to Aggression May Have Lasting Effects." *American Psychological Association Monitor*, Vol. 30, No. 9, October 1999.

Aziz-Zadeh, Lisa, Marco Iacoboni, and Eran Zaidel. "Hemispheric Sensitivity to Body Stimuli in Simple Reaction Time." *Experimental Brain Research*, Vol. 170, No. 1, March 2006, pp. 116–121.

SELECTED SOURCES AND REFERENCES

Bar, Hervé. "Wood Traffickers Devastate Afghan Forests." Agence France-Presse, March 5, 2003.

Barry, John, and Michael Hirsh. "Chopper Down over Kunar: A Special Ops Unit Calls for Help, and a Rescue Goes Awry." *Newsweek*, July 11, 2005, p. 31.

Blumenfeld, Laura. "The Sole Survivor: A Navy Seal, Injured and Alone, Was Saved by Afghans' Embrace and Comrades' Valor." *Washington Post*, June 11, 2007.

Botwinick, Jack, PhD, and Larry W. Thompson, PhD. "Age Difference in Reaction Time: An Artifact?" *Gerontologist*, Vol. 8, No. 1, Spring 1968, pp. 25–28.

Bourne, Peter G., ed. *The Psychology and Physiology of Stress, with References to Special Studies of the Viet Nam War.* Academic Press, 1969.

Boyer, Maud, Arnaud Destrebecqz, and Axel Cleeremans. "The Serial Reaction Time Task: Learning Without Knowing, or Knowing Without Learning?" In *Proceedings of the 20th Annual Conference of the Cognitive Science Society.* Erlbaum, 1998, pp. 167–172.

Coates, Stephen. "Moves to Oust Taliban Gain Momentum." Agence France-Presse, September 27, 2001.

SELECTED SOURCES AND REFERENCES

Costa, Paul T., Jr., Antonia Terracciano, and Robert R. McCrae. "Gender Differences in Personality Traits Across Cultures: Robust and Surprising Findings." *Journal of Personality and Social Psychology*, Vol. 81, No. 2, 2001, pp. 322–331.

Daddis, Maj. Gregory A. "Understanding Fear's Effect on Unit Effectiveness." *Military Review*, Vol. 84, No. 4, July–August 2004, pp. 22–27.

Darack, Ed. "The Kunar Province of Afghanistan." *Weatherwise*, May–June 2006.

———. *Victory Point: Operations Red Wings and Whalers—the Marine Corps' Battle for Freedom in Afghanistan*. Berkeley Caliber, 2009.

Deaner, Robert O. "More Males Run Fast: A Stable Sex Difference in Competitiveness in U.S. Distance Runners." *Evolution and Human Behavior*, Vol. 27, 2006, pp. 63–84.

Feng, Jing, Ian Spence, and Jay Pratt. "Playing an Action Video Game Reduces Gender Differences in Spatial Cognition." *Psychological Science*, Vol. 18, No. 10, 2007.

Fontenot, Gregory. "Fear, God, and Dreadnought." *Military Review*, Vol. 75, Issue 4, July–August 1995.

Gall, Carlotta. "War-Scarred Afghanistan in Environmental Crisis." *New York Times*, January 30, 2003.

SELECTED SOURCES AND REFERENCES

Geary, David C., and M. Catherine DeSoto. "Sex Differences in Spatial Abilities Among Adults from the United States and China: Implications for Evolutionary Theory." *Evolution and Cognition*, Vol. 7, No. 2, 2001.

Glatzer, Bernt. "War and Boundaries in Afghanistan: Significance and Relativity of Local and Social Boundaries." *Die Welt des Islams*, New Series, Vol. 41, Issue 3, November 2001, *The Making and Unmaking of Boundaries in the Islamic World*, pp. 379–399.

Grossman, Lt. Col. Dave, with Loren W. Christensen. *On Combat: The Psychology and Physiology of Deadly Conflict in War and in Peace.* Warrior Science Publications, 2004.

"Health Facilities Elude Kunar—Thanks to Insecurity." Pajhwok Afghan News, February 18, 2006.

Helmus, Todd C., and Russell W. Glenn. *Steeling the Mind: Combat Stress Reactions and Their Implications for Urban Warfare.* Rand Corporation, 2005.

Henry, James P. "Psychological and Physiological Responses to Stress: The Right Hemisphere and the Hypothalamo-Pituitary-Adrenal Axis, An Inquiry into Problems of Human Bonding." *Acta Physiologica Scandinavica, Supplementum*, Vol. 640, 1997, pp. 10–25.

Jones, Franklin D., Linette R. Sparacino, Joseph M. Rothberg, and James W. Stokes, eds. *War Psychiatry*. Produced by the Borden Institute, Walter Reed Army Medical Center, April 2000.

Kalin, Ned H. "The Neurobiology of Fear." *Scientific American*, May 1993.

Kanazawa, Satoshi. "Male Brain vs. Female Brain II: What Is an 'Extreme Male Brain'? What Is an 'Extreme Female Brain'?" *Scientific Fundamentalist*, March 21, 2008.

Kaur, Prabhjot, Maman Paul, and Jaspal Singh Sandhu. "Auditory and Visual Reaction Time in Athletes, Healthy Controls, and Patients of Type 1 Diabetes Mellitus: A Comparative Study." *International Journal of Diabetes in Developing Countries*, Vol. 26, Issue 3, September 2006.

Kemp, Robert. "Counterinsurgency in Eastern Afghanistan." NATO paper, from Foreign Service officer posted as a political officer to the U.S. Mission to NATO in Brussels and, prior, a political adviser to a U.S. brigade commander in the Provincial Reconstruction Team in Khost, Afghanistan.

Kosinski, Robert J. "A Literature Review on Reaction Time." Clemson University online publication, September 2008.

SELECTED SOURCES AND REFERENCES

Kryklywec, Sam, Kimitake Sato, and J. G. Cremades. "Differences in Closed-Loop Control of Cutting Movements Between Collegiate Athletes and Non-Athletes." In M. A. Cleary, L. E. Eberman, and M. L. Odai, eds., *Proceedings of the Fifth Annual College of Education Research Conference: Section on Allied Health Professions*, April 2006, pp. 26–31.

Lang, Peter. Interview with Sebastian Junger, February 21, 2009.

LeDoux, Joseph E. Interview with Sebastian Junger, 2009.

———. "Emotion: Clues from the Brain." *Annual Review of Psychology*, Vol. 46, 1995, pp. 209–235.

Luttrell, Marcus. Transcript of interview with Peter Berg, July 1, 2008.

Luttrell, Marcus, with Patrick Robinson. *Lone Survivor: The Eyewitness Account of Operation Redwing and the Lost Heroes of SEAL Team 10*. Little, Brown, 2007.

Maren, Stephen. "The Threatened Brain." *Science*, Vol. 317, August 24, 2007.

Maren, Stephen, and Chun-hui Chang. "Recent Fear Is Resistant to Extinction." *Proceedings of the National Academy of Sciences*, Vol. 103, No. 47, November 21, 2006, pp. 18020–18025.

SELECTED SOURCES AND REFERENCES

McGirk, Tim. "How the Shepherd Saved the SEAL." *TIME*, July 11, 2005.

Miller, Lt. Robert G., USN, Robert T. Rubin, MD, Brian R. Clark, AB, Lt. Cdr. William R. Crawford, MC, USN, and Capt. Ransom J. Arthur, MC, USN. "The Stress of Aircraft Carrier Landings." *Psychosomatic Medicine*, Vol. 32, No. 6, November–December 1970.

Milne, David. "Can People Really Be Scared to Death?" *Psychiatric News*, Vol. 37, No. 11, June 7, 2002.

Mobbs, Dean, Predrag Petrovic, Jennifer L. Marchant, Demis Hassabis, Nikolaus Weiskopf, Ben Seymour, Raymond J. Dolan, and Christopher D. Frith. "When Fear Is Near: Threat Imminence Elicits Prefrontal-Periaqueductal Gray Shifts in Humans." *Science*, Vol. 317, August 24, 2007.

Moran, Lord. *The Anatomy of Courage*. Constable & Robinson Ltd., 1945.

Morgan, Andrew. Interview with Sebastian Junger, February 26, 2009.

Morgan, Charles A. II, John H. Krystal, and Steven M. Southwick. "Toward Early Pharmacological Posttraumatic Stress Intervention." *Biological Psychiatry*, Vol. 53, 2003, pp. 834–843.

Mujica-Parodi, Lilianne R., PhD, and Helmut Strey, PhD. "Identification and Isolation of

Human Alarm Pheromones." State University of New York at Stony Brook Research Foundation, Progress Report: Phase 0, April 30, 2006.

Nasrat, Amanullah, and Bashir Babak. "Saving Afghanistan's Precious Trees." Environment News Service, March 29, 2005.

North, Andrew. "US Navy Seals' Afghan Disaster." BBC News, July 25, 2005.

"PTS Chief, Provincial Leaders Address Kunar Elders." US Fed News, May 15, 2006.

Rachman, S. J. *Fear and Courage*. W. H. Freeman and Company, 1978.

Roth, Beatrice, and Elaine Snell. "Sex Differences in the Brain." *EuroBrain*, Vol. 1, No. 3, December 1999.

Sargent, Roger. "Afghanistan Crippled, Scarred and Undefeated." *Toronto Star*, December 28, 1985.

Smeets, Jeroen B. J., and Eli Brenner. "The Difference Between the Perception of Absolute and Relative Motion: A Reaction Time Study." *Vision Research*, Vol. 34, No. 4, 1994, pp. 191–195.

Strand, Richard F. "The Current Political Situation in Nuristan." Richard Strand's Nuristân Site, July 17, 2007.

SELECTED SOURCES AND REFERENCES

"Taliban Crush Tribal Revolt in Eastern Afghanistan: Report." Agence France-Presse — English, February 23, 1997.

Thorpe, Simon, Denis Fize, and Catherine Marlot. "Speed of Processing in the Human Visual System." *Nature*, Vol. 381, June 6, 1996.

United Nations Environment Programme Post-Conflict Environmental Assessment press release. "UNEP Report Chronicles Environmental Damage of the Afghan Conflict," January 29, 2003.

"UN: Pakistan Sets Up Environmental Tribunals to Examine Major Offenses Such as Industrial Pollution." M2 Presswire, June 7, 1999.

"U.N. Voices Worry Over on Afghan Deforestation." Reuters, June 4, 1999.

U.S. Agency for International Development, with the Afghanistan Geological Survey. "Preliminary Non-Fuel Mineral Resource Assessment of Afghanistan." USGS Open-File Report, 2007–1214.

Wilson, Duff. "Effort to Get Metal to Act Like Wood." *New York Times*, October 18, 2008.

Yaqub, Nadeem. "Afghanistan: Conflict and Greed Threaten Ancient Forests." Inter Press Service, April 27, 2001.

SELECTED SOURCES AND REFERENCES

Book Two: KILLING

Cooper, Helene. "As Ills Persist, Afghan Leader Is Losing Luster." *New York Times*, June 7, 2008.

Gall, Carlotta. "Marines Push Back Taliban in 4 Days, and a Town's Optimism Grows." *New York Times*, May 27, 2008.

————. "Old-Line Taliban Commander Is Face of Rising Afghan Threat." *New York Times*, June 17, 2008.

Gall, Carlotta, and Abdul Waheed Wafa. "Afghan Officials Abashed at Attempt to Kill Karzai." *New York Times*, April 28, 2008.

Gray, J. Glenn. *The Warriors: Reflections on Men in Battle*. Bison Books, 1959.

Grossman, Lt. Col. Dave. *On Killing: The Psychological Cost of Learning to Kill*. Back Bay Books, 1995.

Keeley, Lawrence H. *War Before Civilization: The Myth of the Peaceful Savage*. Oxford University Press, 1996.

Levav, Itzhak, MD, Haim Greenfeld, and Eli Baruch, MD. "Psychiatric Combat Reactions During the Yom Kippur War." *American Journal of Psychiatry*, Vol. 136, No. 5, May 1979.

Marlowe, David H. "Psychological and Psychosocial Consequences of Combat and Deployment with Special Emphasis on the Gulf War." Rand Corporation, 2000.

Rohde, David, and David E. Sanger. "How the 'Good War' in Afghanistan Went Bad." *New York Times*, August 12, 2007.

Shah, Taimoor, and Carlotta Gall. "NATO and Afghan Troops Clash with Taliban in Strategic Area Near Kandahar." *New York Times*, June 18, 2008.

Shalit, Ben. *The Psychology of Conflict and Combat*. Praeger, 1988.

Smucker, Philip G. "Afghanistan's Eastern Front: Along the Pakistani Border, al Qaeda and Taliban Fighters Take Their Best Shots." *U.S. News & World Report*, April 1, 2007.

Snee, Lawrence W., Stephen G. Peters, and Great J. Orris. "Precious and Semi-Precious Stones." U.S. Geological Survey: Afghanistan Project Products, Section 12.0, May 20, 2008.

Vermetten, Eric, Martin J. Dorahy, and David Spiegel, eds. *Traumatic Dissociation: Neurobiology and Treatment*. American Psychiatric Publishing, 2007.

Weinberg, S. Kirson. "The Combat Neuroses." *American Journal of Sociology*, Vol. 51, No. 5, *Human Behavior in Military Society*, March 1946, pp. 465–478.

Book Three: LOVE

Becker, Selwyn W., and Alice H. Eagly. "The Heroism of Men and Women." *American Psychologist*, Vol. 59, No. 3, April 2004, pp. 163–178.

Belenky, Gregory, ed. *Contemporary Studies in Combat Psychiatry*. Greenwood Press, 1987.

Blake, Joseph A. "The Congressional Medal of Honor in Three Wars." *Pacific Sociological Review*, Vol. 16, No. 2, April 1973, pp. 166–176.

Bowles, Samuel. "Group Competition, Reproductive Leveling, and the Evolution of Human Altruism." *Science*, Vol. 314, December 8, 2006.

Breznitz, Shlomo, PhD, ed. *Stress in Israel*. Van Nostrand Reinhold, 1983.

Burkart, Judith M., Ernst Fehr, Charles Efferson, and Carel P. van Schaik. "Other-Regarding Preferences in a Non-Human Primate: Common Marmosets Provision Food Altruistically." *Proceedings of the National Academy of Sciences*, Vol. 104, No. 50, December 11, 2007, pp. 19762–19766.

Catignani, Sergio. "Motivating Soldiers: The Example of the Israeli Defense Forces." *Parameters*, Autumn 2004.

SELECTED SOURCES AND REFERENCES

Centers for Disease Control and Prevention, National Center for Injury Prevention and Control. "WISQARS Injury Mortality Reports, 1999–2006."

Choi, Jung-Kyoo, and Samuel Bowles. "The Coevolution of Parochial Altruism and War." *Science*, Vol. 318, October 26, 2007.

Cubbison, Douglas R. "Battle of Wanat Historical Analysis." Combat Studies Institute, based at Fort Leavenworth, Kansas, 2009.

Dawkins, Richard. *The Selfish Gene*. Oxford University Press, 1976.

De Waal, Frans B. M., ed. *Tree of Origin: What Primate Behavior Can Tell Us About Human Social Evolution*. Harvard University Press, 2001.

Dunbar, R. I. M. "Coevolution of Neocortical Size, Group Size, and Language in Humans." *Behavioral and Brain Sciences*, Vol. 16, No. 4, 1993, pp. 681–735.

Dyer, Gwynne. *War: The Lethal Custom*. Carroll & Graf, 1985.

Fisher, Richard. "Why Altruism Paid Off for Our Ancestors." *New Scientist*, December 2006.

Gal, Col. Reuven, PhD. "Unit Morale: From a Theoretical Puzzle to an Empirical Illustration — An Israeli Example." *Journal of Applied Social Psychology*, Vol. 16, No. 6, 1986, pp. 549–564.

SELECTED SOURCES AND REFERENCES

Gintis, Herbert, Samuel Bowles, Robert Boyd, and Ernst Fehr. "Explaining Altruistic Behavior in Humans." *Evolution and Human Behavior*, Vol. 24, 2003, pp. 153–172.

Griffith, James. "Further Considerations Concerning the Cohesion-Performance Relation in Military Settings." *Armed Forces & Society*, Vol. 34, 2007.

———. "Measurement of Group Cohesion in U.S. Army Units." *Basic and Applied Social Psychology*, Vol. 9, No. 2, 1988, pp. 149–171.

Grinker, Lt. Col. Roy R., MC, and Maj. John P. Spiegel, MC. *Men Under Stress*. The Blakiston Company, 1945.

Gross, Edward. "Primary Functions of the Small Group." *American Journal of Sociology*, Vol. 60, No. 1, July 1954, pp. 24–29.

Haidt, Jonathan. "The New Synthesis in Moral Psychology." *Science*, Vol. 316, May 18, 2007.

Honess, P. E., and C. M. Marin. "Behavioural and Physiological Aspects of Stress and Aggression in Nonhuman Primates." *Neuroscience Biobehavioral Reviews*, Vol. 30, 2006, pp. 390–412.

Johnson, George E. "The Fighting Instinct: Its Place in Life." *The Survey*, Survey Associates, Charity Organization of the City of New York, Vol. XXXV, October 1915–March 1916.

SELECTED SOURCES AND REFERENCES

Kellett, Anthony. *Combat Motivation: The Behavior of Soldiers in Battle*. Kluwer-Nijhoff Publishing, 1982.

Lang, P. J., and M. Davis. "Emotion, Motivation, and the Brain: Reflex Foundations in Animal and Human Research." *Progress in Brain Research*, Vol. 156, 2006, pp. 3–34.

Lehmann. L., and L. Keller. "The Evolution of Cooperation and Altruism — A General Framework and a Classification of Models." *Journal Compilation, European Society for Evolutionary Biology*, Vol. 19, 2006, pp. 1365–1376.

Lieberman, Harris R., Gaston P. Bathalon, Christina M. Falco, Charles A. Morgan III, Philip J. Niro, and William J. Tharion. "The Fog of War: Decrements in Cognitive Performance and Mood Associated with Combat-Like Stress." *Aviation, Space, and Environmental Medicine*, Vol. 76, No. 7, Section II, July 2005.

Löw, Andreas, Peter J. Lang, J. Carson Smith, and Margaret M. Bradley. "Both Predator and Prey: Emotional Arousal in Threat and Reward." *Psychological Science*, Vol. 19, No. 9, 2008.

Moore, J. "The Evolution of Reciprocal Sharing." *Ethology and Sociobiology*, Vol. 5, 1984, pp. 5–14.

SELECTED SOURCES AND REFERENCES

Moskos, Charles C., Jr. "Why Men Fight: American Combat Soldiers in Vietnam." *Trans-Action*, Vol. 7, No. 1, November 1969, pp. 13–23.

Pepper, John W., and Barbara B. Smuts. "A Mechanism for the Evolution of Altruism Among Non-Kin: Positive Assortment Through Environmental Feedback." Santa Fe Institute, *Working Papers 0-12-065*, December 2000.

Pinker, Steven. "The Moral Instinct." *New York Times*, January 13, 2008.

Rogers, Michael. "How Social Can We Get?" MSNBC, September 10, 2007.

Salo, Mikael, and Guy L. Siebold. "Cohesion Components as Predictors of Performance and Attitudinal Criteria." *Armed Forces & Society*, Vol. 33, No. 2, 2007, pp. 286–295.

Shils, Edward A., and Morris Janowitz. "Cohesion and Disintegration in the Wehrmacht in World War II." *Public Opinion Quarterly*, Summer 1948.

"Social Networks: Primates on Facebook." *The Economist*, February 28, 2009, pp. 84–85.

Solomon, Zahava, Mario Mikulincer, and Stevan E. Hobfoll. "Effects of Social Support and Battle Intensity on Loneliness and Breakdown During Combat." *Journal of Personality and Social Psychology*, Vol. 51, No. 6, 1986, pp. 1269–1276.

SELECTED SOURCES AND REFERENCES

Stouffer, S. A., A. A. Lumsdaine, M. H. Lumsdaine, R. M. Williams, Jr., M. B. Smith, I. L. Janis, S. A. Star, and L. S. Cottrell, Jr. *The American Soldier: Combat and Its Aftermath*. Princeton University Press, 1949.

Trivers, Robert L. "The Evolution of Reciprocal Altruism." *Quarterly Review of Biology*, Vol. 46, March 1971, pp. 35–57.

U.S. Department of Labor, Bureau of Labor Statistics. Census of Fatal Occupational Injuries, 2009.

Wansink, Brian, Collin R. Payne, and Koert van Ittersum. "Profiling the Heroic Leader: Empirical Lessons from Combat-Decorated Veterans of World War II." *Leadership Quarterly*, 2008.

Whitham, Jessica C., and Dario Maestripieri. "Primate Rituals: The Function of Greetings Between Male Guinea Baboons." *Ethology*, Vol. 109, 2003, pp. 847–859.

Wilson, Michael L., William R. Wallauer, and Anne E. Pusey. "New Cases of Intergroup Violence Among Chimpanzees in Gombe National Park, Tanzania." *International Journal of Primatology*, Vol. 25, No. 3, June 2004.

Wrangham, Richard W. "Evolution of Coalitionary Killing." *Yearbook of Physical Anthropology*, Vol. 42, 1999, pp. 1–30.

SELECTED SOURCES AND REFERENCES

Wrangham, Richard W., and Dale Peterson. *Demonic Males: Apes and the Origins of Human Violence.* Houghton Mifflin, 1996.

Wrangham, Richard W., and Michael L. Wilson. "Intergroup Relations in Chimpanzees." *Annual Review of Anthropology,* Vol. 32, 2003, pp. 363–392.

———. "Collective Violence: Comparisons Between Youths and Chimpanzees." *Annals of the New York Academy of Sciences,* Vol. 1036, 2004, pp. 233–256.

Wrangham, Richard W., Michael L. Wilson, and Martin N. Muller. "Comparative Rates of Violence in Chimpanzees and Humans." *Primates,* Vol. 47, 2006, pp. 14–26.

Zegwaard, Gerard A. "Headhunting Practices of the Asmat of Netherlands New Guinea." *American Anthropologist,* New Series, Vol. 61, No. 6, December 1959, pp. 1020–1041.

Zhou, W. X., D. Sornette, R. A. Hill, and R. I. M. Dunbar. "Discrete Hierarchical Organization of Social Group Sizes." *Proceedings of the Royal Society B: Biological Sciences,* Vol. 272, No. 1561, February 22, 2005, pp. 439–444.

ACKNOWLEDGMENTS

FIRST AND FOREMOST I WOULD LIKE TO THANK my wife, Daniela, for accepting my long absences and giving me such a wonderful home to come back to. Her editorial help was amazing and essential to the writing of this book. My parents, Ellen and Miguel, and my sister, Carlotta, provided much encouragement and heartfelt advice. Among my close friends Rob Leaver put a lot of thought into my manuscript and helped me with numerous conversations about men, war, and violence; and Austin Merrill gave me great advice about the overall narrative structure.

In the fall of 2007 I took a long walk in the woods with my dear friend Joanna Settle, and I told

ACKNOWLEDGMENTS

her about my experiences in the Korengal. Our conversation that bright, beautiful October day guided me in ways that are difficult to articulate but utterly essential to the nature of this book. Joanna passed away before she could read the results of our conversation, but her friendship and that of her husband, Ellis, are woven into almost everything I have ever written.

Many thanks must go to Graydon Carter of *Vanity Fair*, who had enough faith in me to underwrite multiple trips to Afghanistan when the story was not particularly hot and magazines were already tightening their belts. I would also like to thank my editor, Doug Stumpf, and his assistant, Christopher Bateman, for their ongoing help and enthusiasm in what became a three-year project. I am also deeply indebted to those at ABC *Nightline* for their hard work on the project: David Scott, Steven Baker, Maddy Sauer, Karen Brenner, James Goldston, Rhonda Schwartz, and Brian Ross. Kerry Smith, head of editorial content for ABC, was incomparable in her support and enthusiasm. My agent, Stuart Krichevsky, and his staff—Shana Cohen, Danielle Rollins, and Kathryne Wick—were critical in helping me with the book. Stuart's advice on everything from editing to jacket design was almost always spot-on and I am very grateful to him. Cathy Saypol was also a source of editorial advice, publicity wisdom, and general encouragement. At Twelve, my editor, Jonathan Karp, gave me feedback early on that set the book in the right direction even though I couldn't quite see it yet; thank you, Jon. Cary Goldstein did an amazing job generating interest in this book among booksellers. Mari Okuda allowed me many more last-minute changes than most authors are allowed, but she still got the book finished in time—I don't know how. And Colin Shepherd was of great help in coordinating all the moving parts.

Throughout the writing of this book I was also making a documentary film on Second Platoon, and I must acknowledge the important roles of editor Michael Levine and associate editor Maya Mumma in the overall project. My researcher and fact-checker, Andrea Minarcek, did an incredible job excavating old studies on the behavior of men in combat, as well as current-day neurological research and psychological studies. Her hard work saved me from numerous errors. Within the U.S. military, I must point out the efforts of the Army public affairs office at Bagram and Jalalabad in getting me in and out of the Korengal Valley so many times—particularly Major Nick Sternberg, Captain Peter Katzfey, Sergeant First Class Jacob

ACKNOWLEDGMENTS

Caldwell, and Sergeant First Class Eric Hendrix. And of course none of this would have been possible without the support of the battalion commander, Lieutenant Colonel Bill Ostlund, as well as Captain Dan Kearney and First Sergeant LaMonta Caldwell of Battle Company. Lieutenants Matt Piosa and Steve Gillespie of Second Platoon, as well as Sergeant First Class Mark Patterson and Staff Sergeant Dave Roels were also great sources of information and support while I was out there. Safa Sediqi, my driver in Kabul, always got me everywhere safely and on time. I remember turning down a ride in a raging snowstorm because he promised that he was coming to get me... and indeed he did.

I must point out that without the friendship and acceptance of the men of Second Platoon this would have been a very different book and possibly not worth writing. My experience with them was one of the most gratifying of my life and changed me in profound ways. I think I finally understand the idea of brotherhood and how—without that—almost nothing else is possible. Thank you, guys, for the humor, the encouragement, the bad food, the good company, and for not making me pull guard duty like you threatened.

Finally there is my friend, partner, and comrade through all of this, photographer Tim Hetherington.

ACKNOWLEDGMENTS

It's hard for me to even begin describing his contribution to this work. The images he captured—both stills and video—have become almost iconic of the war in Afghanistan. But more than that, his humor, courage, and companionship during our trips helped make this project psychologically possible for me. It was difficult out there, and Tim's attitude about those difficulties was crucial. I was once asked about our collaboration, and my answer was something to the effect that working with Tim was like climbing into a little sports car and driving around really, really fast. He saw this story in startling new ways, and I learned a tremendous amount from just talking to him. Thanks, Tim. I hope we get to do many more like this.

ABOUT THE AUTHOR

SEBASTIAN JUNGER is the *New York Times* bestselling author of *The Perfect Storm* and *A Death in Belmont*. He is a contributing editor to *Vanity Fair*, and has been awarded a National Magazine Award and an SAIS Novartis Prize for journalism. With Tim Hetherington he directed the documentary *Restrepo*, which won the Grand Jury Prize at Sundance. He lives in New York City. For more information, you can visit www.sebastianjunger.com.

BE SURE TO LOOK FOR

RESTREPO

ONE PLATOON, ONE YEAR, ONE VALLEY

A Film by Sebastian Junger and Tim Hetherington

"An extraordinary, shattering depiction of war."
—Jada Yuan, *New York* Magazine

GRAND JURY PRIZE
DOCUMENTARY
2010
SUNDANCE
FILM FESTIVAL

FOR MORE INFORMATION, VISIT
WWW.RESTREPOTHEMOVIE.COM

AN OUTPOST FILMS PRODUCTION
IN ASSOCIATION WITH
NATIONAL GEOGRAPHIC CHANNEL

ABOUT TWELVE

TWELVE was established in August 2005 with the objective of publishing no more than one book per month. We strive to publish the singular book, by authors who have a unique perspective and compelling authority. Works that explain our culture; that illuminate, inspire, provoke, and entertain. We seek to establish communities of conversation surrounding our books. Talented authors deserve attention not only from publishers, but from readers as well. To sell the book is only the beginning of our mission. To build avid audiences of readers who are enriched by these works—that is our ultimate purpose.

For more information about forthcoming TWELVE books, please go to www.twelvebooks.com